ELITES AND PEOPLE

COMPARATIVE SOCIAL RESEARCH

Series Editor: Fredrik Engelstad

Recent Volumes:

COMPARATIVE SOCIAL RESEARCH   VOLUME 34

ELITES AND PEOPLE: CHALLENGES TO DEMOCRACY

EDITED BY

FREDRIK ENGELSTAD

University of Oslo, Norway/Institute for Social Research, Norway

TRYGVE GULBRANDSEN

Institute for Social Research, Norway

MARTE MANGSET

Oslo Metropolitan University, Norway/Institute for Social Research, Norway

MARI TEIGEN

Institute for Social Research, Norway

United Kingdom – North America – Japan
India – Malaysia – China

Emerald Publishing Limited
Howard House, Wagon Lane, Bingley BD16 1WA, UK

First edition 2019

Reprints and permissions service
Contact: permissions@emeraldinsight.com

British Library Cataloguing in Publication Data
A catalogue record for this book is available from the British Library

ISBN: 978-1-83867-916-3 (Print)
ISBN: 978-1-83867-915-6 (Online)
ISBN: 978-1-83867-917-0 (Epub)

ISSN: 0195-6310 (Series)

Printed and bound by CPI Group (UK) Ltd, Croydon, CR0 4YY

ISOQAR certified
Management System,
awarded to Emerald
for adherence to
Environmental
standard
ISO 14001:2004.

Certificate Number 1985
ISO 14001

INVESTOR IN PEOPLE

CONTENTS

PART III   ELITES AND POPULISM

ABOUT THE CONTRIBUTORS

Fredrik Engelstad is a Professor (em) in Sociology at the University of Oslo, and formerly the Director of the Institute for Social Research in Oslo. He has published widely on organizations, power, sociology of culture and sociological theory. Recently, he headed a large-scale project on institutional change in Scandinavia, materialising in three books, of which the most recent is *Democratic State and Democratic Society* (2018).

Anja Gibson is a Postdoctoral Researcher at the Department of Educational Sciences at the Martin-Luther-University Halle-Wittenberg, Germany. Her research focusses on qualitative educational research, including biographical, organisational and classroom research. She has conducted studies on elite education and elite (boarding) schools, on educational inequality, and family and school socialisation. Currently, she is working on a qualitative longitudinal study on elite school students from their mid-teens to mid-twenties.

Trygve Gulbrandsen is a Research Professor (em) at the Institute of Social Research and formerly the Adjunct Professor in Sociology at the University of Oslo. His research covers a broad range of topics including elites, ownership, power, trust, professions and civil society. His most recent publication on elites is the book *Elites in an Egalitarian Society* (2019).

Borbála Göncz is a Research Fellow at the Institute of Sociology and Social Policy at the Corvinus University of Budapest. Her research interests include attitudes towards the European integration process and European identity. Related to these topics, she has recently co-edited *National Political Elites, European Integration and the Eurozone Crisis* published by Routledge in 2018, co-authored an article published in *Historical Social Research* and authored several book chapters.

John Higley is an Emeritus Professor of Government and Sociology, University of Texas at Austin, where he was the Chair of the Government Department and holder of the Jack S. Blanton Chair in Australian Studies. He also chaired the IPSA Research Committee on Political Elites. He has (co)edited a large number of books on elites, the most recent being *The Palgrave Handbook of Political Elites* (2018, with Heinrich Best). He is also the co-author of *Elite Foundations of Liberal Democracy* (2006, with Michael Burton).

Ursula Hoffmann-Lange is a Professor Emerita of Political Science at the University of Bamberg. Her fields of research are elites, political culture and democratisation. She is a member of an international research network studying political culture in democratic countries, coordinated by the Transformation Research Unit at the University of Stellenbosch, South Africa. She has published numerous articles in the field of elite studies, along with the book *Eliten, Macht und Konflikt in der Bundesrepublik* (*Elites, Power, and Conflict in the German Federal Republic, 1992*).

Farida Jalalzai publishes works related to women national executives including *Shattered, Cracked and Firmly Intact: Women and the Executive Glass Ceiling Worldwide* (Oxford University Press, 2013) and *Women Presidents of Latin America: Beyond Family Ties?* (Routledge, 2016). Dr Jalalzai's current book project is *Senhora Presidenta: Women's Representation in Brazil during Dilma Rousseff's Presidency* (with Pedro dos Santos, under contract with Temple University Press). She has also authored several articles and book chapters on this topic.

György Lengyel is a Professor at the Corvinus University of Budapest, where he is the Head of the *Centre for Empirical Social Research* and the Editor-in-Chief of the *Corvinus Journal of Sociology and Social Policy*. Among his recent publications is the "Irresponsible elites in opposition and government" In L. Vogel et al. (Eds.), *The Contested Status of Political Elites. At the Crossroads. Routledge*, N.Y., 2019 (with G. Ilonszki).

Marte Mangset is a Senior Research Fellow at the Institute for Social Research, Oslo, Norway. She holds a PhD from Sciences Po Paris and from the University of Bergen, and specialises in international comparative sociological studies of knowledge, education and power. She has studied bureaucratic elites in Norway, France and Britain and engaged in theoretical discussions in elite theory. She is the Co-editor of *Comparative Social Research*.

Jules Naudet is a CNRS Research Fellow at the CEIAS (EHESS), Paris, France. He is the Co-editor-in-Chief of *La Vie des Idées/Books and Ideas* as well as the Co-editor, along with Surinder Jodhka, of the book series "Exploring India's Elite". Naudet is also the author of *Stepping into the Elite* (2018). He now dedicates his research to an ethnographic study of the role of sociability in power and wealth dynamics, doing fieldwork both in Paris and in New Delhi.

Kjetil Selvik is a Senior Research Fellow at the Norwegian Institute of International Affairs. His research focusses on the sources of authoritarian resilience in Iran and the Arab world. His articles have appeared in journals like *Democratization*, *The International Journal of Middle East Studies*, *World Development*, *The Middle East Journal, Comparative Sociology* and *Middle Eastern Studies*. He is the Co-author of *Stability and Change in the Modern Middle East* (IB Taurus, 2011, with Stig Stenslie) and the Co-editor of *Oil States in the New Middle East: Uprisings and Stability* (Routledge, 2016, with Bjørn Olav Utvik).

Shirin Shahrokni is an Assistant Professor of Sociology at York University's Glendon College. Her research bridges the sociology of immigration and race relations, with a focus on the trajectories and identities of descendants of immigrants in France and Canada. Shahrokni's current project examines the settlement pathways of francophone immigrants in Canada, outside Quebec. She is also part of a

SSHRC-funded collaborative research on the racialisation process experienced by Asian international students across several Canadian universities.

Stig Stenslie is a Professor at the Norwegian Defence Intelligence College. He has published a number of books on the Middle East and China, including *49 Myths About China* (Rowman & Littlefield, 2014, with Marte K. Galtung), *Regime Stability in Saudi Arabia: The Challenge of Succession* (Routledge, 2011) and *Stability and Change in the Modern Middle East* (IB Taurus, 2011, with Kjetil Selvik).

Laura Szabó, is a Research Fellow in the Hungarian Demographic Research Institute. In collaboration with the Centre for Empirical Social Research, Corvinus University of Budapest, she had worked as a Researcher and Survey Analyst in the European National Elites and the Crisis 2014 project. Her main topic of analysis was the trust of the Hungarian national elites in national and supranational institutions of the European Union.

Mari Teigen is a Research Professor at the Institute for Social Research, Oslo, Norway. She is Head of the Centre for Research on Gender Equality and the Centre for Research on Gender Equality in Research and Innovation. Her research engages with change and stability in gender relations, through analysis of gender equality policy, social elites and gender segregation in the labour market and in academia. Teigen is the Editor of the Norwegian *Journal of Gender Research* and the Co-editor of *Comparative Social Research*.

EDITORIAL BOARD

LIST OF REVIEWERS

Johannes Bergh	Institute for Social Research, Norway
Nils A. Butenschøn	University of Oslo, Norway
Peter Munk Christiansen	Aarhus University, Denmark
Daniel Gaxie	University of Paris 1 Pantheon-Sorbonne, France
Atle Hennum Haugsgjerd	Institute for Social Research, Norway
Anirudh Krishna	Duke University, Durham, USA
Kuldeep Mathur	Jawaharlal Nehru University, India
Claire Maxwell	University of Copenhagen, Denmark
Rita Nikolai	Humboldt-Universität zu Berlin, Germany
Arnfinn H. Midtbøen	Institute for Social Research, Norway
Ilkka Ruostetsaari	University of Tampere, Finland
John Scott	University of Plymouth, UK
Signe Bock Seegaard	Institute for Social Research, Norway
Jessi Streib	Duke University, USA
Luca Verzichelli	University of Siena, Italy
Lena Wängnerud	University of Gothenburg, Sweden
Øvyind Østerud	University of Oslo, Norway

ELITES AND PEOPLE: CHALLENGES TO DEMOCRACY

Fredrik Engelstad, Trygve Gulbrandsen,
Marte Mangset and Mari Teigen

The past decade has been a period of severe crises centred in the West but with significant repercussions for the rest of the world: the financial crisis, euro crisis, populist resurgence, immigration crisis, gender revolt, cracks in the European Union and dramatic backlash against the Arab Spring. All of these crises have involved elites in various ways and raised questions about the roles of elites in existing forms of social and political governance. Although these issues have significant transnational aspects, crucial differences among them also exist due to national variations in institutions and socio-political traditions. To avoid facile generalisations, thorough comparative studies are crucial.

Numerous contemporary tensions concern not only elites as governing groups but also elites' relationship to democracy, which always has been strained. Over time, the discussion on elites and democracy has taken several turns. The pioneers of elite theory in the early twentieth century were sceptical and sometimes outright dismissive of the possibility of democratic governance. In the second half of the twentieth century, this theme was reintroduced from a different angle underscoring the concentration of power in unified elite as a threat to democracy (Mills, 1956). This perspective was further elaborated by the emphasis on democratic participation as a contrast to Schumpeterian versions of elite democracy (Bachrach, 1969; Bottomore, 1966). The debate recently took a new turn with the proposal of the argument that elites should be regarded as a precondition for democracy (Burton & Higley, 1987; Higley & Burton, 2006), supported by explorations of various types of elite democracy (Best & Higley, 2010; Gulbrandsen, 2019). Undoubtedly, good reasons for questioning the blending of elites with democracy exist. Indeed, the very concept of elites – of chosen people – blatantly contradicts the democratic ideal of political equality. However, strong reasons for regarding elites as necessary parts of democratic societies also exist.

Elites and People: Challenges to Democracy
Comparative Social Research, Volume 34, 1–13
Copyright © 2019 by Emerald Publishing Limited
All rights of reproduction in any form reserved
ISSN: 0195-6310/doi:10.1108/S0195-631020190000034001

From a structural perspective, in any large-scale society, democracy is unthinkable without large organisations, whether political bodies, bureaucracies, enterprises or voluntary organisations. Inevitably, power becomes concentrated at the top positions of these organisations (Michels, 1959 [1911]), and the incumbents who exert this power potentially constitute groups that may be termed elite groups. Power and the concentration of power are multi-faceted phenomena. They obviously can be a source of repression but equally can be a source of innovation and new opportunities, initiating cooperation and overcoming problems of collective action.

From a process perspective, the plurality of organisations consolidates elites to differing degrees into acting groups, even if they are caught in ambivalent positions. They may engage in open conflict with each other or act in relatively loose cooperation. Some sort of interdependence, though, is nearly inevitable (Aron, 1950). The modes of cooperation among elites are circumscribed by the limitations and resources of the organisations they command, the institutions within which they operate and their varying scopes of action within their general institutional frameworks.

From a comparative perspective, the study of elites invites a large set of research questions in addition to the well-established questions concerning elites' structure and integration. Elites may be a precondition for the initial constitution of democracies (Higley & Burton, 2006) or contribute to processes of further democratisation (Engelstad, 2018; Schmitter, 2018). Processes of democratisation are rarely due to the actions of a single elite group but rather results from agreements among competing elites. However, elites may also, and often do, stage the destruction of democracy, most fatefully in the Weimar Republic (Hoffmann-Lange, 1998). In the contemporary world, the resilience of democracy to attacks from elites has been put to trial in Turkey and Hungary, among other nations, also manifested in a flood of books with titles such as *How Democracies Die* (Levitsky & Ziblatt, 2018). In the age of globalisation, elites are no longer limited within the borders of nation-states. International treaties and conventions and intergovernmental organisations indicate the emergence of transnational elites anchored in national contexts but simultaneously transcending the limits of nation-states. The constellation of the European Union and its member states is a significant case.

If elites are to exert power, they are dependent on their non-elite constituency in the long term. In democratic societies, elites' legitimacy is contingent on the degree of their social distance from the general population and thus the degree of the openness of the elite structure. Social distance involves opportunities for mobility into elites, hindrances to be overcome (e.g. gender and class background) and the socialisation and education required to enter elite positions. In another sense, social distance refers to the social and political gaps between elites and ordinary citizens, ranging from elites' attitudes and self-presentation to their ability to develop and present policies furthering the welfare of large segments of the population. If a common feeling that elites live in a bubble and do not take popular interests seriously develops, then populism lies close at hand.

In the present volume of *Comparative Social Research*, all of these aspects are prominent. Moreover, this volume examines a broad set of relationships between elites and non-elites, including ordinary citizens, popular protest movements and prospective elite members. In democratic societies, elites constitute a wide range of social groups, as mentioned; as presented in this volume, from the Arab Spring in Tunisia and Egypt to women's political leadership in Brazil and Germany, via attainment of elite positions among minorities in France and the US.

This diversity needs to be stressed, even if a main focus in the volume is political elites in democratic societies, particularly in European contexts. The quality of democratic governance seems to be declining in many parts of the contemporary world, but political elections, even when far from free and fair, nevertheless remain a main source of legitimacy. Most of today's well-established democracies, as found in Europe and North America, resulted from social processes taking place over more than a century and even longer in some cases. In contrast, societies where democratic governance is developing today face various and often intractable problems, not the least because institutional changes are more condensed in time. These uncertainties justify a close study of how new democracies are constituted, reinforced, succeed and fail in the contemporary world. Here, the aftermath of the Arab Spring may yield important insights. In the present volume, this focus is expanded to elites in the so-called third-wave democracies mostly established around 1990. How do they fare several decades later? Other chapters turn to elite recruitment, socialisation and consolidation in terms of both class and gender. The volume concludes by highlighting elites' various entanglements with populism: on the one hand, underlying reasons for the recent populist expansion, on the other, various images of elites in populist movements.

THE ARAB SPRING – FEASIBLE TRANSITION TO DEMOCRACY?

A major contribution to understanding the emergence of democracy comes from Robert Putnam's *How Democracy Works* (1993), comparing political development in northern and southern Italy over several hundred years. In line with the Tocquevillian tradition, the core notion of Putnam's work is that civil society is a precondition for democracy. A broad set of voluntary organisations becomes an arena for interactions among citizens and thus functions as a source of social capital and trust. The variations in civil society organisations in northern and southern Italy are assumed to be the determinant of the high quality of democracy in northern Italy and the low quality in southern Italy. Social trust certainly is a salient, if also precarious, component of democracies. However, Putnam (1993) proposes a structural, bottom-up model, stressing the impacts of organisations as meeting places for citizens and downplaying the significance of social and political institutions and the actions of elite groups. Consequently, the crucial dynamics of conflict and compromise among elite groups slip out of sight.

Closer to the present, the Arab Spring and its aftermath may serve as a prism for understanding core preconditions for democratisation. At the outset, the Middle East was exceptional as no Arab country had been a democracy (Diamond, 2016, p. 160ff). In its most visible examples, Tunisia and Egypt, two of the most authoritarian countries in the Arab world (Diamond, 2016, p. 162), the aims of democratisation have taken very different roads. Why does the former still have a promise of success, whereas the latter has ended in complete failure? Stig Stenslie and Kjetil Selvik's detailed analysis in this volume points to the quality of civil society as a key to understanding, much in line with Putnam (1993). Their concept of civil society, though, is much broader and includes three closely related factors: civil society organisations with potential relevance to politics, relatively independent social institutions and, accordingly, a set of forceful elite groups. Egypt presents a negative case that supports Putnam's (1993) theory. Egypt possessed few arenas where social trust could develop (but see Kindt, 2013), civil society was very weak, and the army had a dominant position in the economy. In contrast, the case of Tunisia makes it clear that in the processes of democratisation, generalised trust was far from sufficient to change the given social order. Other elites outside the purely political elites also turned out to be necessary to counteract a full return to the old order (see also Schmitter, 2018, p. 598).

POLITICAL ELITES AND RESILIENCE OF DEMOCRACY

If the Arab Spring reflected a crisis in authoritarian societies with pseudo-democratic façades, the financial crisis originating in 2008 can be regarded as a crucial test of the resilience of democracy. The financial crisis was the deepest economic crisis since the Great Depression in the early 1930s. Seymour Martin Lipset's (1959) classic conception, still relevant in political science, holds that stable democracies rest on a combination of economic efficiency and political legitimacy. The crucial question is the shape of the dynamic interdependence of these factors: When an economic crisis occurs, does it undermine legitimacy, or, to the contrary, does robust legitimacy provide confidence in the handling of the crisis? Since the mid-2000s, the world has seen a backlash against democracy. Nevertheless, studies have indicated that the crisis has had only moderate effects on political legitimacy, partly as most strongly affected countries have been rich nations with well-established democratic traditions (Diamond, 2016, pp. 101ff). Such general observations call for more detailed studies considering variations in the sources of legitimacy and the effects on institutional changes within a broad definition of democracy.

These questions are examined in several contributions in this volume in both a broad comparative and an intra-European perspective. They all present analyses of large-scale survey data from recent decades that together yield a picture of the present situation *in statu nascendi*, revealing some preconditions for later developments.

In one chapter, Ursula Hoffmann-Lange discusses variations in support for democracy in seven countries and whether the financial crisis affected that support. The objects of study are the electorates and members of parliament in two well-established democracies (Germany and Sweden) and five third-wave democracies (Chile, Poland, South Korea, South Africa and Turkey). Assessing support for democracy with three different measures finds only weak traces of the financial crisis. Changes from 2007, before the crisis exploded, through 2013 are virtually negligible in both the political elites and the general population (with the exception of South Africa).

Not surprisingly, members of parliaments in the seven countries all express high support for democracy, with the highest support in Sweden and Germany. In general, parliamentarians tend to have a high degree of confidence in democracy independent of the political context, whereas citizens stand more aloof from political processes. While significant differences among countries and between the political elite and citizens are found, the general picture is of noticeably lower support for democracy in the general population than in the political elite. In the new democracies, considerable segments of the general population favour non-democratic modes of governance. The substantial cross-country variations in citizens' confidence in democracy are due foremost to internal political factors. If elites are carriers of the democratic creed, as pointed out by Hoffmann-Lange, they also bear a heavy responsibility for handling challenges to democracy. Even in the absence of economic recession and regardless of a country's economic situation, the gap between the political elite and the general population can deepen and develop into a legitimacy crisis due to significant cultural changes in the concentration of power and privilege. A prosperous country such as Norway demonstrates how rising economic inequality may increase the gap between the elites and the people.

EUROPEAN CRISIS – A CRISIS OF EUROPEANISATION?

In the European Union, the financial crisis took a special turn as the banking crisis fed into the regional euro crisis. In the rest of the world, political authorities managed the banking crisis at the national level, but in the Eurozone, the crisis had to be handled both at the European and the national levels. The whole EU system thus came into play, revealing the complexities of both EU institutions and the EU elite structure. Standard federal systems have a clear division of authority between the individual state level and the federal level, but the EU is a peculiar version of a federal system: individual states are sovereign nations but nevertheless are subordinate in certain aspects to a comparatively weak federal power (Cotta, 2012). Consequently, what may be termed the European elite system is haunted by inconsistencies and relatively low potential for political action (Cotta, 2014). The instabilities of such a system call for changes towards either stronger federal institutions and increased supranationalism or a more intergovernmental system in which bargaining between nation-states constitutes an important part of the *modus operandi*.

Confusing as it might seem, the aftermath of the euro crisis was a slow but nevertheless decisive strengthening of EU institutions, even if measures came late and were mostly reactive (for closer descriptions, see, e.g. Best & Higley, 2014; Cotta, 2012, 2014). Even so, the operation of the EU system remains largely dependent on the preferences and strategies of EU political elites anchored in national parliaments. Two contributions in this volume analyse different aspects of national parliamentarians' visions of the EU's future. Both contributions are based on survey data on parliamentarians in nine European countries, some inside the Eurozone (France, Germany, Greece, Italy, Lithuania, Portugal and Spain) and some outside the Eurozone (Bulgaria and Hungary).

Borbála Göncz studies changes in support for models of EU development due to the financial and euro crises. She finds that all members of these political elites express strong support for EU membership as a useful instrument, and this support did not decline due to the crisis, which may indicate general, stable support for EU institutions. However, views on the future of the EU changed considerably, and from 2007 to 2014, the intergovernmental model of limited EU integration generally gained support alongside the growing significance of identity politics. The expansion of parties on both the right and the left extreme accounts for the growing support for the intergovernmental option, whereas members in mainstream parties express feelings of attachment to Europe and more favour supranationalism.

Given diverse political elites' growing emphasis on the nation-state as constitutive of the future EU, it seems that the financial crisis affected political elites' level of trust in EU institutions. This becomes more precarious as trust generally refers to the present, not so much to a distant future. Trust in different EU institutions also varies. In this volume, György Lengyel and Laura Szabó show that among the political elites in the same nine countries as analysed by Gönsz, trust was not strongly affected, albeit with some variation between institutions. Trust in the European Parliament even slightly increased from 2007 to 2014, whereas trust in the European Commission and the Council of Ministers slightly declined. These findings underscore the tensions within the EU system as unlike the latter two institutions, the European Parliament has members elected at the national level.

Tensions become more visible when hearing the voice of the general population. Using data from Eurobarometer surveys for the same years, Lengyel and Szabó show that voters in the same countries do not share the political elites' rather optimistic views; popular trust in the European Parliament fell quite drastically from 2007 to 2014. Thus, developments after the euro crisis have taken a paradoxical turn. On one hand, scepticism of core EU institutions has increased among both parliamentarians and the general population. On the other hand, core EU institutions have been extended and reinforced. What has emerged from the crisis is what Cotta (2014) terms a compound system, with both intergovernmental and supranational elements more solidly present.

The changes described reflect quite general tendencies to which one exception is Hungary, which was hit hard by the crisis. In 2009, 'the GDP contracted by more than 6 per cent. ... Total external debts, including the debts of households, amounted to 158 per cent in 2009' (Fric, Lengyel, Pakulski, & Somolányi, 2014, p. 94). When the Fidez Government came into power in 2010, it moved to the right and introduced drastic austerity measures, including nationalisation of private pension funds, changes in the tax system and revisions of the labour law. These austerity measures were masked by attacks on foreign forces, profit-hungry private firms and the EU bureaucracy (Fric et al., 2014, p. 95). Lengyel and Szabó show that during this time, the Hungarian political elite's trust in the EU declined drastically; in 2007, they consistently had higher average scores for trust than the other eight EU countries, but seven years later, their scores were well below average. It is worth noting that the most recent data were from 2014, so developments in the past five years are not recorded.

The Hungarian situation is not without paradoxes when compared to the other eight countries studied. The general tendency is that the political elite are more supportive of the European Parliament than the general population, but the opposite is the case in Hungary. Despite a decline, the trust of the general population was significantly higher than that of the political elite, as of 2014. Moreover, consistently higher trust in EU institutions than that held by the political elite is also found in other prominent groups, including the economic, media and administrative elites. Thus, changes in the political elites' trust stem from processes internal to the political milieu rather than pressures from other segments of society.

ELITE RECRUITMENT AND SOCIAL IDENTITY

Filling elite positions in complex, modern societies obviously presupposes a wide filter of learning and socialisation processes for potential incumbents. Not surprisingly, a general finding in empirical studies is that elite members disproportionately have upper and upper-middle class backgrounds. One important reason is the conformation of social identity in these strata closely connected to class habitus, as propounded by Pierre Bourdieu (1992) in *The Logic of Practice*. Bourdieu (1998) and Bourdieu and Passeron (1990) showed how school systems value the knowledge and skills nurtured by specific social groups, such as the middle and upper classes. Elite families invest in their children's social careers, and attending elite schools is a salient resource in the creation of elite identity (Mangset, Maxwell, & van Zanten, 2017; van Zanten, 2018). In line with Bourdieu's insights, Sheamus Kahn's (2011) study of an elite prep school demonstrated that an important part of the hidden curriculum is social intelligence and the social aptitude to connect to people in unconstrained ways. Nevertheless, in democratic societies, a necessary condition for entering elite positions is an education yielding professional competence. Admittedly, there is a high correlation between family background and school attendance, but the connection might not always be straightforward. Rather than simply pointing out that middle- and upper-class children attend elite schools, we should investigate more closely the different social profiles developed by elite schools that, to some extent, cater to different social strata. Family background, thus, has variable effects on recruitment into schools and subsequent elite attainment.

Anja Gibson elucidates both these points in her chapter in the present volume. Her analysis of two elite boarding schools in Germany, one private and one public, brings out significant contrasts in both recruitment and learning processes. She depicts the construction of schools as elite institutions via mechanisms that shape social exclusivity. The private school caters to a socially homogenous upper-class group, and its main outcome is not so much outstanding academic results but more the cultural integration of the student body. The public school, however, is characterised by a less homogenous student group and thus has a more mixed class composition, giving rise to a strongly competitive culture among students far more individualistic than in the private school. These findings relate to the central issue of how elites in modern democratic societies seek to legitimise their power and privilege through (at least seemingly) meritocratic selection systems. Which of the two student groups has higher chances of making it to the top in their occupational careers remains an open question, but it will not be surprising if those who have the most solid social identity attain the highest degree of success.

The scope of analysis may be shifted from family and educational institutions to the persons who are candidates to and later do enter into elite positions. It is quite commonly assumed that prospective elite members constitute a relatively homogenous group by social class, ethnic affiliation and gender and can slide effortlessly into top positions. This stereotype obviously is not true for elite members with working class and ethnic minority backgrounds, who become marginal groups in relation to elite culture; in Bourdieu's (1999, p. 511) expression, with 'a habitus divided against itself'. This has been discussed and empirically demonstrated in several studies on recruitment to elite schools (e.g. Reay, Crozier, & Clayton, 2009). Typically, minority affiliates experience various types of ambivalence with differing positive and negative emphases. This runs parallel with expectations of change, termed anticipatory socialisation by Robert Merton (1957, p. 293), in relation to the group of destination.

In Scandinavia, the incongruity of origin and destination is summarised in the concept of class travel, proposed in the memoir *My First Name is Ronny* by Swedish university professor Ronny Ambjörnsson (1996). More recent and more widely read is the French contribution, *Returning to Reims*, an autobiography by Didier Eribon (2013). Regardless of whether incumbents with minority backgrounds feel less at ease in their achieved positions, they commonly experience a strong sense of belonging in two worlds. This, however, does not necessarily mean that these elite members handle their professional responsibilities differently and develop special political and social attitudes. A study of Norwegian elites, for instance, showed that in this respect, class of origin is not relevant to elites' professional orientation (Gulbrandsen & Engelstad, 2005).

Jules Naudet and Shirin Shahrokni's study in the present volume concentrates on the ambiguities related to ethnic minority status at work in elite recruitment. Comparing upwardly mobile racial minorities in the United States and France, the authors point to similar ambiguities in the recruitment pattern between the origin and destination groups in the two countries. Racial discrimination is part of daily life, so ambiguities in these minority groups are more significant than in the case of pure class inequality. Ties to the groups of origin become more crucial. In both countries, strong attachments to the family and social group of origin are present. However, the ways in which mobility patterns are structured and experienced vary among societies. In France, the mobility of sons (and daughters) in minority groups is very much a family project, whereas in the United States, norms of racial equality, even if still unaccomplished at the societal level, give upward mobility a stronger political flavour connected less to family relationships and more to larger ethnic groups. However, whether neutrality towards the group of origin becomes the main trait after entry into elite positions, similar to class differences in racially homogenous societies, remains to be seen. Either way, this cross-country study demonstrates the value of taking institutional and cultural dimensions into account when analysing minorities' possibilities to obtain elite positions.

GENDER DISPARITIES IN ELITE RECRUITMENT?

Male dominance in top positions exerting political authority and corporate power is among the most visible signs of unequal gender relations globally. Gender disparities in elite recruitment can be viewed from the position of not only the upwardly mobile but also those already at the summit who act as gate-keepers in recruiting new members. The literature on male dominance assumes that homosocial reproduction is an important mechanism; people tend to prefer those similar to themselves, so men tend to prefer other men (Kanter, 1977). Consequently, the presence of more women in elite positions should have positive impacts on women's career opportunities. Accordingly, in the corporate world, Kunze and Miller (2017) found a smaller gender gap in promotions at companies with more women as top managers. They concluded that increased gender balance in corporate management positively affects recruitment of women in lower ranks of organisations. In politics, a study on female role models showed that women politicians have an important motivating effect, especially on adolescent women who become more interested in and more motivated to participate in politics (Wolbrecht & Campbell, 2007).

In contrast, comparative political studies generally assume that same-gender preferences, whether held by men or women, do not play a substantial role in recruitment to the top. Another research stream holds that women managers in male-dominated organisations reproduce rather than challenge the gender hierarchy (Derks, Van Laar, & Ellemers, 2016). The argument is that the few women who make it to the top may choose to distance themselves from junior women because they feel a need to reduce their associations with less successful women in the organisation (Kanter, 1977). In other words, having a few additional women does not necessarily produce a mechanism of homosocial reproduction among women.

In a detailed comparative case study in this volume, Farida Jalalzai addresses the gatekeeping role of women in top elite positions who allocate resources to challenge the gender hierarchy. Jalalzai's study of two top politicians, German Prime Minister Angela Merkel and Brazilian President Dilma Ruosseff, demonstrates that female top politicians may indeed be important for recruitment of women to political office. Over time, both politicians have increased recruitment of women as members of their governments. These findings are not directly generalisable but yield material for reflection and further studies. They can be taken to support the thesis of peer recruitment: men recruit men, and more women help recruit more women. However, given the generally low representation of women in top political positions, an alternative hypothesis that women are recruited to balance gender representation is equally plausible. This study demonstrates that the promotion of gender balance in politics may also be advanced by committed persons at the top of institutions.

ELITES, ELITISM AND POPULISM

An aspect of the relationship between elites and the general population that has suddenly come into focus is the growing tensions created by populism as a prominent anti-elite movement. Scholars studying populism have given much attention to uncovering possible sources of the emergence of populism (e.g. Kaltwasser, Taggart, Espejo, & Ostiguy, 2017): Are they primarily economic, or are they rooted in cultural factors? Does populism have its roots in those left behind when capital and workplaces were exported from the western world to the global south and east? Or have the dynamics of cultural value changes affected hegemonic ideas of what constitutes a good society? The assumption that globalisation is a main cause of populism has gained a certain popularity and at least superficially seems plausible. However, it has been countered by several comparative studies demonstrating a lack of a clear correlation between economic problems and the rise of populism, as shown by Ivarsflaten as early as 2008 and supported by Norris and Inglehart (2016) nearly a decade later.

However, the interaction of culture and the economy is worth further reflection. Norris and Inglehart (2016) proposed a simple, effective model: as pluralist values rise around the world, what explains the present growth of populism is not stronger support for authoritarian values; instead, their decline has triggered a backlash and counter-mobilisation. Appealing as this model is, its underlying mechanisms might be conceived too simplistically. Many types of indirect connections are certainly at work, and the crucial point is not variations in perceptions of macro-economic measures, as tested and rejected by Ivarsflaten (2008). More recently, Norris and Inglehart (2019) nuanced their views to point out that authoritarian values are reinforced by the prevalence of economic changes, which have primarily affected the lifeworld of the working class and rural groups, causing experiences of social and economic insecurity and even fear.

In a comparative historical analysis in this volume, John Higley broadens the focus on the relationship between social fear and insecurity in working life. The meaning of economic factors as an explanation for populism has been discussed and generally rejected in the literature. In this volume, Ursula Hoffmann-Lange shows that the financial crisis in 2008 had negligible effects on support for democracy. Higley, however, locates economic effects differently and points to changes in employment types and work security for the general population, which have gradually deteriorated in the Western world. Drawing on long historical lines, Higley highlights present-day elites' inattention to securing participation in stable work for all citizens, pushing much of the population to the margins. These broad trends generate political alienation and subsequently resistance to foreigners and distrust in national elites. If these same elites show little concern for the problems of the common man, it will, in the long term, result in forceful demands for alternative, strong leadership promising immediate, efficient solutions – in one word, populism.

The problems of populism are discussed in this volume from a different angle by Marte Mangset, Fredrik Engelstad, Mari Teigen and Trygve Gulbrandsen. Their focus is neither on populist movements and their causes (the most common perspective in the literature) nor on the roles of elites as such. Instead, the authors consider the ways in which populism understands the relationship between elites and people, a topic given surprisingly little attention by researchers. The authors' main point is that even if populism is an expression of anti-elitism, it also has a deeply elitist requirement of strong, charismatic leadership. Populists tend to attack the elite as a unitary group – to be replaced with another, even narrower elite devoted to serving the people. However, populism's monist perception of the elite is surprisingly flexible. For Ernesto Laclau (2005), the concept of elites becomes an empty signifier; it may refer to not only political elites but also to media, cultural, artistic and bureaucratic elites and highly qualified experts. Populism, thus, thrives on simultaneously attacking elites as a unitary enemy of the people while making any selected group its main target. Insights from elite theory may illuminate this paradox. Despite considerable theoretical diversity in interpretations of elites, a common assumption in elite studies is the necessity of elite pluralism in democratic societies. Even classical elite theories rejecting democracy offer the germ of the possibility of elite pluralism. Discussions on elite integration and elite pluralism in elite theory shed light on what in populist elite critiques deserves attention and how populist ideological understandings of political leadership challenge democracy.

CONCLUDING REMARKS

The present volume of *Comparative Social Research* concentrates on political elites in democratic and not-so-democratic societies. In parallel, extensions are drawn to other groups, including other elite groups and the general population. Behind the choice of focus lies no intent to diminish the importance of elite pluralism and its complexities. The concentration on political elites, however, raises special questions about the legitimacy of elite power. Legitimacy is a core concern in democracy, but in the age of globalisation, it has inevitably become more diffuse and even opaque as elites and populations are linked in unexpected ways, as demonstrated in the present volume. Desires for meritocracy lead to more diverse institutional pathways and trajectories into elite positions; yet traditional structural obstacles such as gender, race and class continue to matter – although possibly in new ways. Even as this makes understanding elite relations more difficult, it necessitates more attention and analyses to evaluating elite power.

REFERENCES

Ambjörnsson, R. (1996). *Mitt förnamn är Ronny*. [*My first name is Ronny*.] Stockholm, Sweden: Bonnier Alba.

Aron, R. (1950). Social structure and the ruling class: Part 2. *British Journal of Sociology, 1*(2), 126–143.

Bachrach, P. (1969). *The theory of democratic elitism*. London: University of London Press.

Best, H., & Higley, J. (Eds.). (2010). *Democratic elitism: New theoretical and comparative perspectives*. Leiden, The Netherlands: Brill.

Bottomore, T. (1966). *Elites and society*. Harmondsworth: Penguin.

Bourdieu, P. (1992). *The logic of practice*. Stanford, CA: Stanford University Press.

Bourdieu, P. (1998). *The state nobility. Elite schools in the field of power*. Stanford, CA: Stanford University Press.

Bourdieu, P. (1999). The contradictions of inheritance. In P. Bourdieu et al. (Eds.), *The weight of the world: Social suffering in contemporary society* (511). Cambridge: Polity Press.

Bourdieu, P., & Passeron, J.-C. (1990). *Reproduction in education, society and culture*. London: Sage.

Burton, M., & Higley, J. (1987). Elite settlements. *American Sociological Review, 52*, 295–307.

Cotta, M. (2012). Political elites and a policy in the making. The case of the EU. *Historical Social Research, 37*, 167–192.

Cotta, M. (2014). Facing the crisis: The European elite system's changing geometry. In H. Best & J. Higley (Eds.), *Political elites in the transatlantic crisis* (pp. 58–80). New York, NY: Palgrave Macmillan.

Derks, B., Van Laar, C., & Ellemers, N. (2016). The queen bee phenomenon: Why women leaders distance themselves from junior women. *The Leadership Quarterly, 27*, 456–469. http://dx.doi.org/10.1016/j.leaqua.2015.12.007

Diamond, L. (2016). *In search of democracy*. Abingdon, UK: Routledge.

Engelstad, F. (2018). Elite compromise as a mode of institutional change: The United States and Norway compared. In F. Engelstad, C. Holst & G. C. Aakvaag (Eds.), *Democratic state and democratic society* (pp. 363–3889). Warsaw, Poland: De Gruyter Open.

Eribon, D. (2013). *Returning to Reims*. Cambridge, MA: MIT Press.

Fric, P., Lengyel, G., Pakulski, J., & Somolányi, S. (2014). Central European elites in the crisis. In H. Best & J. Higley (Eds.), *Political elites in the transatlantic crisis* (pp. 81–100). New York, NY: Palgrave Macmillan.

Gulbrandsen, T. (2019). *Elites in an egalitarian society: Support for the Nordic model*. London: Palgrave Macmillan.

Gulbrandsen, T., & Engelstad, F. (2005). Elite consensus on the Norwegian welfare state model. *West European Politics, 28*(4), 899–919.

Higley, J., & Burton, M. (2006). *Elite foundations of liberal democracy*. Lanham, MD: Rowman & Littlefield.

Hoffmann-Lange, U. (1988). Germany: Twentieth-century turning points. In M. Dogan & J. Higley (Eds.), *Elites, crises and the origins of elites* (pp. 169–188). Lanham, MD: Rowman & Littlefield.

Ivarsflaten, E. (2008). What unites right-wing populists in Western Europe? Reexamining grievance mobilization in seven successful cases. *Comparative Political Studies, 41*, 3–23.

Kahn, S. (2011). *Privilege: The making of an adolescent elite at St. Paul's School*. Princeton, NJ: Princeton University Press.

Kaltwasser, C. R., Taggart, P. Espejo, P. O., & Ostiguy, P. (2017). (Eds.), *The Oxford handbook of populism*. Oxford: Oxford University Press

Kanter, R. (1977). *Men and women of the corporation*. New York, NY: Basic Books.

Kindt, K. T. (2013). *Unintentional democrats. Independent unions in post-Mubarak Egypt*. M.A. thesis, Department of Sociology and Human Geography. University of Oslo, Oslo. Retrieved from https://www.duo.uio.no/bitstream/handle/10852/38177/KRISTIANTAKVAMKINDT.pdf?sequence=1

Kunze, A., & Miller, A. R. (2017). Women helping women? Evidence from private-sector data on workplace hierarchies. *Review of Economics and Statistics, 99*, 769–775. https://doi:10.1162/REST_a_00668

Laclau, E. (2005). *On populist reason*. London, UK: Verso.

Levitsky, S., & Ziblatt, D. (2018). *How democracies die*. New York, NY: Broadway Books.

Lipset, S. M. (1959). Some social requisites of democracy: Economic development and political legitimacy. *American Political Science Review, 53*, 69–105.

Mangset, M., Maxwell, C., & van Zanten, A. (2017). Knowledge, dispositions and skills: The socialization and training of elites. *Journal of Education and Work, 30*(2), 123–129.

Merton, R. K. (1957). Continuities in the theory of reference groups and social structure. In R. K. Merton (Ed.), *Social theory and social structure* (pp. 281–386). Glencoe, IL: The Free Press.

Michels, R. (1959 [1911]). *Political parties*. New York, NY: Dover.

Mills, C.W. (1956). *The power elite*. Oxford, UK: Oxford University Press.

Norris, P., & Inglehart, R. (2016). *Trump, Brexit and the rise of populism. Economic have-nots and cultural backlash.* Faculty Research Working Paper Series. Cambridge, MA: Harvard Kennedy School.

Norris, P., & Inglehart, R. (2019). *Cultural backlash. Trump, Brexit and authoritarian populism.* Cambridge: Cambridge University Press. Retrieved from https://www.cambridge.org/core/books/cultural-backlash/3C7CB32722C7BB8B19A0FC005CAFD02B

Putnam, R. (1993). *How democracy works.* Princeton, NJ: Princeton University Press.

Reay, D., Crozier, G., & Clayton, J. (2009). 'Strangers in paradise'? Working-class students in elite universities. *Sociology, 43*(6), 1103–1121.

Schmitter, P. C. (2018). Democratization: The role of elites. In: H. Best & J. Higley (Eds.), *The Palgrave handbook of political elites* (pp. 593–610). New York, NY: Palgrave Macmillan.

Van Zanten, A. (Ed.). (2018). *Elites in education.* London, UK: Routledge.

Wolbrecht, C., & Campbell, D. E. (2007). Leading by example: Female members of parliament as political role models. *American Journal of Political Science, 51,* 921–939. https://doi.org/10.1111/j.1540-5907.2007.00289.x

PART I

POLITICAL ELITES
AND POPULATIONS

ELITE SURVIVAL AND THE ARAB SPRING: THE CASES OF TUNISIA AND EGYPT

Stig Stenslie and Kjetil Selvik

ABSTRACT

The chapter compares the survival of old regime elites in Tunisia and Egypt after the 2011 uprisings and analyses its enabling factors. Although democracy progressed in Tunisia and collapsed in Egypt, the countries show similarities in the old elite's ability to survive the Arab Spring. In both cases, the popular uprisings resulted in the type of elite circulation that John Higley and György Lengyel refer to as 'quasi-replacement circulation', which is sudden and coerced, but narrow and shallow. To account for this converging outcome, the chapter foregrounds the instability, economic decline and information uncertainty in the countries post-uprising and the navigating resources, which the old elites possessed. The roots of the quasi-replacement circulation are traced to the old elites' privileged access to money, network, the media and, for Egypt, external support. Only parts of the structures of authority in a political regime are formal. The findings show the importance of evaluating regime change in a broader view than the formal institutional set-up. In Tunisia and Egypt, the informal structures of the anciens régimes *survived – so did the old regime elites.*

Keywords: Elite survival; regime change; revolution; Arab uprisings; Tunisia; Egypt

INTRODUCTION

The so-called Arab Spring triggered a euphoria of optimism, and in hindsight, it is obvious that many academics and observers grossly exaggerated the consequences of the uprisings that shook the Arab world in the spring of 2011.

Elites and People: Challenges to Democracy
Comparative Social Research, Volume 34, 17–34
Copyright © 2019 by Emerald Publishing Limited
All rights of reproduction in any form reserved
ISSN: 0195-6310/doi:10.1108/S0195-631020190000034002

Mark Wasserman (1993, p. 71) believes this is a general trend, which applies to observers of revolutions. Often, the overthrow of a political system does not lead to deep transformations. The society and the economy go on as before. A revolution may seem like a catalyst for more long-term and subtle changes, but it is difficult to isolate the changes that the revolution led to and those that would have happened anyway. Also, the political consequences are often exaggerated. Did the revolution actually destroy the ruling elites associated with the old regime? To what extent did the new elite and the new regime change the way in which the country is governed? Have the people become more involved in the governance?

The fate of the old rulers is an overlooked topic in the history of revolutions, with a few exceptions: Albert Soboul (1989, p. 15) finds, in his study of the French Revolution 1789–1799 that aimed at destroying the formerly dominant class, that a 'great many nobles lived through the revolution without coming to much harm and kept their property intact'. Wasserman (1993, p. 71), emphasising the persistence of the old elite in revolutionary Mexico 1910–1940, makes a similar observation:

> the old elite ... survived through a combination of the weakness of the revolutionary regime ..., the growing compatibility of economic and political interests with the emerging new elite, and the considerable skills and sound strategies of its own members.

Likewise, parts of the elite survived the fall of Communism in Eastern Europe in the late 1980s/early 1990s, and re-established themselves in different important sectors. Dobrinka Kostova (2012, p. 166) notes with reference to post-Communism Bulgaria that

> [...] part of the old elite has merged with the newly arising one and is managing to survive, transfer from one sphere to another and adopt to the new structures and institutions.

These studies indicate that a revolution is not necessarily a 'clean break' with the past, where the old elite is replaced by a new one. The old elite, or parts of this elite, might survive and thrive under the new regime. This is a useful lesson for all who strive to understand regime changes in the Middle East and North Africa in the wake of the Arab uprisings. A study of elite survival could help shed light on the nature of these changes, their depth and breadth and help us understand why the uprisings took the direction they took. All countries in the Arab world witnessed protests and unrest but to varying degrees and with very different consequences. The most troubled countries experienced three different outcomes: In Syria and Bahrain, the uprising was brutally suppressed by the sitting regime, not least thanks to military support from external powers. In Libya and Yemen, the uprisings led to total collapse, and no new elite has succeeded in consolidating power in the vacuum that arose after the fall of the old regime. In Tunisia and Egypt, revolutionary forces toppled the regimes of Ben Ali and Hosni Mubarak, respectively, and new regimes were eventually established. Accordingly, Egypt and Tunisia are the interesting cases for studying the survival of the *anciens régimes'* elites.

It is important to emphasise that the Arab uprisings produced very different results in Tunisia and Egypt. With regard to democratic development, Tunisia has unarguably progressed while Egypt has moved in the opposite direction. Despite the huge differences, this chapter observes parallels concerning the elites' ability to reproduce themselves. This makes it interesting to try to understand how. To study the degree of elite survival, we will map and compare the political elite before and after the Arab uprisings. It is not possible to present a comprehensive account within the chapter's scope so we will focus on main features such as the relative strength of different elite groups and the composition of the 'inner circle'. We shall compare the resources that the old elite had privileged access to, maintained and used to reactivate core elements of its pre-2011 power basis: money, networks, media and external support.

The chapter starts with a brief theoretical perspective that is useful for the further discussion of the rise and fall, and eventual re-emergence of elites in the cases of Tunisia and Egypt.

TYPES OF ELITE CIRCULATION

A key topic within elite research is 'the rise and fall of elites' (Gulbrandsen, 2017, p. 2). The history of the Middle East and North Africa is indeed a history about the constant rise and fall of elites – or dynasties, brilliantly described by the medieval Arab scholar Ibn Khaldun (2015/1377), who formulated an early version of the theory of circulation of elites. Vilfredo Pareto (1963/1916) was concerned with the same issue. He introduced the concept of 'elite circulation', which is a dialectical theory of an endless competition between elites with one elite group replacing another repeatedly over time.

More recently, based on in-depth studies of the replacement of the old Communist elites by new elites in Eastern Europe in the late 1980s/early 1990s, John Higley and György Lengyel have made important contributions to our theoretical understanding of elite circulation. Higley and Lengyel (2000) argue that elite circulation might take different patterns, with regard to, first, its *scope*, which is the horizontal range of the positions affected and the vertical depth from which those entering elite positions come, and, second, its *mode*, which is the speed and manner in which it occurs (p. 4). The scope of circulation can be 'wide and deep' or 'narrow and shallow', while its mode can be 'gradual and peaceful' or 'sudden and coerced' (Higley & Lengyel, 2000, pp. 4–5).

On the basis of these dichotomies, Higley and Lengyel derive four types of elite circulation: the first is 'classic circulation', which is gradual and peaceful, wide and deep. This type of elite circulation is essential for elite renewal, and thus stable and effective governance. The second is 'reproduction circulation', which is gradual and peaceful but narrow and shallow. Through this type of circulation, the elite is preserving its control of central power positions. The third is 'replacement circulation', which is sudden and coerced, wide and deep. This type of wholesale replacement of an old kind of elite might be the outcome of coups or revolutions. The fourth, and final, is 'quasi-replacement circulation', which is sudden and coerced, but narrow and shallow (Table 1). This type of circulation is the result of a dramatic regime change in which parts of the elite associated with the old regime manage to survive (Higley & Lengyel, 2000, pp. 5–6).

Table 1.   Patterns of Elite Circulation (Higley & Lengyel, 2000, p. 5).

		SCOPE	
		Wide and Deep	*Narrow and Shallow*
MODE	*Gradual and Peaceful*	Classic circulation	Reproduction circulation
	Sudden and Coerced	Replacement circulation	Quasi-replacement circulation

THE CASE OF TUNISIA

Tunisia was the birthplace of the Arab Spring and is the country that has fared best in its aftermath. Ben Ali's fall on 14 January 2011, after 23 years in power, set off a democratic transition. A constituent assembly elected on 23 October 2011 voted a new constitution on 26 January 2014, overcoming deep political divisions. It created a semi-presidential ruling system based on free elections, fundamental human rights and the separation of powers. The constitution guarantees personal and public freedoms and defines Tunisia as 'a civil state based on citizenship, the will of the people, and the supremacy of law' (Tunisia's Constitution of 2014). Underneath this success lay an elite compromise between the Islamist al-Nahda party that had won the largest share of votes in the constituent assembly election (37 per cent, gaining 89 out of 217 seats) and the secular-leaning coalition Nidaa Tounes. Led by Tunisia's president, Beji Caid Essebsi, Nidaa Tounes united opponents of al-Nahda from leftist revolutionary forces to members of the old elite.

Pre-Arab Spring

The pre-revolutionary elite had grown out of Tunisia's two regimes after independence, Habib Bourguiba's party-state (1956–1987) and Ben Ali's police state (1987–2011). The first was built on a revolutionary break with the past that profoundly upset the pre-existing elite configurations. The second left more room for continuity because it presented itself as a reformist continuation of the first. Habib Bourguiba came to power as the leader of the Neo Destour party that broke with traditional elites and spearheaded the battle for independence. Its cadres were French-educated and shared a secular modernising vision that pitted it against the religious class (Henry, 2017). Geographically, the majority originated from the Eastern part of the Mediterranean coast. Contrary to strongmen in other Arab republics, such as Gamal Abdel Nasser in Egypt, Bourguiba was a civilian and distrusted the military. Like his contemporaries, on the other hand, he pursued a state-led, temporarily socialist, development model that left little room for private economic actors. The elite resided in the state bureaucracy, the ruling party apparatus and corporatist organisations such as the General Union of Tunisian Workers (UGTT) and the Tunisian Union of Industrialists, Merchants and Artisans (UTICA; Erdle, 2004, pp. 207–236).

Ben Ali staged a medical coup against Bourguiba in 1987, whose health problems raised concern in the elite about the president's ability to lead – in a context of economic crisis. The new president was of military background and had built his networks and career in the secret police and the Ministry of Interior. Ben Ali had served as Director General of national security in two periods and was Interior Minister when assigned the premiership in 1987. He lacked a genuine power base in the ruling party. Ben Ali tried liberalisation of the regime as a tactic to win popular support, but retreated in 1989 when the Islamist movement showed its strength in national elections. He doubled down on networks in the security apparatus for the twin purpose of quelling criticism from Islamists and strengthening his position vis-à-vis the party elite, which dominated the state bureaucracy.

Ben Ali used his loyal cohorts in the security services to create a person-dominated regime where power laid in his personal entourage of political advisors, close friends and relatives. He recruited technocrats to leading positions in the palace, creating a parallel government that ruled outside the formal political institutions. Steffen Erdle (2004) identified security experts, economic experts and administrative experts as the main players in the core elite. Despite his background, Ben Ali did not entrust most power to the officer corps. A key reason was Interior Minister 'Abd Allah Qallal's announcement in May 1991 – probably staged – that he had discovered an Islamist military coup plot (Nassif, 2015). The military lost out in the internal regime competition with the secret service and the police. When the popular protests of the 2011 uprising broke out, it did not come to the president's rescue.

Accelerating a trend begun towards the end of Bourguiba's rule, Ben Ali liberalised the economy in response to the economic crisis. This created opportunity for a rising group of business elites with connections to the president. The number one benefactor was the family of his second wife, Layla al-Tarablusi, who became the symbol of the growing corruption. As per a World Bank study, 662 firms belonging to the Ben Ali family were confiscated in the aftermath of the 2011 uprising (Rijkers, Freund, & Nucifora, 2017). Other families gained sector-based prominence under coverage of the Tarablusi-Ben Ali superstructure. Some entered politics through organisations representing the private sector, such as UTICA, led by the wealthy textile manufacturer Hadi Jilani and the Institute Arabe des Chefs d'Entreprises, run by Shakib Nuira (Erdle, 2004).

Post-Arab Spring

The 2011 uprising brought new political actors to power and changed the rules of the game for Tunisia's elites. The name of the game was no longer to position oneself for influence in a ruling party or in the proximity of a dictator, but to compete for votes in democratic elections. This opened for the rise of elites that had been the regime opposition under Ben Ali's opposition and enjoyed popular credibility. First and foremost, the al-Nahda party capitalised on its decades-long resistance to oppression and patient endeavours to Islamise society from below. Leftist and liberal parties also had considerable appeal in society. After the Constituent Assembly election, a tri-party government was formed including al-Nahda, the secular social-democratic Ettakatol and the liberal Congress for the Republic.

However, the uprising did not uproot the old elite profoundly. The regime change was not accompanied by a social revolution. As Asef Bayat argues, the swift and relatively peaceful power shifts in 2011 Egypt and Tunisia are better described by the term 'refolution'. The civic-inspired popular movements that enforced them sought to neither change society's class structure nor capture the state. They pushed for reforms in the existing institutions and left the state to the politicians, relying on the established counter-elite to lead the change. Consequently, Bayat explains,

the possibility of genuine transformation through systematic reforms and social pacts will depend on the perpetual mobilization and vigilance of social organizations – popular layers, civil associations, trade unions, social movements, political parties – exerting constant pressure. Otherwise, 'revolutions' carry the constant danger of counter-revolutionary restoration, precisely because the revolution has not made it into the key institutions of state power. (Bayat, 2013, p. 53)

Following the uprising, the fate of individuals associated with the old regime became a matter of political dispute. Activists pressed for the prosecution of former regime officials and their exclusion from politics, but faced resistance from the state administration and the interim government led by Beji Caid Essebsi. Some key figures of Ben Ali's repressive apparatus were tried before military courts. The head of the presidential guard, 'Ali Sariati, the Minister of Defence, Ridha Qarira and former Interior Ministers Rafiq Bi-l Hajj Kadhim and 'Abd Allah Qallal received prison sentences. However, the prosecution of old elite members did not go deep. While the old ruling party, the Democratic Constitutional Rally, known by its French acronym RCD, was disbanded, most of its leaders were authorised to leave the country. The military tribunals tried 23 security officials for crimes against civilians during the uprising. But in parallel, Essebsi reappointed former security officials to the Ministry of Interior (Boubekeur, 2016, pp. 112–113). In terms of electoral participation, an agreement was reached to exclude regime officials having served in the past 10 years. It concerned approximately 8,000 individuals in the 2011 election (Gobe, 2016).

As the strongest political party coming out of the 2011 uprising, al-Nahda's position vis-à-vis the old elites was of importance. Al-Nahda chose a careful approach, eschewing radicalism, to preserve its gains and protect against a counter-revolution. It had burned its fingers the last time it participated in elections in 1989, when success at the ballots lead to repression, and drawn lessons from similar Muslim Brothers' setbacks across the region – from the Islamic Salvation Front in Algeria in the early 1990s to Hamas in Palestine in 2006. The 2013 military coup against Muhammad Mursi's government in Egypt further strengthened its belief in the necessity of compromise and prudence. As Amel Boubekeur (2016) has described, al-Nahda's relation with the old elite took the form of a 'bargained competition'. The two entered negotiations and, from 2014, a power sharing arrangement despite rivalry and mutual distrust.

The old elites' hand was strengthened in this competition by polarisation along the Islamist–secularist divide. During the years of the al-Nahda-led Troika Government, tensions grew high over the role of Islam in the constitution, the rights and position of women and the 2013 assassination of two secular-left political activists. Civil society and secular-left opposition parties mobilised against the Islamists on these issues. The result was a triangular conflict constellation that tied al-Nahda's hands and counterworked political reform.

Tunisia has a vibrant civil society that serves as a veritable check on the government. Organisations like the labour union (UGTT), the Tunisian National Order of Lawyers, the Tunisian Human Rights League, the Tunisian Association of Democratic Women and the National Syndicate of Tunisian Journalists were pillars of the 2011 uprising. With the unprecedented freedom of organisation and expression that came with Ben Ali's fall, the non-governmental organisation (NGO) sector gained in sophistication and strength. It pushes for genuine democratic development and accountability for crimes committed in the past. However, with al-Nahda in government, many secular-leaning activists shifted attention from the old regime elites to the perceived Islamist danger. In the political realm, Essebsi took advantage of the anti-al-Nahda mood to create Nidaa Tounes as a platform for secular forces. It brought together socialists, leftists, liberals, environmentalists and, crucially, members of the old regime ruling party. From 2014, when a draft law that had suggested excluding former RCD members from political participation was abandoned, the latter group started to take over leadership positions in the party (Bobin & Haddad, 2018).

Nidaa Tounes became the biggest party in the 2014 elections, with 85 against al-Nahda's 69 seats. The latter agreed to support a Nidaa Tounes-led government in exchange for continued influence in the state apparatus and one of two vice presidential posts. Al-Nahda became a loyal collaborator to a government that had an old regime flavour and started to restrict civil liberties (Boukhars, 2017). When Salafi-inspired gunmen attacked the Bardo National Museum on 18 March 2015, killing 22 people, the government reacted by introducing a new counter-terrorism law that gave security forces wide authorities. President Essebsi also seized the opportunity to present a 'reconciliation law' which, when adopted in September 2017, would give impunity to civil servants implicated in corruption under Ben Ali and allow them to return to positions of power.

Inside Nidaa Tounes, President Essebsi was promoting his son Hafidh Essebsi who became national secretary in charge of the executive administration in 2016. Hafidh spearheaded the old elite's influence in the party, supported by former secretary general of the RCD, Muhammad Ghariani. Following a September 2017 cabinet reshuffle, the old elite put its unmistakable mark on the government. According to *Le Monde*, 18 out of 43 of the nominated ministers and secretaries of state – 40 per cent – had been ministers, RCD party officials or affiliates under Ben Ali (Bobin & Haddad, 2018). The Minister of Education Hatim bin Salam and the Minister of Finance Ridha Shalghum were two prominent examples. They had held the exact same positions before the uprising.

THE CASE OF EGYPT

Following the ousting of Tunisian president Ben Ali after mass protests, Egypt was the next country to witness an uprising. It began on 25 January 2011 and took place across all of Egypt. On 11 February 2011, President Hosni Mubarak's resignation was announced. Egypt was set for a turbulent ride: The Supreme Council of Egyptian Armed Forces (SCAF) was entrusted with the temporary leadership of the country. Then, on 30 June 2012, Muhammad Mursi of the Muslim Brotherhood was sworn in as Egypt's first democratically elected president. On 3 July 2013, the Minister of Defence, General 'Abd al-Fattah al-Sisi, deposed Mursi. Sisi was sworn into office as President of Egypt on 8 June 2014.

Pre-Arab Spring

Hazem Kandil (2012) read the deposition of Mubarak, as when it happened seemed dramatic and abrupt, as yet another episode in the never-ending power struggle between the three elite groups that have dominated Egypt's authoritarian regime: 'soldiers' (the military), 'spies' (the security services) and 'statesmen' (the government). This is a particularly helpful framework for understanding elite politics in Egypt, and Kandil shows how the complex and changing relationship between these three elite groups has defined Egyptian politics ever since the revolution of 1952 – a watershed in Egyptian politics. The revolution ended the monarchy, and brought the Free Officers and eventually Gamal Abdel Nasser to power.

Based on a study of the power of, and relationship between, the three mentioned elite groups, Kandil divides Egypt's political history since the revolution into three epochs: The first is the 'militarist state' from the 1950s to the early 1970s, under the Free Officers, which ruled with the support of the military cadres. The second era is 'police state' from the late 1970s to the 90s, where the interior ministers and their ever-expanding internal security apparatus gained influence in the political life at the expense of the military. The third epoch is the 'capitalist state' in the 2000s when business tycoons became among the most powerful elite groups in Egyptian politics (Roll, 2013, p. 5).

Economic liberalisation gave private companies a greater role in the Egyptian economy and a significant concentration of capital was taking place. The result was that several sectors of the Egyptian economy towards the end of Mubarak's rule were totally dominated by individual private companies. As examples, the steel sector was monopolised by Ezz Industries, the automotive production by Ghabbour Auto and the food sector by Juhayna Food (Roll, 2013, p. 8). A number of business tycoons were given key ministerial positions, among them Rashid Muhammad Rashid and Muhammad Mansur, and positions in parliament and the ruling National Democratic Party (NDP), such as Ahmad 'Izz. Mubarak's NDP served as an effective nationwide system for distributing benefits in exchange for political support, which was especially important for winning support from the rural areas. It welcomed wealthy individuals to its ranks. Other businesspersons avoided direct political involvement, but could nevertheless exercise political influence and secure their interests through business partnership with leading politicians and ownership in the media sector. Among those with significant informal influence were the Coptic Sawiris, Egypt's richest. In addition, business families gained influence under Mubarak as a result of Gamal Mubarak being groomed as his father's successor from the late 1990s. Unlike his father, Sadat and

Nasir, Gamal was a civilian – and he had no reliable power base in the military. He, therefore, needed support from other actors, and the business elite was an ideal ally. The relationship between Gamal and the business elite was a typical marriage of convenience; the former got a much-needed political support base, while the latter got a powerful political alliance that could promote their financial interests. Several businesspersons connected to Gamal were awarded government positions (Roll, 2013, p. 9; Abdelnasser, 2004).

If we move from elite groups to the level of individuals, at the end of Mubarak's regime, the president's inner circle, or the core of the political elite relevant, included the following prominent persons: On the informal side, his wife, Egypt's 'first lady' Suzanne, along with his sons Gamal and Ala'. On the technocratic side, the closest advisors for the president were Ahmad Abu-al Ghayt, Foreign Minister; Ahmad Nazif, Prime Minister; Husayn Tantawi, Minister of Defence and Military Production; 'Umar Sulayman, Intelligence Chief; and Habib al-'Adli, Minister of Interior. On the political side, Safwat Sharif, General Secretary of the NDP and Minister of Information and Kamal al-Shazli, NDP Vice-General Secretary (Abdelnasser, 2004, p. 119).

Post-Arab Spring

On 11 February 2011, Hosni Mubarak stepped down as the President of Egypt following massive demonstrations. The Egyptians did not only protest against oppression and despotism, but also against social injustice and corruption. In particular, the masses' anger was directed at the 'fat cats', the businessmen who had profited from privatisation and ties to the political leadership. When unrest broke out, cracks within the elite soon came to the surface. Lack of unity in the elite arguably contributed to the fall of the Mubarak regime. Many state elites, and especially the generals, were frustrated that they had been politically and economically marginalised in favour of the business actors. They reacted negatively to the growing power of the civilian Gamal Mubarak. When the protesters gathered in Tahrir Square, the army portrayed itself as a 'neutral actor' and failed to save Mubarak and his inner circle. The generals, thus, arguably helped create a situation they could use to renegotiate the existing power distribution between Egypt's political elites for their own benefit (Kandil, 2012, p. 245).

Immediately after Mubarak left office, SCAF took temporary leadership of the country. The military kept existing formal state structures intact and largely retained key personnel, including in the military and the domestic security apparatus. Only Mubarak, his family and some members of his innermost circle were charged with abuse of power and corruption. Within a few years, the leaders were also pardoned, including Hosni Mubarak, his sons Gamal and Ala', and Habib al-'Adli (*The Guardian* 2015). Since being released in 2015, Gamal and Ala' have reportedly become more popular among the Egyptians, contrary to Sisi (Meky, 2017). Feeling threatened by the increasingly public profile of the brothers, the president ensured that they were arrested again in September 2015 (*Fanack,* 2017). The comeback of the Mubarak brothers still illustrates the persistence of old regime elites, even the most discredited.

A presidential election was held in Egypt in two rounds in 2012. The Muslim Brotherhood's candidate, Muhammed Mursi, won the presidential election. While Mursi sought to marginalise and exclude as much of the NDP as possible, he carefully avoided confrontation with the security apparatus and the military. Probably, the generals initially considered it opportune that Egypt had a civilian government under a friendly-minded Brotherhood so that they could retain their political influence and economic interests while at the same time not being blamed for unpopular political decisions (Roll, 2013, p. 5). The Brotherhood, in turn, regarded the military as both a powerful ally and a useful tool for retaining power. Several top leaders in the military and security establishment were deposed under Mursi, among these Defence Minister Husayn Tantawi and Intelligence Chief Murad Mawafi. However, these moves were probably agreed in advance by Mursi and the general of the SCAF, and the latter could control the appointment of new military leaders (Kandil, 2012, p. 246). Among these were Sisi, who took over as defence minister. Some observers believed that Sisi had Islamic sympathies, and considered him the hand of the Muslim Brothers (Roll, 2015, p. 24). This was far from the truth. The military teamed up with the judiciary, businessmen and the media to undermine and eventually overthrow Mursi's Government.

When taking power, Sisi recruited many Mubarak-era politicians in his government. As many as 11 out of 34 cabinet ministers were veterans of Mubarak's regime (Hauslohner, 2013). Critics referred to them as *feloul*, that is, 'remnants' from the Mubarak-era. The military leadership had replaced the Mubarak family at the apex of the patronage system.

After Sisi came to power, there has been significant within-regime turbulence, making it difficult to identify his very closest supporters. His former closest allies, Muhammad Farid al-Tuhami, former head of intelligence, and Mahmud Hijazi, former Chief of Staff of the Egyptian Armed Forces and Sisi's in-law (Sisi's son is married to Hijazi's daughter), have both been pushed out of the innermost circle (*Mada Masr,* 2017; *Middle East Observer,* 2017a; *Middle East Monitor,* 2014). Moreover, Sidqi Subhi was removed as defence minister in June (*Egypt Independent,* 2018). Now, Sisi's immediate sphere seemed to be made up of 'Abbas Kamil, the President's Chief Of Staff; Khalid Fawzy, Head of the General Intelligence; Muhammad Sa'id al-Assar, Minister Of Military Production, who, according to some sources, serves as acting prime minister alongside Prime Minister Sharif Isma'il; Muhammad Faraj al-Shahat, Director Of Military Intelligence; and newly appointed Defence Minister Muhammad Ahmad Zaki. Sisi's sons are also part of his inner circle. Mahmud and Hassan have been appointed to key roles in General Intelligence (*Marsad,* 2018), while Mustafa is an officer in the important oversight-body, the Administrative Control Authority (*Middle East Observer,* 2017b).

While Mubarak's core elite included generals, security officials, technocrats, politicians and businessmen, the elite around President Sisi is drawn almost exclusively from the military and the General Intelligence. Like Nasser, Sadat and Mubarak, Sisi has moved the centre of gravity of his repressive apparatus to General Intelligence, thus extending the intelligence over both the military and civilians. The business tycoons that had joined the military and intelligence elites in the 1990s were never able to establish control over the deep state. They, therefore, fell victim to it post-2011. Consequently, the core elite in Egypt has both shrunk in size and increased its power (*Middle East Eye*, 2015; Roll, 2015, p. 37; Email correspondence with Robert Springborg January–February and October 2018).

THE TWO CASES COMPARED

Although the differences between Tunisia and Egypt are legion – and democratic progress has only been recorded in the first – the above country analyses show similarities in the old regime elites' ability to survive the Arab Spring. To account for this converging outcome, one must take into consideration the post-uprising context and the elites' survival strategies. Important parallels exist between the cases in both respects. Moreover, one must adopt a broader view of a political regime than a narrow focus on the formal institutional set-up. David Easton conceived of a regime as a set of constraints on political interaction that may be broken down into values, norms and structures of authority (Easton, 1965, p. 193). Only part of the structures of authority is formal. This is particularly true in the Middle East, where regimes rule trough informal networks and mechanisms of patronage (Selvik & Stenslie, 2011). Regime change alters the system of government as defined in a country's constitution. It transforms the formal distribution of authority, but not necessarily the informal power sources.

The 2011 uprisings changed the rules of the political game in Tunisia and Egypt and provoked a sudden reshuffle of elites. At the same time, they created conditions under which the elites could capitalise on resources accumulated under the previous ruling systems. The post-uprising context was marked by instability, economic decline and information uncertainty. To start with, the weakening of the central power created a security vacuum where ordinary citizens began to feel unsafe. Street violence increased dramatically in Egypt and, in Tunisia, the 2013 political assassinations had a chilling effect. Large-scale terrorist attacks occurred in both countries. Consequently, the economic situation deteriorated sharply. Egypt went into recession and Tunisia's GDP/capita decreased. Investors flew, unemployment rates soared and the poverty increased. Moreover, the development of new media technologies created a confusing and combustible information flow. Rapidly circulating images, revelations, rumours and accusations opened avenues for manipulation and added to the transitional uncertainty.

For the sake of navigating in this context, the old regime elite had the benefit of three essential power resources.

First, it had the money, as the accumulation of wealth under Ben Ali and Mubarak had been contingent on proximity to the ruler. The weight of capital increased as the transition progressed and Tunisia and Egypt grew ever more dependent on new investments. Economic decline fuelled popular disillusionment with the uprising and opened a room for old elites to attack the transitional governments and present themselves as the alternative. In Tunisia, the drift was visible in the 2015–2017 debate over the 'reconciliation law'. Opponents of the 'reconciliation' initiative, a coalition of civil society activists, anti-corruption groups and the parliament-launched independent truth and dignity commission, argued that it blocked movement toward transitional justice by granting amnesty to public officials involved in corruption during the previous regime (The International Center for Transitional Justice, 2017). Proponents responded that the hunt for corrupt agents of the past was feeding investor uncertainty and hindering economic growth (*The Guardian,* 2017). It was the latter group that eventually prevailed.

The new regime's dependency on the old economic elite is also clearly illustrated in Egypt. SCAF, while taking power after Mubarak's fall, initiated investigation against several members of the business elite, who were among the most hated members of the old regime. Nevertheless, they had little to fear. Only four members of the 21 richest Egyptian families were sentenced to prison, Rashid Muhammad Rashid, Ahmad al Maghribi, Husayn Salim and Ahmed 'Izz, respectively (Roll, 2013, pp. 10–11). The latter was sentenced to more than 30 years for corruption, but he was soon released on bail.

Second, the old regime elite had well-founded networks, created by the elaborate patronage systems of the old regimes. Ben Ali and Mubarak used patron–client ties to mobilise political support by handing out 'privileges'. The networks also served as levers of corruption with investors linked with politicians and state officials in murky business deals (Heydemann, 2004). The most powerful networks span around security officials. After the uprisings, vested interests stood in the way of public sector reform and the lack of reform made corruption networks possible to preserve. The weight of security networks also grew with the spread of instability and terrorism. According to Yezid Sayegh (2016), Tunisia's 'security sector – the various police forces, internal security agencies and customs branches under the control of the ministry of interior – has resisted all subsequent attempts to restructure or reform it. The ministry is run by shadowy networks of officials and competing police unions that act as clientilistic 'lobbies' or 'clans' working for their own separate interests'. The same is true in Egypt, where Sisi's inner circle is totally dominated by the military and now by General Intelligence. Also other patron-client networks of the Mubarak-era have been fully reactivated under Sisi. The network of the now forbidden National Democratic Party, serves as a good example. Former members who helped running the party's large patron-client network have partly reactivated themselves, partly been reactivated, especially in the Egyptian countryside, where local notables with money and contacts distribute goods in exchange for political support for Sisi. Like Mubarak, Sisi understands that the support of the countryside is key to retaining power in Egypt and that it is crucial to team up with local elite figures (Fick, 2014).

Third, the old regime elite had strong influence in the media. Investors that had benefitted from Ben Ali and Mubarak's licensing of private TV stations in the 2000s were able to uphold their sector dominance after the uprising. The high costs of running a TV channel put the old 'networks of privilege' in a comparatively favourable position. The media often played a destructive role, fanning rumours, inciting hatred against political adversaries and fuelling divisive and demonising narratives (Lynch, 2015). The media campaigns against al-Mursi's Islamist government in Egypt and the al-Nahda-led Troika in Tunisia were particularly harsh. Media-driven polarisation along the Islamist-secularist divide opened a room for old elites to re-enter the political game. The old elites presented themselves as the solution to the poor economic situation, the deteriorating security situation and the Islamist threat. In Tunisia, polarising discourse often emanates from TV and radio commentators knows as *chroniqueurs* who argue with invited guests and turn up the heat in political talk shows. Several prominent *chroniqueurs* were part of Ben Ali's propaganda machine in the past (*Nawaat* 2016). Private investors own the two most-viewed TV stations in Tunisia – *Elhiwar Ettounsi* and *Nessma* – and most of the radio stations. Many made their fortunes in the shadow of Ben Ali's regime. The owner of *Nessma*, Nabil Karwi, Essebsi and was a founding member of the Nidaa Tounes party. In a voice recording leaked in April 2017, he could be heard ordering his staff to slander the anti-corruption watchdog IWatch. Karwi prompted his journalists to run a smear campaign against the NGO's founder and his wife, and to refer to the anti-corruption activists as 'thieves', 'traitors' and 'liars' (*The New Arab*, 2017).

In Egypt, the old elite used media polarisation to prepare for the 2013 coup. According to Fatima el-Issawi (2014, p. 299), '[n]ational Egyptian media shifted from an excess of attack dog journalism under the rule of the deposed Muslim Brotherhood President to an excess of lapdog journalism post coup'. El-Issawi argues that this U-turn, from fiercely attacking Mursi to applauding the military, reflects that Egyptian journalists largely perceive their role as guardians of the regime. For decades, the state media was directed to play this role leaving no room to dissenting voices. By re-introducing private media in the later years of the Mubarak regime, the regime tried to create a notion of 'modern' and 'independent' media in Egypt. Behind the façade, these media were largely owned by business tycoons linked to the regime and served as a complimentary mouthpiece of the regime.

Under Sisi, the state has tightened control over the media. His regime has acquired leading media houses through businessmen close to the government and the intelligence services (*Middle East Eye*, 2017). In December 2017, Eagle Capital, headed by former Minister of Investment Dalia Khurshid, acquired a large stake in Egyptian Media Group, which owns 16 media subsidiaries including the *Youm7* daily newspaper, *Synergy* and *ONTV*, as well as a number of marketing and advertising agencies. According to Egyptian online newspaper *Mada Masr*, Eagle Capital is a front that manages the General Intelligence's private sector projects and companies (Bahgat, 2017). Earlier the same year, the TV channel *al-Hayat* was taken over by Falcon, an Egyptian security company whose director is a former senior military intelligence officer. In addition, *ONTV*, a part of the Eagle Capital portfolio, was taken over by Ahmad Abu Hashima, a powerful millionaire steel magnate close to Sisi. Abu Hashima also controls the pro-Sisi *DMC* TV network (*Middle East Eye*, 2017).

In addition to money, networks and media, external support has been a fourth important resource for the old elite's survival in Egypt.

Egypt is heavily dependent on financial aid. Since 1979, following the peace deal with Israel, the country has been receiving uninterrupted US aid at an average of $1.6bn a year, the bulk of which goes to the military (Najjar, 2017). Egypt also received substantial economic support from Europe, the Middle East and Japan (Sowa, 2013). After Mursi's election, US aid continued to go to the military rather than to the new government that was in a deep economic crisis. Saudi Arabia and its regional allies withdrew financial support, leaving the Brotherhood-led government with the sole support of Qatar (Daragahi, 2013). The old establishment worked behind the scene to worsen the economic crisis under Mursi (Hubbard & Kirkpatrick, 2013). In the wake of Sisi's takeover, the external aid to Egypt suddenly peaked. Washington was careful not to label Sisi's power grab as a 'military coup' to maintain the economic transfers to Egypt. Under US law, aid must stop to 'any country whose duly elected head of government is deposed by military coup d'état or decree' (Ghattas, 2013). But the big money came from Saudi Arabia, UAE and Kuwait, which provided an aid package worth $ 12bn, four times the size of total assistance from the US and European countries (Hearst, 2013). These three rich Gulf monarchies wanted to eliminate both the Brotherhood and the influence of the rival Qatar in Egypt. Undoubtedly, the generous support helped Sisi to consolidate the power of his army-dominated new government.

Tunisia also relies on foreign aid, but compared to Egypt, this aid has not benefitted the old regime elite to the same degree. For one, more of the aid has gone to democracy promotion and civil society organisations. The EU is a major donor and has conditioned its economic support on Tunisia not reverting to authoritarian rule. US military assistance has increased substantially following a series of terrorist attacks in 2015 (Kimball, 2016). However, contrary to Egypt, the military is not a major stronghold of Tunisia's old elite. Regional players like Saudi Arabia and the UAE have also been less actively supporting the old guard in Tunisia. Saudi Arabia did not consider developments in the small North African country a potential threat to its security and treated Tunisia with benign disinterest (Tansey, Koehler, & Schmotz, 2017).

CONCLUSION

Based on our findings, the Arab Spring in Egypt and Tunisia both resulted in the type of elite circulation that John Higley and György Lengyel refer to as 'quasi-replacement circulation', which is sudden and coerced, but narrow and shallow. This being said, there are significant differences between the two cases.

In Tunisia, democratic progress has pluralised the political scene and widened the circle of politically relevant elites. Formerly excluded opposition politicians from the left, liberal centre and Islamist right have entered the game. The al-Nahda party has gained a prominent position. This political renewal has also had knock-on effects in other spheres. For example, in the military, the 2011–2013 troika government replaced officers from the traditional elite areas in the capital and the Eastern coast with officers from the interior. The aim was to weaken the old regime security networks and reduce the likelihood of a military coup. Tunisia's external security threats also led successive governments to allocate more resources to the military. Consequently, the military elite has come out of the Ben Ali era's marginalisation and strengthened its hand relative to the police (Grewal, 2016).

However, the overall movement toward elite renewal was reversed with the rise of Nidaa Tounes and Essebsi's presidency December 2014-July 2019. Essebsi spearheaded efforts to clear the old elite from accusations related to the past and appointed a growing number of its members to leadership positions in the state and the party. The limited degree of public sector reform after 2011 facilitated his endeavour. The Interior Ministry, which formed the core of Ben Ali's repressive apparatus, remains a powerhouse as well as 'an unreconstructed bastion of secrecy and unaccountability' (Boukhars, 2017, p. 263). In the economic sphere, the established bourgeoisies of the Eastern coast, the Jarba Island and provincial capitals such as Sfax and Tuzir continue to maintain their predominant positions. They block access to newcomers from the southeast, centre and west interior regions through corruption networks in the state bureaucracy (International Crisis Group, 2017).

In the case of Egypt, there is far more continuity than change. The uprising did not destroy the ruling elites associated with the old regime. Hosni Mubarak and the members of his inner circle are out of political life, but beyond that, the elite circulation has been limited. The uprising did not produce any new elites. The only new group that was included for a short while in the political elite were members of the Muslim Brotherhood. Today, the Brothers are further from political power than ever in Egypt's modern history. The major change the uprising brought was that it rocked the relative influence of each of the different elite groups dominating Egyptian politics. Sisi has reduced the importance of governmental and economic elites and upgraded the role of military and, to a lesser extent, security elites. Like under the old regime, the president is still the centre of gravity of the entire system. Last but not the least the new regime has not in any substantial way changed the way in which Egypt is governed. The Egyptian people have definitively not become more involved in the governance after the Arab Spring. In fact, Robert Springborg notes, 'Egypt is more authoritarian under Sisi than it was under Mubarak' (Springborg, 2018, p. 61).

We have traced the roots of the quasi-replacement circulation to the old elites' privileged access to resources, focussing on money, network, the media and external support. Except the latter, which mostly applies to Egypt, the resources have favoured the old elites in both cases. Though democracy progressed in Tunisia and regressed in Egypt, both countries' elites were able to reproduce themselves. This is not to say that democracy does not matter. Democracy makes a huge difference in the ability of aspiring social forces to countermobilise. In Tunisia, the people and civil society have far more resources in their hand to counter the old elites' power strategies than in Egypt. Consequently, they have been able to steer the outcome of the Arab Spring in a more favourable direction.

Nonetheless, our cases show the importance of evaluating regime change in a broader view than just the formal institutional set-up. In Tunisia and Egypt, the informal structures of the *anciens régimes* survived – so did the old regime elites.

REFERENCES

Abdelnasser, G. (2004). Egypt: Succession politics. In V. Perthes (Ed.), *Arab elites: Negotiating the politics of change* (pp. 117–39). London: Lynne Rienner Publishers.

Bahgat, H. (2017). Looking into the latest acquisition of Egyptian media companies by general intelligence. *Mada Masr*, December 21. Retrieved from https://www.madamasr.com/en/2017/12/21/feature/politics/looking-into-the-latest-acquisition-of-egyptian-media-companies-by-general-intelligence/

Bayat, A. (2013). Revolution in bad times. *New Left Review* (80), 47–60.

Bobin, P. F., & Haddad, M. (2018). En Tunisie, les anciens bénalistes passent de l'ombre à la lumière. *Le Monde*, January 29. Retrieved from http://www.lemonde.fr/afrique/article/2018/01/29/en-tunisie-les-anciens-benalistes-passent-de-l-ombre-a-la-lumiere_5248856_3212.html

Boubekeur, A. (2016). Islamists, secularists and old regime elites in Tunisia: Bargained competition. *Mediterranean Politics*, *21*(1), 112–113.

Boukhars, A. (2017). The fragility of elite settlements in Tunisia. *African Security Review*, *26*(3), 257–270.

Daragahi, B. (2013). Qatar gives Egypt $3bn aid package. *Financial Times*, April 10. Retrieved from https://www.ft.com/content/790a7d52-a1f4-11e2-8971-00144feabdc0

Easton, D. (1965). *A systems analysis of political life*. New York, NY: John Wiley & Sons.

Egypt Independent. (2018). Egypt replaces ministers of defense, interior, finance in new cabinet. *Egypt Independent*, June 14. Retrieved from https://www.egyptindependent.com/egypt-replaces-ministers-defense-interior-finance-new-cabinet/

Erdle, S. (2004). Tunisia: Economic transformation and political restoration. In V. Perthes (Ed.), *Arab elites: Negotiating the politics of change* (pp. 207–236). London: Lynne Rienner.

Fanack. (2017, September 27). Surprise arrests a 'message' for Mubarak's sons to back off. Retrieved from https://fanack.com/egypt/history-past-to-present/surprise-arrests-of-mubarak-sons/

Fick, M. (2014). Insight: Mubarak-era networks return for new military man in Egypt. *Reuters*, January 29. Retrieved from https://uk.reuters.com/article/uk-egypt-patronage-insight/insight-mubarak-era-networks-return-for-new-military-man-in-egypt-idUKBREA0S0CS20140129

Ghattas, K. (2013). Egypt is still not a coup in Washington. *BBC*, July 18. Retrieved from https://www.bbc.com/news/world-us-canada-23351997

Gobe, E. (2016). Système électoral et révolution: la voie tunisienne [Electoral System and Revolution: The Tunisian Way]. *Pouvoirs*, *156*, 71–82.

Grewal, S. (2016, February 24). *A quiet revolution: The Tunisian military after Ben Ali*. Carnegie Middle East Center. Retrieved from http://carnegie-mec.org/2016/02/24/quiet-revolution-tunisian-military-after-ben-ali-pub-62780.

The Guardian. (2015). Egypt court orders release of Hosni Mubarak's sons. *The Guardian*, October 12. Retrieved from https://www.theguardian.com/world/2015/oct/12/egypt-court-hosni-mubarak-sons-gamal-alaa-release-corruption-conviction

The Guardian. (2017). 'Amnesty of the corrupt': Tunisia's move to heal old wounds branded a sham. *The Guardian*, October 27. Retrieved from https://www.theguardian.com/global-development/2017/oct/27/tunisia-reconciliation-act-dismissed-amnesty-of-the-corrupt

Gulbrandsen, T. (2017). Rise and fall of elites: Professionals as movers? *European Societies*, *20*(2), 159–182.

Hauslohner, A. (2013). After Morsi's ouster, Egypt's old guard is back – And Muslim brotherhood is out. *The Washington Post*, July 19. Retrieved from https://www.washingtonpost.com/world/after-morsis-ouster-egypts-old-guard-is-back--and-muslim-brotherhood-is-out/2013/07/19/28ae563c-efd1-11e2-8c36-0e868255a989_story.html?utm_term=.6c7f03397a03

Hearst, D. (2013). Why Saudi Arabia is taking a risk by backing the Egyptian coup. *The Guardian*, August 20. Retrieved from https://www.theguardian.com/commentisfree/2013/aug/20/saudi-arabia-coup-egypt

Henry, C. M. (2017). Political elites in the Middle East and North Africa. In H. Best & J. Higley (Eds.), *The Palgrave handbook of political elites* (pp. 181–202). London: Palgrave Macmillan.

Heydemann, S. (2004). *Networks of privilege in the Middle East: the politics of economic reform revisited.* New York, NY: Palgrave Macmillan.

Higley, J., & Lengyel, G. (2000). *Elites after state socialism: Theories and analysis.* Lanham, MA: Rowman & Littlefield Publishers.

Hubbard, B., & Kirkpatrick, D. D. (2013). Sudden Improvements in Egypt Suggest a Campaign to Undermine Morsi. *New York Times*, July 10. Retrieved from https://www.nytimes.com/2013/07/11/world/middleeast/improvements-in-egypt-suggest-a-campaign-that-undermined-morsi.html

The International Center for Transitional Justice. (2017, September 14). ICTJ denounces the passage of Tunisia's new 'Administrative reconciliation' law that grants amnesties to public officials for corruption. Retrieved from https://www.ictj.org/news/ictj-denounces-passage-tunisia%E2%80%99s-new-%E2%80%98administrative-reconciliation%E2%80%99-law-grants-amnesties

International Crisis Group. (2017, May 10). *La transition bloquée: corruption et régionalisme en Tunisie.* Rapport Moyen-Orient et Afrique du Nord N°177. Retrieved from https://www.crisisgroup.org/fr/middle-east-north-africa/north-africa/tunisia/177-blocked-transition-corruption-and-regionalism-tunisia

El-Issawi, F. (2014). The role of Egyptian media in the coup. In *IEMed mediterranean yearbook 2014* (pp. 299–304). Barcelona, Spain: European Institute of the Mediterranean (IEMed). http://repository.essex.ac.uk/21411/1/ElIssawi_egypt_media_military_coup_IEMed_yearbook_2014_EN.pdf

Kandil, H. (2012). *Soldiers, spies, and statesmen: Egypt's road to revolt.* New York, NY: Verso.

Khaldun, I. (2015). *The Muqaddimah: An introduction to history.* Princeton, NJ: Princeton University Press (Original work published in 1377).

Kimball, S. (2016). Tunisia's getting more guns than democracy. *Foreign Policy*, April 21. Retrieved from https://foreignpolicy.com/2016/04/21/tunisias-getting-more-guns-than-democracy/

Kostova, D. (2012). Dynamics of the 1990s: Change and continuity of the Bulgarian economic Elite. In D. Lane, G. Lengyel & J. Tholen (Eds.), *Restructuring of the economic elites after state socialism: Recruitment, institutions and attitudes* (pp. 153–168). Stuttgart, Germany: ibidem-Verlag.

Lynch, M. (2015). How the media trashed the transitions. *Journal of Democracy*, 26(4), 90–99.

Mada Masr. (2017). Lieutenant General Hegazy II: Egypt's new chief-of-staff. *Mada Masr*, October 28. Retrieved from https://www.madamasr.com/en/2017/10/28/feature/politics/the-new-hegazy-at-the-head-of-egypts-military/

Marsad. (2018, July 23). Sisi appoints sons in key roles to 'protect his throne'. Retrieved from https://marsad-egypt.info/en/2018/07/23/sisi-appoints-sons-key-roles-protect-throne/

Meky, S. (2017). Egypt's comeback kids: Why are Mubarak's sons being spotted everywhere? *Al Arabiya*, February 13. Retrieved from http://english.alarabiya.net/en/features/2017/02/13/Gently-testing-waters-Mubarak-sons-under-media-glare-once-again-.html

Middle East Eye. (2017). Egyptian intelligence services front acquires leading media houses: Reports. *Middle East Eye*, December 22. Retrieved from http://www.middleeasteye.net/news/egyptian-intelligence-services-front-acquires-leading-media-houses-reports-2056424970

Middle East Eye. (2015). The military: Sisi's real political support base. *Middle East Eye*, November 1. Retrieved from http://www.middleeasteye.net/news/military-sisis-real-political-support-base-477364529

Middle East Monitor. (2014). Egypt relieves spy chief for 'health reasons'. *Middle East Monitor*, December 21. Retrieved from https://www.middleeastmonitor.com/20141221-egypt-relieves-spy-chief-for-health-reasons/

Middle East Observer. (2017a). The confound dismissal of Egypt's Chief of Staff. *Middle East Observer*, December 11. Retrieved from https://www.middleeastobserver.org/2017/12/11/the-confound-dismissal-of-egypts-chief-of-staff/

Middle East Observer. (2017b). Egyptian sovereign body involved in 'Killing' former State Council secretary 'Wael Shalabi': New Khalij. *Middle East Observer*, January 13. Retrieved from https://www.middleeastobserver.org/2017/01/13/egyptian-sovereign-body-involved-in-killing-former-state-council-secretary-wael-shalabi-new-khalij/

Najjar, F. (2017). Why US aid to Egypt is never under threat. *Al-Jazeera*, October 3. Retrieved from https://www.aljazeera.com/news/2017/10/aid-egypt-threat-171002093316209.html

Nassif, H. B. (2015). A military besieged: The armed forces, the police, and the party in Ben Ali's Tunisia, 1987–2011. *International Journal of Middle East Studies*, *47*(1), 65–87.

Nawaat. (2016). Médias: Les attaques terroristes, brise-glace de la propagande benaliste. *Nawaat*, March 17. Retrieved from https://nawaat.org/portail/2016/03/17/medias-les-attaques-terroristes-brise-glace-de-la-propagande-benaliste/

The New Arab. (2017). Leaked recording highlights Tunisian establishment 'bullying tactics' against activists. *The New Arab*, April 23. Retrieved from https://www.alaraby.co.uk/english/indepth/2017/4/23/leaked-recording-highlights-tunisian-establishment-bullying-tactics-against-activists

Pareto, V. (1963). *Treaties on general sociology*. New York, NY: Dover Press (Original work published in 1916).

Rijkers, B., Freund, C., & Nucifora, A. (2017). All in the family: State capture in Tunisia. *Journal of Development Economics*, *124*(C), 41–59.

Roll, S. (2013). *Egypt's business elite after Mubarak*. SWP Research Paper. Retrieved from https://www.swp-berlin.org/fileadmin/contents/products/research_papers/2013_RP08_rll.pdf

Roll, S. (2015). Managing change: How Egypt's military leadership shaped the transformation. *Mediterranean Politics*, *21*(1), 23–43.

Soboul, A. (1989). *The French Revolution, 1787–1799: From the storming of the Bastille to Napoleon*. London: Routledge.

Sayegh, Y. (2016, February 5). *Bringing Tunisia's transition to its security sector*. Carnegie Middle East Center. Retrieved from http://carnegie-mec.org/2016/02/05/bringing-tunisia-s-transition-to-its-security-sector-pub-62563

Selvik, K., & Stenslie, S. (2011). *Stability and change in the modern Middle East*. London: I. B. Tauris.

Sowa, A. (2013, July 19). *Aid to Egypt by the numbers*. Center for Global Development. Retrieved from https://www.cgdev.org/blog/aid-egypt-numbers

Springborg, R. (2018). *Egypt*. Cambridge: Polity Press.

Tansey, O., Koehler, K., & Schmotz, A. (2017). Ties to the rest: autocratic linkages and regime survival. *Comparative Political Studies*, *50*(9), 1221–1254. http://dx.doi.org/10.1177/0010414016666859

Tunisia's Constitution of 2014, Article 2. Constituteproject.org. Retrieved from https://issafrica.org/ctafrica/uploads/TunisiaConstitution2014Eng.pdf

Wasserman, M. (1993). *Persistent oligarchs: Elites and politics in Chihuahua, Mexico, 1910–1940*. Durham, NC: Duke University Press.

THE DEVELOPMENT OF POLITICAL LEGITIMACY AMONG MPs AND CITIZENS IN OLD AND YOUNG DEMOCRACIES

Ursula Hoffmann-Lange

ABSTRACT

The contribution starts out from the question whether the political legitimacy of the Third Wave democracies has suffered in the wake of the Great Recession. The expectation of a damaging effect of an economic or political crisis on legitimacy is based on Lipset's assumption that established democracies with a high degree of political legitimacy are better capable of coping with such crises than young democracies. The database includes two surveys of members of parliament conducted in 2007 and 2013 in Sweden, Germany and five Third Wave democracies located in different world regions (Chile, South Korea, Poland, South Africa and Turkey). Waves 5 and 6 of the World Values Survey that were conducted at about the same time were used for comparing the legitimacy beliefs among MPs and citizens. The data show that the scores for all indicators of political legitimacy are higher among MPs than among citizens and that the differences between the two groups of respondents are considerably larger in the five young democracies. Confidence in political parties is fairly low, especially among citizens, while the evaluation of the quality of democracy in the respondents' country is much higher. Both evaluations have been rather stable over time. In the two established democracies, support for democracy among citizens is nearly as high as among MPs. In the five young democracies, the MP-citizen differential is larger and support for democracy in the population shows a steady increase only in Chile, while it has remained low in Poland and Turkey and even decreased in Korea and South Africa. This indicates that democracy has not taken deep roots in four of the five new democracies included in the study. In Korea and South Africa, the decline in support for democracy

Elites and People: Challenges to Democracy
Comparative Social Research, Volume 34, 35–59
ISSN: 0195-6310/doi:10.1108/S0195-631020190000034003

started already before the onset of the economic crisis and therefore cannot be attributed to the recession. This is confirmed by the lack of a statistical relationship between political legitimacy on one side and economic evaluations on the other side. A multiple regression analysis shows strong country-specific effects, while individual-level variables have only minor effects.

Keywords: Political legitimacy; support for democracy; confidence in political parties; elite-mass differences; consolidation of democracy; political effects of the Great Recession

INTRODUCTION

Concerns about the damaging effects of a deep economic crisis on the viability of democracy are particularly pertinent in the light of the European experience during the *Great Depression* of the early 1930s when democracy collapsed in several European countries and was replaced by authoritarian or totalitarian regimes. It is, therefore, not surprising that the global economic and financial crisis that started in 2008, the *Great Recession*, revived those memories, especially as some of the repercussions of the current crisis are similar: Rising levels of unemployment, widespread public protests, increasing voter volatility, dwindling support for traditional parties and a rise of populist and extremist parties. The comparative analysis of democratic stability and breakdown in inter-war Europe by Berg-Schlosser and colleagues (Berg-Schlosser & Mitchell, 2002) confirms these similarities.

However, although all 15 European democracies included in Berg-Schlosser's study suffered from economic distress and political conflicts, democracy survived in 8 of the 15. In six of the seven breakdowns of democracy, the economic problems caused by the Great Depression played a major role.

The situation in today's democracies differs in many important respects however. First, and most importantly, the Great Recession was less severe and could be overcome must faster than the Great Depression. This was primarily owing to the fact that the available economic policy tools for dealing with economic crises have become more elaborate. Moreover, since World War II, global institutions have been created that allow for swift international responses to such crises. Most democracies also have established welfare policies that contribute to alleviating the economic hardships associated with unemployment, inflation or other crisis-related consequences for the livelihood of the less well-to-do.

Moreover, support for democracy is more deeply rooted in the political culture of most European democracies than it was in the 1930s. Last but not least, most of their political elites are convinced that democratic institutions are the only acceptable way of governing. These factors have not only contributed to easing the economic downturn associated with the recession and bringing most European countries quickly back onto the path of economic recovery, but also prevented economic dissatisfaction from evolving into anti-democratic mass movements, the success of populist parties in the last decade notwithstanding. The latter is caused primarily by genuinely political problems such as public resistance against mass immigration, pervasive corruption and the inability of governments in dealing with the rapid changes in labour markets owing to globalisation. At the same time, all populist parties and leaders try to capitalise on economic dissatisfaction by denouncing governments' lack of willingness to address the economic woes of the 'victims of globalisation' and of 'neoliberalism'.

The following analysis will primarily focus on the legitimacy of democracy among citizens and members of parliament (MPs) in five young and two established democracies to determine whether democratic legitimacy suffered in the wake of the economic and financial crisis. The analysis is based on data collected in the context of a larger comparative project on the development of political culture after democratisation.

ELITES, CITIZENS, ECONOMIC CRISES AND POLITICAL LEGITIMACY IN YOUNG DEMOCRACIES

The Role of Elites in Democratic Transition and Consolidation

Many studies on democratisation have emphasised the importance of elites for democratic transitions and the consolidation of democracy (Albertus & Menaldo, 2018; Haggard & Kaufman, 2016; Higley & Burton, 2006). Transitions to democracy usually are the result of an agreement among both elites of the non-democratic regime and the leaders of dissident movements to end long and inconclusive conflicts over the character of the previous authoritarian regime. They involve the implementation of a new constitution defining a set of institutions for political decision-making, electoral laws, as well as rules for government-formation and legislation. During the stage of democratic consolidation, it is crucial that the elites learn to trust each other and to develop informal rules of managing emerging conflicts. This involves the formation of a functioning party system with a limited number of major players. At this stage, the new elites have to convince citizens that democracy is capable of producing political stability and of delivering successful policies.

It is obvious that young democracies are more vulnerable than consolidated democracies to experience challenges to their democratic institutions, especially as most of them have to grapple with the legacies of their authoritarian past such as economic problems and corruption (Haggard & Kaufman, 2016). Their party systems tend to be more volatile, while citizens are inclined to accept the new democracy only if it is able of producing stable and decisive governments and economic development. In such a situation, an economic recession may severely impair the consolidation process and lead to an increase in political dissatisfaction that can be exploited by populist movements.

Economic Crises and Political Legitimacy

The question of how much the legitimacy of political regimes depends on economic success has for long been a central concern of political philosophers and

social scientists. Lipset's (1959) analysis of effectiveness and legitimacy as preconditions of democratic stability is still an authoritative statement on this matter.
Lipset (1959) defined effectiveness as the extent to which a political system

> satisfies the basic functions of government as defined by the expectation of most members of
> a society, and the expectations of powerful groups within it which might threaten the system.
> (p. 86)

He assumed that 'such effectiveness means primarily constant economic development' (Lipset, p. 91) and also claimed that the presence of a high level of
legitimacy constitutes a safety valve, stabilising democracy even in times of poor
economic performance or other crises.

While gaining legitimacy presupposes a long period of political and economic
stability, a decline in political effectiveness may happen quickly during an economic or political crisis, although it does not necessarily lead to a fast breakdown
of democracy and may drag on for quite some time. Even where democratisation
was originally supported by a majority of both citizens and elites, new democracies usually do not only lack the broad legitimacy of consolidated democracies,
but also frequently suffer from dismal economic conditions that had often been a
major cause for the demise of the previous authoritarian regime. Inevitable conflicts over basic provisions of the new constitution, a lack of informal norms for
conflict regulation and an insufficiently institutionalised party system may impair
the effectivity of governments of new democracies.

Empirical studies have confirmed that a deep and prolonged economic crisis
is apt to produce a destabilisation or even a breakdown of democracy and young
democracies are especially prone to democratic breakdown (Møller, Schmotz, &
Skaaning, 2015; Morlino & Quaranta, 2016). They also show that reducing
regime effectiveness to purely economic success is unsatisfactory. This assumption is supported by the study of Haggard and Kaufman (2016), who found that
in the democratic reversals of the last decades a *weak democracy syndrome* played
a more important role than economic failures. In these countries 'adherence to
rules is less valued, more contingent, and therefore more uncertain' (Haggard &
Kaufman, p. 227), and citizens assume that governments use their electoral majority 'to strengthen executive authority at the expense of institutions of horizontal
accountability such as legislatures, judiciaries, opposition parties, NGO's and the
media' (Haggard & Kaufman, p. 228). Under these conditions an economic crisis
may further aggravate the situation by triggering elite defections and a general
disaffection among the public (Haggard & Kaufman, p. 229).

The political repercussions of the recent financial and economic crisis, which
was the worst recession in Europe since the Great Depression and the first global
financial crisis (Tooze, 2018), have been extensively analysed. Many studies have
confirmed that satisfaction with democracy, confidence in political institutions
and support for democracy, but also electoral support for the incumbent parties suffered during the crisis (e.g. Armingeon & Guthmann, 2013; Cordero &
Simón, 2015; Gangl & Giustozzi, 2018; Hernández & Kriesi, 2016; Polavieja,
2013; Wroe, 2016). Different authors identified a number of causally relevant
factors. Studies relying exclusively on macro-data found a direct impact of the

depth of the recession on the quality of democracy, especially a detachment from the institutional channels of representation and an increase in political protest that only subsided after economic recovery (Morlino & Quaranta, 2016). Some macro-factors such as bailout measures and the type of welfare regime were also shown to have had some influence. Berg-Schlosser (2015) additionally emphasised that developments in the party system may impair the functioning of party competition and the quality of democracy.

OBJECTS AND TYPES OF POLITICAL SUPPORT

Legitimacy theories distinguish between different objects of legitimacy. The distinction between support for authorities, support for the democratic performance of the political system and support for democracy involves a hierarchy of objects from political actors to value orientations, which at the same time constitutes a hierarchy from specific to diffuse support (Fuchs, 2007; Klingemann, 2018; Norris, 1999). At the lowest level, the electoral mechanism allows voters to withdraw electoral support if they are dissatisfied with the performance of the political actors. This mechanism is designed to shield democracies from a loss of legitimacy in situations of perceived deficits in government performance. The intermediate level involves the perception of deficits in the institutional structure and in the performance of the political system. The highest level finally is a belief in the value of democracy as the best type of regime. It is easy to imagine that it takes time for a young democracy to gain legitimacy at higher levels. This requires experience with different democratically elected governments and is a precondition for grasping the analytical distinction between the performance of the current government, the performance of the political system and the appreciation of democratic principles.

Economic crises that cause a decline in standards of living can be expected to impair political support, especially if the crisis persists and government policies to cope with it turn out to be ineffective. While such dissatisfaction will primarily affect specific support for the current government, after a while it may spill over to higher levels of support. This raises the question whether the third-wave democracies have already achieved a sufficiently broad support for their democratic institutions to prevent anti-democratic movements from successfully mobilising against the democratic institutions.

Theoretical Assumptions

The following analysis will study political beliefs and value orientations among MPs and the general population in two established and five Third Wave democracies that democratised in the late 1980s or early 1990s. The MP surveys were conducted in 2007 and 2013, the citizen surveys between 2005 and 2007 and from 2010 to 2013. The first wave of surveys took place before the onset of the global economic crisis, the second wave after the crisis had crested. This is a quasi-experimental design, although it will of course not be possible to claim that observed declines in political legitimacy have been caused by the crisis.

Herbert McClosky's (1964) classic study was the first to demonstrate a considerable gap in support for democratic principles between politicians and ordinary citizens. While he found broad support for general principles in both groups, support for more specific principles, especially political tolerance was much lower in the population, McClosky concluded that elites have to be considered as the main *carriers of the democratic creed*. His basic results have been confirmed by a host of later studies (Hoffmann-Lange, 2008; McClosky & Brill, 1983). Therefore, the inclusion of elites in the analysis will provide a more differentiated account of democratic legitimacy.

The first theoretical assumption regards differences between MPs and citizens. Because of the division of labour between the two groups, MPs can be expected to accept the rules for political decision-making and to be more familiar with the limits of what can be achieved by politics. Therefore, they also should be more satisfied with the performance of the political system than citizens who are outside observers of the legislative process.

The second assumption is about differences between old and young democracies. The MP–citizen differential should be larger in young democracies as their citizens are less well acquainted with the political implications of democratic institutions that have not existed long enough to instil confidence in their proper functioning.

A third assumption regards the impact of the economic crisis. Dissatisfaction with performance of the economy should have the largest effect on confidence in political actors (Diamond, 2016, chapter 5). In the established democracies, it should have less influence on satisfaction with the democratic performance of the political system and even less on support for democracy, however. In young democracies, it is more likely to impair legitimacy also on the two higher levels of support.

The fourth and last assumption looks at differences within the party systems. It can be expected that elite dissensus about the legitimacy of the existing democratic institutions and rules may impair the effectiveness of democracy. This assumption is based on a study of Sniderman et al. (1991), which demonstrated that a simple elite-citizen comparison may conceal considerable differences within the party system. Even if populist or anti-democratic parties are small, they can have a disruptive influence (Sartori, 1976, p. 123). Therefore, a breakdown of the data by political party affiliation promises to provide additional insights.

DATABASE

The Two MP Surveys and the World Values Survey

The two MP surveys were conducted within the context of an on-going comparative project on the consolidation of new democracies that started in the mid-1990s. The five new democracies, Chile, South Korea, Poland, South Africa and Turkey, were selected according to a most-different systems design to study the impact of different historical and cultural backgrounds on the process of democratisation and consolidation of democracy. These countries democratised between the late 1980s and the early 1990s and were chosen because they were the front-runners among the Third Wave democracies in their respective regions. Sweden and Germany were included as benchmark cases of consolidated democracy.[1] Another reason for the inclusion of Germany was the country's peculiar historical experience as a divided country from 1945 to 1990.[2]

The first MP survey had been conducted in 2007 with the intention to broaden the focus of the project by studying the role of elites and political representation in democratic consolidation (Van Beek, 2010). The economic recession that started shortly after that survey had been completed, offered a welcome opportunity to conduct a follow-up survey in 2013 that was supposed to provide information on the MPs' perceptions of the crisis and the impact of the crisis on their political beliefs and value orientations (Klingemann & Hoffmann-Lange, 2018).[3] For both waves, roughly 100 interviews based on random samples of all MPs were conducted in each of the participating countries.

Most of the questions included in the MP surveys are directly comparable to questions asked in the fifth and sixth waves of the World Values Survey (WVS; Inglehart et al., 2014) that were conducted in the seven countries at about the same time (2005–2007 and 2010–2013). Table 1 provides the respondent numbers for all four surveys.

Germany will be treated as a special case in the analysis because the experience of the political and economic transition deeply affected the personal lives of most East Germans, and persistent economic disparities between the two regions have left their mark in the political culture. While a considerable convergence in value orientations has taken place over the years (Holtmann et al., 2015), political dissatisfaction is still higher in the eastern part of the country and manifests itself for instance in a considerably higher electoral support for

Table 1. Number of Respondents in the Surveys.

Country	MP Surveys		WVS			
	TRI Survey 2007	CMP Survey 2013	Wave 5, 2005–2007		Wave 6, 2010–2013	
	n	*n*	*N*	Year	*n*	Year
Chile	99	105	1,000	2006	1,000	2012
Germany	101	112	2,064	2006	2,044	2013
Western Germany			988	2006	1,032	2013
Eastern Germany			1,076	2006	1,012	2013
Korea	100	105	1,200	2005	1,200	2010
Poland	99	150	1,000	2005	966	2012
South Africa	100	142	2,821	2006	3,443	2013
Sweden	101	107	1,003	2006	1,206	2011
Turkey	148	152	1,346	2007	1,605	2012
Total	748	873	10,434		11,464	

Source: MP surveys 2007 and 2013; WVS cumulated file, Waves 5 (2005–2007) and 6 (2010–2013).
Note: Western Germany: territory of the former Federal Republic of Germany plus West Berlin: Eastern Germany territory of the former German Democratic Republic (including East Berlin).

the Left party and the right-wing *Alternative für Deutschland* (AfD). Therefore, the residents of the two German regions will be treated separately for those indicators that show substantial divergences. The same is not possible, however, for the MPs because of two reasons. First, the political attitudes and value orientations of the MPs are primarily determined by their party affiliation while their regional identity is much less relevant. The second reason is that the small number of MPs from the eastern German states does not permit to treat them as a separate group.

As the selection of the five new democracies in the study was based on their performance during the democratisation process, it could not be expected that these countries were at the same time the best choice for studying the impact the economic crisis on the legitimacy of democracy. In fact, Poland did not experience any economic recession at all, and the impact of the crisis in the other four young democracies was less severe than in other countries with similar socio-economic backgrounds. This does not seriously diminish the validity of the results, though. The results of the 2013 MP survey show that these retrospective evaluations of the impact of the economic crisis did not mirror the macro-economic severity of the recession (Hoffmann-Lange, 2018). This supports the conclusion that such perceptions take on a reality of their own and influence the attitudes of people regardless of the actual impact of the crisis on their own country. Moreover, the crisis has been widely perceived as revealing fundamental flaws of the global financial markets and as endangering countries around the globe. Thereby, it contributed to a rise in political dissatisfaction with governments regardless of the actual economic impact of the crisis on individual countries (Tooze, 2018).

Indicators

Confidence in government, parliament and political parties was measured by offering respondents four answering categories: 'a great deal', 'quite a lot', 'not very much' and 'none at all'. Following Klingemann's (2018) suggestion, confidence in political parties was chosen as an indicator of trust in political actors out of two reasons. First, political parties usually receive the lowest score for political confidence because many people assume that parties pursue their own particularistic interests and do not really care about the needs and wishes of their voters. Therefore, they are most likely to be blamed when voters are dissatisfied with government performance. At the same time, confidence in government is usually much higher among voters of the parties in government, which makes that indicator less suitable for studying changes in political legitimacy.

Two questions measure the perceived democratic performance (the 'democraticness') of the political system. The first is 'And how democratically is this country being governed today?' with an answering scale from 1 'not at all' to 10 'completely'.

Support for democracy at the value level, finally, was measured by asking the respondents to evaluate three regime types on a four-point scale as very good, fairly good, fairly bad or very bad:

- 'having a strong leader who does not have to bother with parliament and elections';
- 'having the army rule'; and
- 'having a democratic political system'.

Diamond (2008, pp. 31–34) questioned the validity of the simple score assigned to democracy and argued that the stimulus 'democracy' evokes mostly positive associations even among respondents who do not understand its institutional implications. Therefore, a more demanding index of *support for democracy* was constructed by subtracting the higher score for either an autocratic or a military regime from the score for democracy.

To increase the comparability of questions using different ranges of scale values, all variables were rescaled to a range between 0 and 1. The only exception is the index support for democracy that has a range from −1 to +1. Weight variables have been applied. In the WVS data they correct for unequal sampling probabilities, in particular for the deliberate overrepresentation of East German respondents in the German sample documented in Table 1, and for biased response rates (redressment weight). In the MP surveys, the weight ensures the correct representation of the party–political composition of the legislatures.

MACRO-INDICATORS OF ECONOMIC GROWTH, UNEMPLOYMENT AND THE QUALITY OF DEMOCRACY

Data on the gross domestic product (GDP) per capita show that the seven countries vary considerably with respect to their level of economic development. Sweden, Germany and Korea are highly developed OECD countries, while the other four countries belong to the so-called emerging markets, with Turkey and South Africa being the poorest in the group. Compared to the overall median of 38 developed countries and emerging markets (5.9%), the impact of the recession was above the median in Germany, Sweden and Turkey. The output gap compared to the long-term GDP growth before the recession was fairly large in Korea, followed by Sweden, while it was below the overall median (−8.5%) in the other five countries. By 2016, Sweden's and South Africa's GDP were still below their 2007 level, while especially Korea and Chile had made remarkable gains (Du Plessis, Freytag, & Boshoff, 2015, pp. 21–26).

Fig. 1 informs about the development of democracy in the seven countries from 1980 to 2018. The two indicators of quality of democracy are taken from the V-Dem data (Lindberg et al., 2014).[4] The *electoral democracy index* measures the existence of basic democratic rights, especially free and fair elections, and the *liberal democracy index* additionally includes the degree to which individual liberty rights and the rule of law are effectively protected in the country. Therefore, the second index is more demanding and its scores are mostly somewhat lower.

Sweden and Germany show the typical pattern of consolidated democracies. Both curves are flat with scores above 0.80 and only slight differences between the two indices. The curves for four of the five new democracies show that

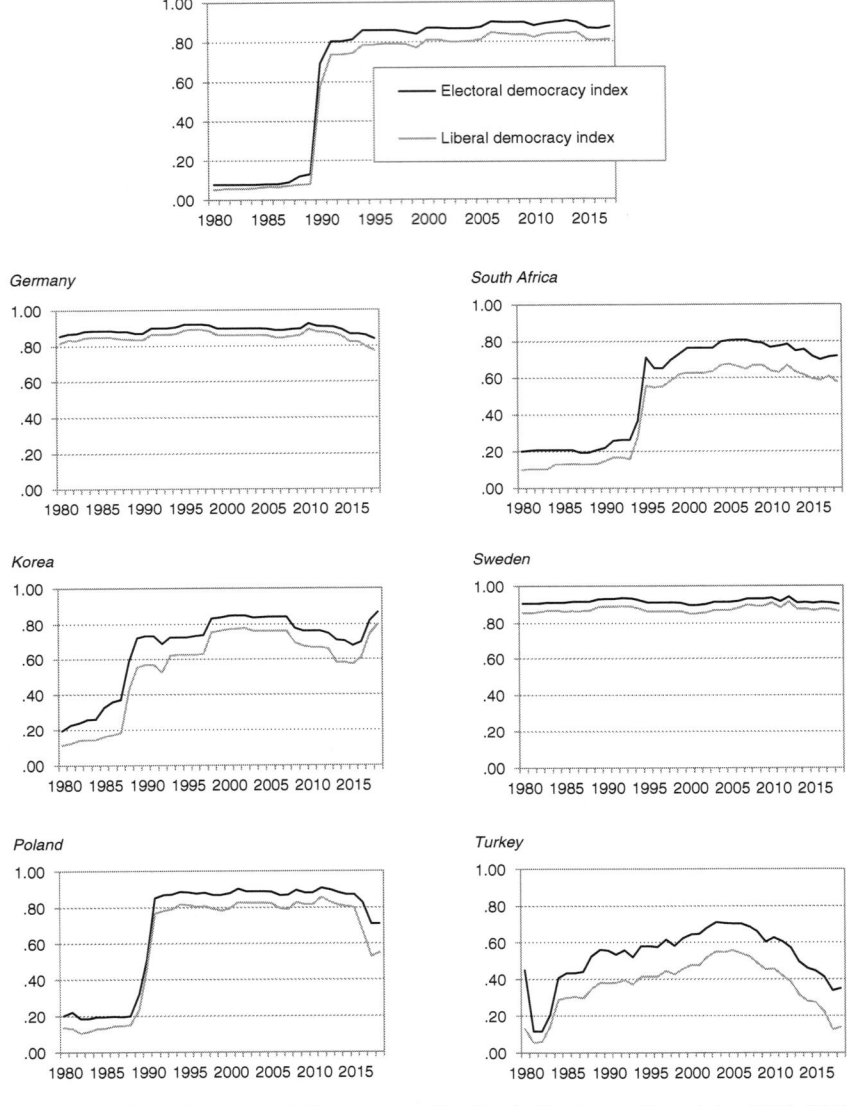

Fig. 1. The Development of Democratic Quality in the Seven Countries 1980–2017.
Source: V-Dem, Release 9 (April 2019).

these started out from rather low levels in 1980. With the exception of Turkey, the quality of democracy steeply increased around 1990, beginning with Korea and ending with South Africa that achieved full democracy only in 1994. Chile's democracy scores have meanwhile reached a level of 0.79 and caught up with the two established democracies. The Korean, Polish and South African scores are somewhat lower and the scores of the latter two countries have slightly declined since the mid-2010s. The great exception among the seven countries is Turkey. After 1983, Turkey started to democratise in several small steps and reached a high of 0.71 for electoral democracy and of 0.55 for liberal democracy in 2004. Afterwards, a steady decline of both scores set in and meanwhile the country is back to its low level of 1980.

EMPIRICAL RESULTS

Effects of the Economic Perceptions of MPs on Political Legitimacy

The second wave of the MP survey (2013) included a set of questions asking for the perceptions and evaluations of the national economy, the impact of the crisis on the country, causes of the crisis and the performance of different national (government and individual parties) and international (IMF, EU, etc.) actors. The correlation coefficients between the perceptions of the economic situation and of the impact of the economic crisis on one side and indicators of political legitimacy on the other side provide a first cue on whether assumed effects of the recession have played a role in the present crisis (Hoffmann-Lange, 2018). It is not surprising that a positive perception of the economic situation is closely associated with a positive evaluation of the performance of the national government in coping with the crisis ($r = 0.64$), with confidence in the government ($r = 0.61$), with satisfaction with democracy ($r = 0.58$) and with the evaluation of the democratic quality of the political system ($r = 0.51$), but not with support for democracy ($r = -0.01$). A positive evaluation of the economic situation is closely related to the participation of the respondents' party in government ($r = 0.61$).

In contrast, the perceptions of the impact of the crisis show a fairly high negative correlation only with the perception of the economic situation ($r = -0.39$), but close to zero correlations with the legitimacy indicators.

Confidence in Political Parties

The development of confidence in political institutions has frequently been studied by political culture research. The empirical results indicate that several indicators of the citizens' confidence in democratic politics (trust in politicians, confidence in public and private institutions and satisfaction with democracy) have declined over the last decades, a trend that already started long before the onset of the economic recession in 2008. The magnitude of the decline varies considerably across countries, however (e.g. Dalton, 2006, 2015; Fuchs, Guidorossi, & Svensson, 1995; Holmberg, 1999; Listhaug & Wiberg, 1995).

Table 2 includes the mean scores for confidence in government, parliament and political parties. It confirms that the latter enjoy the lowest reputation among citizens. Fig. 2 shows that confidence in political parties is considerably higher among the MPs than among the citizens. The average difference is 0.21. The higher confidence ratings of the MPs are not really surprising as MPs are actively

Table 2. Mean Citizen Confidence in Government, Parliament and Political Parties.

	Confidence in Government		Confidence in Parliament		Confidence in Political Parties	
	Wave 5	Wave 6	Wave 5	Wave 6	Wave 5	Wave 6
Chile	0.46	0.38	0.32	0.33	0.25	0.27
Germany	0.36	0.47	0.35	0.47	0.29	0.37
West Germany	0.37	0.47	0.36	0.47	0.30	0.38
East Germany	0.31	0.47	0.30	0.46	0.23	0.34
Korea	0.46	0.48	0.35	0.36	0.33	0.36
Poland	0.31	0.30	0.27	0.28	0.22	0.23
South Africa	0.64	0.47	0.60	0.46	0.45	0.42
Sweden	0.45	0.53	0.52	0.54	0.42	0.45
Turkey	0.59	0.57	0.56	0.53	0.39	0.41

Source: WVS cumulated file, Waves 5 and 6.
Note: Scores on a four-point scale (none at all, not very much, quite a lot, and a great deal), rescaled to range 0–1.

involved in policymaking while most of the citizens are only bystanders. The results support the conclusion that confidence in political parties has not suffered in the wake of the economic recession. The lower scores of the citizens do not necessarily imply a lower level of democratic legitimacy, however. Instead, they should be interpreted as resulting from the division of labour between MPs and citizens. Because most citizens are not actively involved in policy-making, they evaluate the parties from a distance and tend to be more sceptical about their

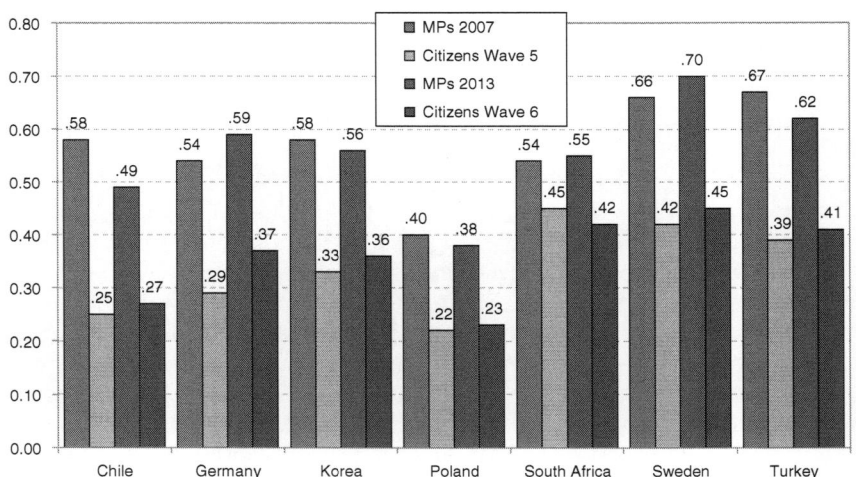

Fig. 2. Mean Confidence in Political Parties among MPs and Citizens.
Source: MP surveys 2007 and 2013, WVS cumulated file, Waves 5 and 6.
Note: Confidence ratings on a 10-point scale, rescaled to range 0–1.

dedication to promote the welfare of the nation and more inclined to assume that parties primarily pursue their own interests. This conclusion is supported by the fact that citizen confidence in political parties is only slightly higher in the two benchmark democracies Sweden and Germany.

The changes between the two survey waves are rather small and do not indicate any negative impact of the economic crisis on confidence in political parties. The differences between the supporters of different parties are not very pronounced either. Some individual results are remarkable though. In Germany, supporters of radical right parties (the Nationaldemokratische Partei Deutschlands (NPD) and the AfD) express a considerably lower confidence in political parties. The same is true for voters in the eastern German states. A control for affiliation with parties in government or opposition parties finally shows that the confidence ratings are systematically lower among the voters of opposition parties among both MPs and citizens. Respondents who failed to express a vote intention showed even lower confidence in political parties than those who intended to vote for opposition parties. It seems that they feel even more distant to the party system. The main result, however, is the overall low level of confidence in political parties and its stability over time.

Evaluation of the Political System's Democratic Performance

Theoretically, the evaluation of the democratic quality of the political system ('democraticness') has an intermediate status between the evaluations of political actors and support for democracy. The results in Fig. 3 support this expectation. Among the MPs, the mean scores for this indicator are somewhat higher than

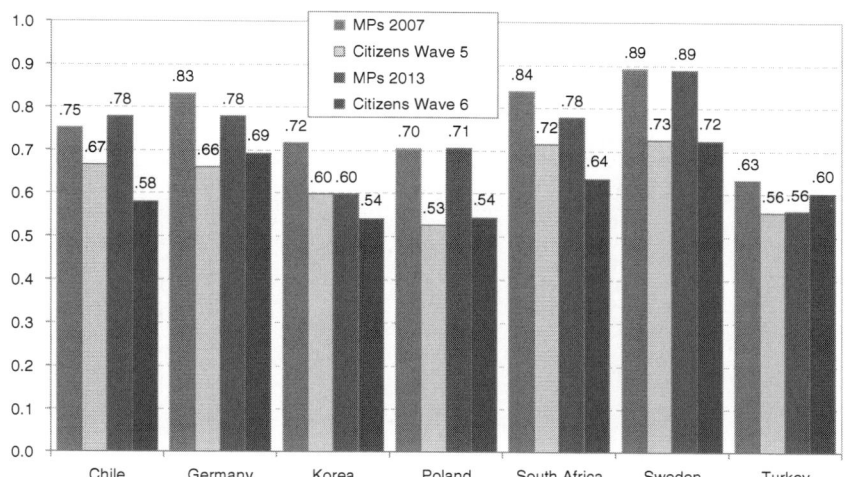

Fig. 3. Mean Evaluations of Political Regime as Democratic (Democraticness).
Source: MP surveys 2007 and 2013, WVS cumulated file, Waves 5 and 6.
Note: Ratings of 'How democratically is this country governed today?' on a 10-point scale, rescaled to range 0–1.

those for confidence in political parties and they are even considerably higher among the citizens. The results are again relatively stable between the two survey waves in four of the seven countries and declined only in Chile, Korea and South Africa.

Among MPs, the difference between members of the parties in government and the opposition parties was more pronounced for the evaluation of democraticness than for confidence in political parties. Moreover, this difference even increased substantially in Korea (from -0.11 to -0.30) and Turkey (from -0.20 to -0.58). Among the party voters in the population, the differences slightly increased as well (Table 3). This shows that the evaluation of the political system's democratic quality are more controversial than confidence in political parties and casts doubt on the assumption that consensus increases at higher levels of political support. It confirms that it is essential to take into account the degree of polarisation within the party system.

Support for Democracy

The mean scores for democracy in Table 4 are uniformly high for both MPs and citizens. All average MP ratings were above 0.80. Those of the citizens were only

Table 3. Mean Evaluation of Political Regime as Democratic by Affiliation with Parties in Government and Opposition Parties.

		MPs 2007	MPs 2013	Citizens' Wave 5	Citizens' Wave 6
Chile	Parties in government	0.85	0.88	0.71	0.73
	Opposition parties	0.66	0.69	0.64	0.56
	No party vote			0.64	0.55
Germany	Parties in government	0.86	0.84	0.66	0.73
	Opposition parties	0.75	0.71	0.54	0.67
	No party vote			0.58	0.66
Korea	Parties in government	0.77	0.73	0.64	0.62
	Opposition parties	0.66	0.43	0.59	0.51
	No party vote			0.63	0.55
Poland	Parties in government	0.89	0.89	0.55	0.63
	Opposition parties	0.52	0.53	0.52	0.51
	No party vote			0.49	0.52
South Africa	Parties in government	0.91	0.87	0.77	0.68
	Opposition parties	0.62	0.56	0.58	0.59
	No party vote			0.65	0.57
Sweden	Parties in government	0.92	0.94	0.70	0.82
	Opposition parties	0.86	0.84	0.75	0.69
	No party vote			0.69	0.70
Turkey	Parties in government	0.70	0.80	0.61	0.66
	Opposition parties	0.50	0.22	0.48	0.52
	No party vote			0.54	0.59

Source: MP surveys 2007 and 2013, WVS cumulated file, Wave 6.
Notes: MP surveys: Party membership of MPs; WVS: Vote intention; respondents without vote intention coded as 'No party vote'.
Evaluation of democratic quality: mean scores on a 10-point scale, rescaled to range 0–1.

Table 4. Mean Evaluation of Autocratic Regime, Military Regime and Democracy.

		Chile	Germany	Korea	Poland	South Africa	Sweden	Turkey
MPs 2007	Autocratic leader	0.25	0.02	0.30	0.24	0.10	0.02	0.40
	Military regime	0.15	0.00	0.05	0.08	0.01	0.01	0.10
	Democracy	0.90	0.99	0.89	0.83	0.98	1.00	0.96
MPs 2013	Autocratic leader	0.27	0.02	0.20	0.16	0.07	0.05	0.22
	Military regime	0.14	0.01	0.02	0.02	0.06	0.02	0.01
	Democracy	0.98	0.99	0.87	0.86	0.95	1.00	0.93
Citizens wave 5	Autocratic leader	0.36	0.22	0.47	0.37	0.40	0.22	0.54
	Military regime	0.25	0.08	0.19	0.29	0.33	0.12	0.38
	Democracy	0.78	0.84	0.66	0.69	0.80	0.91	0.83
Citizens wave 6	Autocratic leader	0.39	0.23	0.49	0.30	0.56	0.27	0.53
	Military regime	0.23	0.08	0.18	0.29	0.48	0.17	0.33
	Democracy	0.83	0.87	0.64	0.67	0.67	0.89	0.80

Source: MP surveys 2007 and 2013, WVS cumulated file, Waves 5 and 6.
Note: Evaluation of regime types: mean scores on a 4-point scale, rescaled to range 0–1.

slightly lower in Chile, Germany, South Africa, Sweden and Turkey, and considerably lower only in Korea and Poland. The stability between the two survey waves is again high, with the exception of the South African citizens whose mean score dropped from 0.80 in 2006 to 0.67 in 2013.

Conversely, support for the two authoritarian regime types is low among the MPs in all seven countries as well as among Swedish and German citizens. The same is not true for the citizens in the five young democracies, however, where the two authoritarian regime types reach much higher scores. This result confirms Diamond's plea for a more demanding index of support for democracy.

As explained above, the index *support for democracy* was calculated by determining the differential between the scores for democracy and those for either an autocratic leader or a military regime.[5] As the WVS has included these questions since the mid-1990s, Fig. 4 shows the development of the index over the last four surveys.[6] The scores for Germany and Sweden show consistently high levels, albeit the East German scores are slightly lower than the West German ones. The curves for Korea and South Africa point downward. They fell from 0.39 to 0.13 in Korea and from 0.39 to 0.02 in South Africa.[7] This indicates that democratic consolidation has suffered a considerable setback in these two countries and that the stability of their democracy depends primarily on the presence of a strong elite consensus. It remains to be seen whether support for democracy will start increasing again after the changes in the presidency from Geun-hye Park to Jae-in Moon in 2017 and from Jacob Zuma to Cyril Ramaphosa in early 2018.

Chile's curve points upward and confirms that the country has considerably diminished the gap to the two established democracies, while support in the other four young democracies remained considerably lower. The figures indicate that many citizens in these countries do not really care whether they live in a democracy or under authoritarian rule.

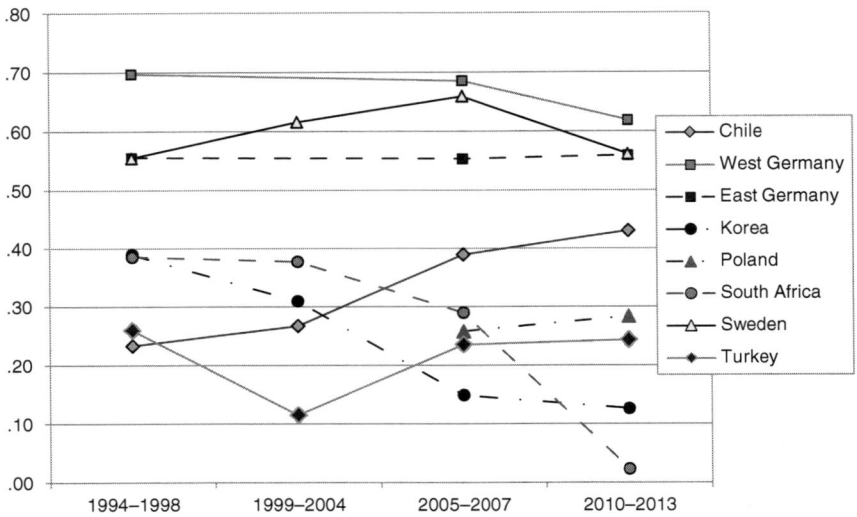

Fig. 4.   Mean Support for Democracy among the Citizens.
Source: WVS cumulated file, Waves 3–6. *Note*: Support for democracy: score for democracy
minus higher score for either autocratic or military regime; original scores measured on a
4-point scale, rescaled to range 0–1; range of difference −1 to +1.

Support for democracy either remained stable or even increased among the
MPs in all seven countries (Fig. 5). The differences between MPs and the popula-
tion are more pronounced than for the evaluation of democraticness. They are
especially large in South Africa (0.59 in 2006 and even 0.81 in 2013), Korea (0.44
and 0.54) and Poland (0.32 and 0.41). The MP-citizen differences increased in
Korea and Poland owing to an increase in support for democracy among the
MPs, while support remained stable among the voters. The increase in South
Africa is entirely owing to a conspicuous decline among the citizens.

A breakdown by party affiliation provides additional information on the level
of consensus about the democratic political order in the five new democracies.
Theoretically, support for democracy should not be associated with party affiliation in consolidated democracies because it is supposed to be a personal value
orientation acquired during political socialisation and reinforced by living in a
long-standing and well-functioning democracy. In countries that democratised
only recently, however, democracy may be contested by populist or anti-democratic
parties harbouring sympathies for authoritarian regime types.

The descriptive results in Table 5 are instructive. In Sweden and Germany, the
scores of the MPs of all parties are similarly high and above 0.85. At the same
time, the voters of these parties have consistently lower scores, mostly ranging
between 0.57 and 0.74. Only the voters of the AfD in Germany and those of the
Sweden Democrats have considerably lower scores of 0.42 and 0.30.

In the five young democracies, the mean scores of the different parties' MPs
are about as high as those in the two established democracies, although the

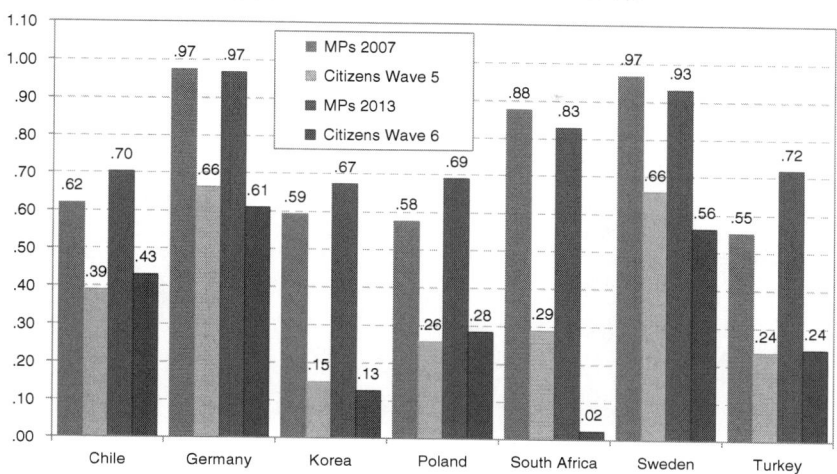

Fig. 5. Mean Support for Democracy among MPs and Citizens.
Source: MP surveys 2007 and 2013, WVS cumulated file, Waves 5 and 6. *Note*: Support for democracy: score for democracy minus higher score for either autocratic or military regime; original scores measured on a 4-point scale, rescaled to range 0–1; range of difference −1 to +1.

MPs of the RN and the PPD in Chile, of the Saenuri Party in Korea, of the PiS in Poland and of the AKP in Turkey show some authoritarian proclivities. Even though none of these parties openly advocates replacing democracy by an authoritarian regime, the results indicate that support for democracy is more ambiguous among the representatives of these parties than one should expect in a consolidated democracy. At the same time, the citizens of all five young democracies lag those of Sweden and Germany by a wide margin, a few exceptions such as the voters of the BDP in Turkey and of the two right-wing parties in Sweden and Germany notwithstanding.

In South Africa finally, the MPs of the two major parties express an exceptionally high commitment to democracy, while the voters of both parties seem to have lost their confidence in democracy.

PRELIMINARY SUMMARY AND MULTIVARIATE ANALYSIS

In this section, the central results of the data analysis will be summarised, followed by a multiple regression analysis to determine whether important individual-level determinants that were disregarded in the previous analysis exert an additional influence on the political legitimacy beliefs.

The results confirm the first theoretical assumption regarding considerable differences between MPs and citizens for all indicators and all seven countries.

Table 5. Mean Support for Democracy[b] among MPs and Citizens by Party Affiliation in the 2010s.

Party Affiliation[a]	MPs 2013	Citizens Wave 6	Difference
Chile			
UDI – Union Democrata Independiente	0.70	0.33	0.37
RN – Renovacion Nacional	0.65	0.47	0.18
PDC – Partido Democrata Cristiano	0.76	0.42	0.34
PPD – Partido por la Democracia	0.62	0.37	0.25
PSC – Partido Socialista	0.70	0.52	0.18
Total	0.70	0.43	0.27
Germany			
CDU/CSU – Christlich Demokratische Union	0.95	0.63	0.32
SPD – Sozialdemokratische Partei Deutschlands	1.00	0.57	0.43
Buendnis 90/Die Gruenen	0.98	0.65	0.33
FDP – Freie Demokratische Partei	0.94	0.74	0.20
Die Linke	0.98	0.58	0.40
AfD – Alternative für Deutschland[c]		0.42	
Total	0.97	0.61	0.36
Korea			
NFP – Saenuri dang	0.59	0.14	0.45
DP – United Democratic Party – Minju ang	0.78	0.17	0.61
Total	0.67	0.13	0.54
Poland			
PiS – Prawo i Sprawiedliwosc	0.59	0.21	0.38
PO – Platforma Obywatelska	0.77	0.35	0.42
SLD – Sojusz Lewicy Demokratycznej	0.75	0.34	0.41
Total	0.69	0.28	0.41
South Africa			
ANC – African National Congress	0.84	0.03	0.81
DA – Democratic Alliance	0.84	0.02	0.82
Total	0.83	0.02	0.81
Sweden			
V – Vaensterpartiet	0.89	0.73	0.16
S – Arbetarepartiet	0.94	0.57	0.37
M – Moderata Samlingspartiet	0.89	0.58	0.31
MP – Miljoepartiet de Groena	1.00	0.72	0.28
Other centrist parties combined (FL + KD + C)	0.96	0.69	0.27
Sverigedemokraterna	0.93	0.30	0.63
Total	0.93	0.56	0.37
Turkey			
AKP – Adalet ve Kalkinma Partisi	0.62	0.22	0.40
CHP – Cumhuriyet Halk Partisi	0.92	0.22	0.70
MHP – Milliyetci Hareket Partisi	0.76	0.30	0.46
BDP – Barış ve Demokrasi Partisi	0.75	0.53	0.22
Total	0.72	0.24	0.48

Source: MP survey 2013, WVS cumulated file, Wave 6.
[a]Support for democracy: score for democracy minus higher score for either autocratic or military regime; original scores measured on a 4-point scale, rescaled to range 0–1; range of difference −1 to +1.
[b]Party affiliation: for MPs party membership; for citizens: vote intention.
[c]The AfD (*Alternative für Deutschland*) was founded in 2013, but gained representation in the German Bundestag only in the elections of 2017.

The differential was least pronounced for confidence in political parties and largest for the value attributed to democracy, with a much broader rejection of authoritarian system types among the MPs.

The second assumption predicting considerably lower scores for the five young democracies is only partly supported by the data. Confidence in political parties is about as high and the evaluation of the democratic performance of the political regime is only slightly lower in the new democracies. The most dramatic differences between the old and new democracies in our study have been found with respect to support for democracy. This violates the assumption of a hierarchical order of the three objects of legitimacy that postulates a linear increase in the level and the stability of political support from specific to diffuse.

Taking the very high sympathy score attributed to democracy in Table 5 alone rather than the scores for the combined index, the results would have preserved the hierarchy of legitimacy beliefs. However, the more demanding index of support for democracy is the more valid indicator because it requires an explicit rejection of non-democratic regimes. The results for this index reveal that many citizens in the five young democracies have ambivalent feelings about different regime types and therefore do not reject authoritarian systems as unequivocally as the Swedish and the German respondents.

The overall temporal stability found in the data does not support the third assumption that the economic crisis has diminished the legitimacy of democracy in the five young democracies. This interpretation is supported by the fact that economic policy attitudes such as support for a reduction of income differences, for an increase in government ownership of industry and for the evaluation of the financial situation of the respondents' household are not statistically related to the legitimacy indicators.

Therefore, the causes for the observed differences between the seven countries in the indicators of political legitimacy and support for democracy should be sought in political rather than economic factors. However, as the WVS includes no questions on satisfaction with the economic situation, it cannot be ruled out that the decline in support for democracy among South African citizens was at least partly caused by the economic conditions in the country. South Africa is the poorest country in our sample. While the economic recession was not as deep as in some of the other six countries, South Africa has still not been able to reach its pre-crisis GDP and its economy is still declining. The advent of democracy has not fulfilled the promise of improving the standard of living for the great majority of the people. On the other hand, it seems doubtful that the sharp decline in support for democracy can be explained by the economic situation alone. The dismal government performance under President Zuma certainly has to take part of the blame. In any case, the increase in support for non-democratic regime types indicates that democratic consolidation has suffered a considerable setback and that the stability of today's South African democracy continues to depend primarily on the presence of a strong elite consensus.

Regarding the fourth assumption about the relevance of political polarisation within the party systems, the MP surveys indicate that polarisation was most pronounced with respect to the evaluation of the democratic quality of the country. In 2013, the differences between the MPs of the government and the opposition parties were below 0.15 in the two established democracies and Chile, but fairly high in South Africa (0.31), Poland (0.36), Korea (0.40) and a staggering 0.58 in Turkey. The differences between the two major parties are less pronounced with respect to support for democracy (0.18 in Poland, 0.19 in Korea and 0.30 in Turkey). Overall, the data point to a considerable polarisation over the regime institutions in these three countries.

To explore whether and to what extent individual-level determinants also affect political legitimacy beliefs, a multiple regression analysis follows. The small number of only seven countries precludes a systematic inclusion of macro-factors such as the level of corruption, persisting deficits in the rule of law or the degree of domestic unrest that frequently have been shown to have an impact on political trust and other aspects of political legitimacy (van der Meer, 2017). The data do allow, however, determining whether individual-level factors that are known to influence political legitimacy beliefs play a role as additional explanatory variables. These are the affiliation with a party in government and ideological orientation (left–right). Additionally, level of education and interest in politics are included as control variables for the population.[8]

The following regression analysis will take into account only one macro-factor, namely, the age of democracy (young vs established democracies). As the evaluation of the democratic quality of the political system showed a relatively high and consistent relationship with confidence in political parties and support for democracy, it was included as an additional independent variable in the regression models for the two other dependent variables.

Instead of a dummy variable for old and new democracies, dummies for the five new democracies were introduced. Their regression coefficients indicate the country-specific deviations from the two established benchmark democracies. The results for the two regression analyses for MPs and citizens are presented in Tables 6 and 7.

Table 6 for the MPs shows that the country effects are strongest for support for democracy and reflect the country means in Fig. 5. Membership in a party in government has a fairly strong effect on the MPs' evaluation of the democraticness of the political system which, in turn, has the largest influence on confidence in political parties but is not a significant predictor of support for democracy. The explanatory power of the independent variables is relatively weak with an r^2 of only 19.2% for confidence in political parties and best with an r^2 of 41.2% for the evaluation of the democraticness of the political system. Support for democracy ($r^2 = 24.6\%$) depends significantly on country-specific factors in four of the new democracies with the exception of South Africa where support for democracy among MPs was nearly as high as in Sweden and Germany. A rightist ideological orientation is highly significant as well and negatively related to support for democracy.

The results in Table 7 for the citizens differ in important ways from those for the MPs. The explanatory power of the models for confidence in political parties and for the evaluation of the democraticness of the political system is rather low, while it is considerably higher for support for democracy. As before, the effects of

Table 6. MPs: Regression Analysis for the three Legitimacy Variables.

Independent Variables	Dependent Variable: Confidence in Political Parties		Dependent Variable: Democratic Quality of the Regime		Dependent Variable: Support for Democracy	
	B	Std.error	B	Std.error	B	Std.error
Constant	0.421***	0.025	0.695***	0.013	1.052***	0.035
Government-opposition[a]	0.006n.s.	0.013	0.215***	0.010	−0.003n.s.	0.018
Ideological orientation[b]	0.024n.s.	0.022	0.071***	0.020	−0.200***	0.030
Democraticness of country[c]	0.223***	0.031			−0.003n.s.	0.042
Chile[d]	−0.068***	0.017	−0.065***	0.015	−0.291***	0.023
Korea[d]	−0.014n.s.	0.018	−0.186***	0.015	−0.325***	0.024
Poland[d]	−0.215***	0.019	−0.147***	0.017	−0.270***	0.026
South Africa[d]	−0.074***	0.017	−0.064***	0.016	−0.127***	0.024
Turkey[d]	0.078***	0.019	−0.273***	0.016	−0.317***	0.026
Explained variance	0.192		0.412		0.246	

Source: MP surveys 2007 and 2013, cumulated file.
Level of significance: n.s. = not significant, * = 0.05, ** = 0.01, and *** = 0.001.
[a]Member of a party in government (1) or an opposition party (0).
[b]Left–right orientation, 10-point scale, rescaled to 0–1.
[c]Evaluation of the democratic quality of the country, 10-point scale, rescaled to range 0–1.
[d]Dummy variables for the five young democracies; Sweden and Germany as benchmark cases.

Table 7. Citizens: Regression Analysis for the three Legitimacy Variables.

	Dependent Variable: Confidence in Political Parties		Dependent Variable: Democratic Quality of the Regime		Dependent Variable: Support for Democracy	
	B	Std.error	B	Std.error	B	Std.error
Constant	0.143***	0.010	0.618***	0.007	0.458***	0.016
Government-opposition[a]	0.037***	0.005	0.078***	0.005	0.013n.s.	0.008
Ideological orientation[b]	0.048***	0.010	0.088***	0.009	−0.139***	0.016
Democraticness of country[c]	0.202***	0.010			0.181***	0.017
Interest in politics[d]	0.117***	0.008	0.014*	0.007	0.128***	0.013
University education[e]	0.002n.s.	0.006	0.023***	0.005	0.112***	0.009
Chile[f]	−0.069***	0.008	−0.058***	0.007	−0.174***	0.013
Korea[f]	0.004***	0.007	−0.132***	0.006	−0.460***	0.012
Poland[f]	−0.107***	0.008	−0.160***	0.007	−0.292***	0.013
South Africa[f]	0.059***	0.008	−0.061***	0.007	−0.457***	0.013
Turkey[f]	0.043***	0.008	−0.132***	0.007	−0.332***	0.013
Explained variance	0.129		0.111		0.243	

Source: WVS cumulated file, Waves 5 and 6.
Level of significance: n.s. = not significant, * = 0.05, ** = 0.01, and *** = 0.001.
[a]Vote intention for a party in government (1) versus vote intention for an opposition party or no vote intention (0).
[b]Left–right orientation, 10-point scale, rescaled to range 0–1.
[c]Evaluation of the democratic quality of the country, 10-point scale, rescaled to range 0–1.
[d]Interest in politics, 4-point scale, rescaled to range 0–1, low to high.
[e]Respondent attended a university (1) versus lower educational level (0).
[f]Dummy variables for the five young democracies; Sweden and Germany as benchmark cases.

country-specific factors are rather strong. Ideological orientation, the evaluation of the democraticness of the political system, interest in politics and a university education are other significant factors influencing support for democracy, while electoral support for the parties in government is insignificant.

CONCLUSIONS

The main result of the foregoing analysis is certainly that the global economic crisis has had no or only a minor effect on the legitimacy of democracy in six of the seven countries. It cannot be ruled out that this is because of the fact that the recession was simply not severe and long enough to have any major effects.

The empirical results instead provide ample support for the assumption that political legitimacy, measured as confidence in political actors, a positive evaluation of the democratic performance of the political system and support for democracy, is higher among MPs – and in elites more generally – than among voters. This is already visible in looking at the country-specific means for the three indicators. The MP–citizen differential is considerably larger in the new democracies. This confirms that the elites' value orientations and actions are highly relevant for the consolidation of democracy.

The strong country-specific effects evident in the data confirm the importance of idiosyncratic factors reflecting the historical legacies and the cultural differences of the diverse set of countries in our study. While research on political legitimacy has mostly dealt with democratic countries sharing a common cultural legacy, the analysis suggests that the growing number of democracies in countries with different cultural backgrounds necessitates the inclusion of countries with different cultural backgrounds in comparative research to find out to what extent such legacies influence the chances for the consolidation of democracy. The fact that it shares a common cultural background with the European countries may explain why the consolidation of democracy has been more successful in Chile than in the other four young democracies of our study. Even though one should expect that the consolidation of democracy in Poland – as a European country – would progress very fast as well, the legitimacy of democracy is still lower there. This may be owing to the long period of communist rule in Poland, which is probably responsible for the very low confidence in political parties in that country. It may also dampen the enthusiasm of the Polish people to embrace democracy as the better system of government.

With respect to South Africa, it is plausible to assume that citizens displeased with the poor political and economic performance of the political system, rather than punishing the party in government for its failures by withdrawing their electoral support, have started questioning whether the democratic model is appropriate for their country. In South Korea, it is likely that the tradition of a strong state and the cultural aversion to social and political conflicts has prevented Koreans from accepting that conflict can be a productive social force.

Looking at the results for Turkey, finally, it is obvious why the consolidation of democracy has failed. The MPs of the AKP are not particularly committed to democracy and support for democracy is low among the voters of both major parties. At the same time, confidence in the parties is rather high, which has given the government wide latitude to change the balance of power in favour of the ruling party. It remains to be seen if the democratic forces in the CHP will be able to gain an electoral majority and to successfully challenge President Erdoğan who has concentrated all governmental power in the presidency.

Finally, given the negligible impact of economic policy attitudes on the indicators of the legitimacy of democracy, it seems insufficient to assume that economic success is the most important precondition for the consolidation of new democracies.

NOTES

1. The project team includes members from all seven countries under the leadership of Ursula van Beek, head of the Transformation Research Unit at the University of Stellenbosch. So far, four monographs on the results of the project have been published. The first volume (Van Beek, 2005) analysed the transition to democracy in only five countries, including the former *German Democratic Republic*. The three ensuing volumes were devoted to monitoring the development of democracy in the seven countries (Van Beek, 2010, 2011, 2019).

2. After the breakdown of communism in the Soviet Union and the democratisation of its former satellite states in Central and Eastern Europe, the *Federal Republic of Germany* (FRG) and the communist *German Democratic Republic* reunited in 1990. This involved the formal accession of the five eastern German states (Länder) and the eastern districts of Berlin by way of adopting the constitutional and legal framework of the Federal Republic. Yet, despite huge public subsidies and private investments over a period of nearly 30 years since German unification, the economic productivity and the salaries in the eastern states still trail those in the western part of the country.

3. The first MP survey was funded by the Daimler Foundation with additional funding by the Fritz Thyssen Stiftung for the German survey. Funding for the second survey was provided by the Swedish Riksbankens Jubileumsfond. The support of these foundations is gratefully acknowledged.

4. The V-Dem data (Release 9) are accessible on the website of the V-Dem project (https://www.v-dem.net/en/), the best and most comprehensive collection of data on the historical development of democracy worldwide.

5. The higher score for one of the two authoritarian regime types was deducted from the score for democracy.

6. Germany did not participate in Wave 4 of the WVS, and in Poland this question was only included in Waves 5 and 6.

7. It should be noted that Lekalage (2016) reports a much higher rejection rate for autocratic regime types in 2015 (80%). The Afrobarometer survey used a different question wording, however. It asked if respondents were in favour of abolishing elections and parliament and letting the president decide everything instead. The broad rejection of this statement was probably caused by the widespread dissatisfaction with President Zuma rather than measuring a general rejection of autocratic rule. Another Afrobarometer question asked if respondents were willing to forego elections in favour of a non-elected government that would guarantee basic services such as safety, rule of law, housing and jobs. The latter question was supported by 61% of the respondents. This confirms that the wording of survey questions is of utmost importance. The second question is probably a better

indicator of regime preference than the first question that primarily measures confidence in the sitting president.

8. These control variables were not included in the regression analysis for the MPs because social background is known to have a negligible effect on elite attitudes.

REFERENCES

Albertus, M., & Menaldo, V. (2018). *Authoritarianism and the elite origins of democracy*. Cambridge: Cambridge University Press.

Armingeon, K., & Guthmann. K. (2013). Democracy in crisis? The declining support for national democracy in European countries, 2007–2011. *European Journal of Political Research, 53*(3), 423–442.

Berg-Schlosser, D. (2015). The impact of the Great Recession on regime change: Economic and political interactions. *Taiwan Journal of Democracy, 11*(1), 37–52.

Berg-Schlosser, D., & Mitchell, J. (Eds.). (2002). *Authoritarianism and democracy in Europe 1919–39: Comparative analyses*. Houndmills: Palgrave Macmillan.

Cordero, G., & Simón, P. (2015). Economic and support for democracy in Europe. *West European Politics, 39*(2), 1–21.

Dalton, R. J. (2006). *Citizen politics* (2nd ed.). Washington, DC: CQ Press.

Dalton, R. J. (2017). Political trust in North America. In S. Zmerli & T. W. G. van der Meer (Eds.), *Handbook on political trust* (pp. 375–394). London: Edward Elgar.

Diamond, L. (2008). *The spirit of democracy*. New York, NY: Henry Holt and Company.

Diamond, L. (2016). *In search of democracy*. Abingdon: Routledge.

Du Plessis, S., Freytag, A., & Boshoff, W. (2015). Deliberate recovery. Policy, politics, the economic recovery from the international financial crisis. *Taiwan Journal of Democracy, 11*(1), 17–36.

Fuchs, D. (2007). The political culture paradigm. In R. J. Dalton & H.-D. Klingemann (Eds.), *The Oxford handbook of political behavior* (pp. 161–184). Oxford: Oxford University Press.

Fuchs, D., Guidorossi, G., & Svensson, P. (1995). Support for the democratic system. In H.-D. Klingemann & D. Fuchs (Eds.), *Citizens and the state* (pp. 323–353). Oxford: Oxford University Press.

Gangl, M., & Guistozzi, C. (2018). *The erosion of political trust in the Great Recession*. CORRODE Working Paper #5, Goethe-Universität, Frankfurt A.M., Germany.

Haggard, St., & Kaufman, R. R. (2016). *Dictators and democrats. Masses, elites and regime change*. Princeton, NJ: Princeton University Press.

Hernández, E., & Kriesi, H. (2016). The electoral consequences of the financial and economic crisis in Europe. *European Journal of Political Research, 55*(2), 203–224.

Higley, J., & Burton, M. (2006). *Elite foundations of liberal democracy*. Lanham, MD: Rowman & Littlefield.

Hoffmann-Lange, U. (2008). Studying elite vs mass opinion. In W. Donsbach & M. W. Traugott (Eds.), *The Sage handbook of public opinion research* (pp. 53–63). London: Sage.

Hoffmann-Lange, U. (2018). Parliamentarians' evaluations of the global economic crisis. *Historical Social Research, 43*(4), 175–202.

Holmberg, S. (1999). Down and down we go: Political trust in Sweden. In P. Norris (Ed.), *Critical citizens. Global support for democratic governance* (pp. 103–122). Oxford: Oxford University Press.

Holtmann, E., Gabriel, O. W., Maier, J., Maier, M., Jaeck, T. & Leidecker, M. (2015). *Deutschland 2014:25 Jahre friedliche Revolution und Deutsche* Einheit [Germany 2014:25 years after peaceful revolution and German unity]. Berlin, Germany: Die Beauftragte der Bundesregierung für die neuen Bundesländer. Retrieved from https://www.bmwi.de/Redaktion/DE/Publikationen/Studien/deutschland-2014-25-jahre-friedliche-revolution-und-deutsche-einheit.html. Accessed on May 27, 2018.

Inglehart, R., et al. (Eds.). (2014). *World values survey: All rounds – Country-pooled datafile*. Madrid, Spain: JD Systems Institute. Retrieved from http://www.worldvaluessurvey.org/WVSDocumentationWVL.jsp

Klingemann, H.-D. (2018). The impact of the global economic crisis on patterns of support for democracy in Germany. *Historical Social Research, 43*(4), 203–234.

Klingemann, H.-D., & Hoffmann-Lange, U. (2018). The impact of the global economic crisis on support for democracy. *Historical Social Research, 43*(4), 164–174.

Lekalage, R. (2016). Support for democracy in South Africa declines amid rising discontent with implementation. *Afrobarometer* 71. Retrieved from http://afrobarometer.org/sites/default/files/publications/Dispatches/ab_r6_dispatchno71_south_africa_perceptions_of_democracy.pdf. Accessed on April 21, 2018.

Lindberg, St., Coppedge, M., Gerring, J., Teorell, J., et al. (2014). V-Dem: A new way to measure democracy. *Journal of Democracy, 25*(1), 159–169.

Lipset, S. M. (1959). Some social requisites of democracy: Economic development and political legitimacy. *American Political Science Review, 53*(1), 69–105.

Listhaug, O., & Wiberg, M. (1995). Confidence in political and private institutions. In H.-D. Klingemann & D. Fuchs (Eds.), *Citizens and the state* (pp. 298–322). Oxford: Oxford University Press.

McClosky, H. (1964). Consensus and ideology in American politics. *American Political Science Review, 58*(2), 361–382.

McClosky, H., & Brill, A. (1983) *Dimensions of tolerance.* New York, NY: Russell Sage Foundation.

Møller, J., Schmotz, A., & Skaaning, S.-E. (2015). Economic crisis and democratic breakdown in the interwar years: A reassessment. *Historical Social Research, 40*(2), 301–318.

Morlino, L., & Quaranta, M. (2016). What is the impact of the economic crisis on democracy? Evidence from Europe. *International Political Science Review, 37*(5), 618–633.

Norris, P. (1999). Introduction: The growth of critical citizens. In. P. Norris (Ed.), *Critical citizens? Global support for democratic governance* (pp. 1–27). Oxford: Oxford University Press.

Polavieja, J. (2013). Economic crisis, political legitimacy, and social cohesion. In D. Gallie (Ed.), *Economic crisis, quality of work and social integration: The European experience* (pp. 256–278). Oxford: Oxford University Press.

Sartori, G. (1976). *Parties and party systems.* Cambridge: Cambridge University Press.

Sniderman, P. M., Fletcher, J. F., Russell, P. H., Tetlock, P. E., & Prior, M. (1991). The fallacy of democratic elitism: Elite competition and commitment to civil liberties. *British Journal of Political Science, 21*(3), 349–370.

Tooze, A. (2018). *Crashed. How a decade of financial crises changed the world.* New York, NY: Viking.

Van Beek, U. J. (Ed.). (2005). *Democracy under construction: Patterns from four continents.* Opladen: Barbara Budrich Publishers.

Van Beek, U. J. (Ed.). (2010) *Democracy under scrutiny: Elites, citizens, cultures.* Opladen: Barbara Budrich Publishers.

Van Beek, U. J. (Ed.). (2011). *Democracy under stress. The global crisis and beyond.* Opladen: Barbara Budrich Publishers.

Van Beek, U. (Ed.). (2019). *Democracy under threat: A crisis of legitimacy?* Basingstoke: Palgrave Macmillan.

Van der Meer, T. W. G. (2017). Political trust and the "crisis of democracy". In *Oxford research encyclopedia of politics.* Retrieved from http://oxfordre.com/politics/view/10.1093/acrefore/9780190228637.001.0001/acrefore-9780190228637-e-77. Accessed on March 30, 2019.

Wroe, A. (2016). Economic insecurity and political trust in the United States. *American Politics Research, 44*(1), 131–163.

UNRAVELLING UNCHANGED SUPRANATIONAL COMMITMENT OF NATIONAL POLITICAL ELITES DURING THE EUROZONE CRISIS

Borbála Göncz

ABSTRACT

The chapter examines the evolution of individual attitudes of the national political (parliamentarian) elite towards a supranational entity such as the European Union in the changing political context during times of economic crisis. General attitudes towards the European integration process and federal/ intergovernmental preferences for governance are analysed with a hierarchical approach taking into account individual level data, party characteristics and the country context with a comparative perspective across three time points during the period of the economic crisis. Contrary to expectations, results show that supranational attitudes of the national political elites remained quite stable and the increasing presence of extremist parties in national parliaments did not have a significant effect, while individual drivers of attitudes, such as an instrumental evaluation of the benefits of EU membership and attachment to Europe remained key determinants.

Keywords: European Union; political elites; attitudes; supranationalism; party positions; economic crisis

INTRODUCTION

The crisis that the European Union (EU) is currently undergoing, also called multidimensional, already has different stages. It started in 2008 with the global financial crisis that lead to the 2009–2010 Eurozone or economic crisis, followed

Elites and People: Challenges to Democracy
Comparative Social Research, Volume 34, 61–89
Copyright © 2019 by Emerald Publishing Limited
All rights of reproduction in any form reserved
ISSN: 0195-6310/doi:10.1108/S0195-631020190000034004

by the 2015 migration or Schengen crisis. The 2016 still not settled Brexit and the recent challenge of illiberalism in certain member states can also be considered different manifestations of the current crisis (Dinan, Nugent, & Paterson, 2017; Hooghe & Marks, 2019). All of these drew the attention to the weak foundations of the EU system of governance (Dinan et al., 2017). While the crisis itself did not create the main dilemmas the EU has been facing, it certainly intensified the issues. Different facets of the crisis brought about different problems of the European integration, also rooted in the way the previous stage of the crisis was handled: how supranational was the intended solution, how politicisation happened and how identities were activated. While the Eurozone or economic crisis seems to have contributed to the strengthening of supranational institutions, supranational delegation was also a way to avoid further politicisation of the problem resulting in the rise of Eurosceptic parties (Börzel & Risse, 2018; Gerhards & Lengfeld, 2015). In this context, the following refugee crisis lead to more politicisation and the activation of identity politics, which made a coordinated response from the member states difficult (Börzel & Risse, 2018); instead of seeking a solution through supranational delegation as in the first case, the refugee crisis triggered national solutions.

Among other dilemmas, the crisis further fuelled the questioning of the democratic legitimacy of the European integration project and contributed to rising Euroscepticism. Austerity measures following the economic crisis also contributed to increased dissatisfaction with the ruling elites that brought about nationalist, populist and anti-EU parties all over Europe. National elites have always been a driving force of the European integration process by shaping institutions and policies of the European Union; it is thus crucial for the European project to see how attitudes of national parliamentarian elites have changed.

While numerous works deal with different angles of attitudes towards the EU among the general public, elite research in this respect is much more limited both in terms of available data and the scope of these research. As far as the national political arena is concerned, it is usually party positions towards European issues that are dealt with. This chapter takes a novel approach in this respect: it combines individual attitudes of members of national parliament (MPs) with their respective party positions. In the chapter, individual opinions of national elite members are analysed building on survey data collected among MPs in 2007 and 2009 in the *Integrated and United? A Quest for European Citizenship in an Ever Closer Union (INTUNE)* project as well as in 2014 in the *European National Elites and the Crisis (ENEC)* project. These data are combined with respective waves (2006, 2010 and 2014) of the *Chapel Hill Expert Survey* (CHES) as far as party attitudes are concerned.

The purpose of this chapter is to examine the evolution of attitudes of the national political (parliamentarian) elite towards the European Union during the period of the Eurozone crisis in nine European countries,[1] that is, to what extent the attitudes have changed in this changing political context of increased criticism and in times of economic recession. This way, only the first stage of the on-going crisis is dealt with. The chapter focusses on the concept of supranationalism. National parliamentarians' supranationalism is approached through two different dimensions: general perceptions of the European integration project and preferences for supranational governance are analysed. The chapter adopts a hierarchical approach: besides individual-level factors of influence, party and country characteristics are taken into account. It is found that individual attitudes of national parliamentarians are explained by their attachment to Europe, their instrumental evaluation of a country's EU membership, while their socialisation to EU institutions does not play an important role. Members of traditionalist/authoritarian/nationalist (TAN) parties, or with a radical position either on the left or the right, are less inclined to support supranationalism, while the effect of regional cleavages seem to disappear if controlled for individual- and party-level predictors. The main result of the chapter, however, is that no significant change was detected in the different dimensions of supranationalism over the studied period. National political elite's attitudes, this way, seem to be quite stable, although there are initial signs that this might be eventually due to polarisation of the attitudes.

The chapter is structured as follows. The first part sums up the theoretical frame and formulates hypotheses. It is followed by the presentation of the methodology of the analysis and the variables used. Then, the factors influencing attitudes are addressed through hierarchical multivariate models. Finally, the main findings are summarised, discussing their implication on the future of the European integration project.

THEORETICAL FRAMEWORK AND HYPOTHESES

According to the new elite paradigm a consensually unified elite produces a stable regime ensuring smoother operation of institutions (Best, Lengyel, & Verzichelli, 2012; Higley & Burton, 1989, 2006). Consensus, in general, is related to shared rules and codes of political conduct, and rests on an integrated structure of interactions to secure cooperation and competition within the democratic regime (Higley & Burton, 1989). Consensus, in the case of the European integration project, might refer to the need for a certain level of integration of national elites in terms of shared concept of European integration to achieve a smooth functioning of EU institutions. The question is what would be a shared idea of the EU, and how this has changed over the period of economic crisis.

Preference for Further Integration without Supranationalism?

Supranationalism is a wide concept that applies to governance arrangements where states delegate some of their sovereignty to an entity that stands above the nation state (Nugent, 2003). It can entail decision-making logics, behavioural norms and decision-making procedures (Schimmelfennig, 2015a). Supranationalism is a key term in the main theories of the integration process. For liberal intergovernmentalists, the baseline theoretical approach by 2000, the European integration is primarily seen as the result of intergovernmental bargaining process along national preferences where supranational actors have little or no influence (Moravcsik, 1998). Neo-functionalism, ideas abandoned by the 1980s, but revived owing to globalisation and the emergence of post-industrial problems (Sandholtz & Stone Sweet, 2012), on the other hand, promotes the idea of delegation of rule-making authority from the national to the EU level, where the latter is increasingly functioning as a supranational governance (Haas, 2004). In terms of the European integration project, supranationalism usually appears in opposition to intergovernmentalism or state–centrism when it comes to the character of the institutional setting of the European Union. Preference for the form of governance in the EU is assumed to appear on a continuum ranging from intergovernmentalism with the bargaining of national representatives to a centralised structure of governance and primary role of supranational organisations on the other end (Stone Sweet & Sandholtz, 1997). On the two ends of this intergovernmental versus federal continuum is the primary role of the member states appearing against the authority of the European Commission. Although federalism often appears as a synonym for supranationalism, in Haas's (2004) original conception of the European integration's institutional and procedural frame supranationalism does not equate to federalism, but is conceived as a hybrid structure between the federal and the intergovernmental approaches.[2] Within this hybrid structure called supranationalism, the European Commission and the member states are complementing institutions, jointly providing political guidance. This governance preference for the complementarity of intergovernmentalism and supranationalism either appears in previous studies as the rejection of the dominance of either the Commission or the member states, called 'institutional pragmatism' (Hooghe, 2012), or alternatively, one can attribute importance to both the Commission and the member states as central actors, also called a 'compound' model (Cotta & Russo, 2012). However, these diverse forms of complementarities can all be interpreted as different levels of supranationalism and incorporated, this way, to the proposed intergovernmental versus federal governance continuum.

Another question is how general acceptance of the European integration project relates to preferences for the form of governance in the EU. While within a neo-functional conception of the integration project, it is a common assumption that the process of European integration is inherently supranational, and thereby, preferences for further integration are tied to preferences for supranational governance, a recent study has questioned this equating of deeper integration and increasing federalism/supranationalism. Bickerton, Hodson, and Puetter (2015) challenged theories that associated integration with transfers of competences from the national to supranational levels of governance with introducing the concept of 'new intergovernmentalism'. Their proposition is that the post-Maastricht era is characterised by integration without supranationalism in which the increasing level of integration is based on intensification of policy coordination of the member states instead of delegation of competences. They argue that member states pursue more integration but resist any further supranationalism, what they call 'integration paradox'. The new intergovernmentalism is assumed to rely on deliberative and consensual behaviour of members states. Although criticised as an idea applicable only for new policies instead of being a new theory (Schimmelfennig, 2015b), it raises the question how this translates to individual preferences or attitudes towards the EU among national political elites. Following the logic of the proposed 'new intergovernmentalism', a sound proposition would be that:

> *H1*. Supporting further European integration does not necessarily translate to preferences for supranational governance.

It is worth, in this way, to deal with these two different aspects of supranationalism separately.

Rising Euroscepticism?

Euroscepticism is not a new phenomenon; the increasingly critical and politicised public opinion needs to be taken into account for a while (e.g. Carrubba, 2001; Steenbergen, Edwards, & De Vries, 2007). This period of 'constraining dissensus', being more pronounced since the Maastricht Treaty, produced diverse forms of Euroscepticism among the general public, which are on the rise since the outburst of the economic crisis with an increased questioning of the legitimacy of the European integration project.

Support for a political system provides legitimacy to it, while it secures stability for its smooth functioning according to system theorists (Easton, 1965; Harteveld, van der Meer, & De Vries, 2013). Support might be understood in two ways: specific support would be based on the perception of the performance of a system, while a diffuse support might represent a reservoir of positive attitudes towards a system making people to accept unfavourable outputs. Indeed, an unfavourable economic environment might have an eroding effect on specific support for a political system, and is, this way, directly affected by economic difficulties (Easton, 1965; Ringlerova, 2015). After a period of economic growth, the financial crisis that developed into a sovereign debt crisis indeed came with economic hardship, rising unemployment rates and slowing economic growth rate in several EU member states, which revealed the lack of the economic convergence of countries with very different economic performance and different capacities to cope with the crisis. The rising political disillusionment and rising Euroscepticism fuelled populist parties and led to shifts in governments in Greece, Ireland, France, Italy, Portugal, Spain, Slovenia, Slovakia, Belgium, the Netherlands and the United Kingdom.

If support for the European integration project is characterised by weighing the economic performance of the EU and its member states, it is quite likely that the national elite's opinion is following similar tendencies as the general public with increasing Euroscepticism. Furthermore, parliamentary elites were also affected by the crisis and the following austerity measures in terms of their capacities to decide and sovereignty of their country. Elites of both debtor and creditor countries might have been affected with the previous group being reluctant to apply the prescribed measures, the latter with their hesitance to provide financial help. This way, it may be supposed that:

H2a. In this period of economic hardship, support for the European integration project among the national political elites has decreased, along with the preferences for supranational governance, giving way to increasing intergovernmentalism.

Nevertheless, the idea that economic factors define support is not unanimously shared; in fact, it is revealed that the link between economic factors and Euroscepticism is weak and other factors than economic hardship might be causing the latter (Rosamond, 2017). Besides, following the logic of diffuse support, positive dispositions towards the EU might as well persist despite bad economic performance and economic challenges.

Furthermore, not all countries of the European Union were equally hit by economic difficulties. In Southern member states before the economic crisis, pro-EU attitudes were exceptionally widespread, linking the idea of European integration to modernisation and democratisation processes (Conti, 2014). However, these countries (and Ireland) were the most seriously affected by the crisis. The financial aid for Eurozone countries that were not able to get their sovereign debts financed (i.e. Greece, Portugal, Ireland, Spain and Cyprus) was conditional on austerity measures that caused further economic and social devastation, which later were blamed for low economic growth in the entire European Union. While Ireland and Portugal managed to exit their bailout programmes in 2014, the tension between Greece and the remaining Eurozone countries prevailed. In creditor countries, on the other hand, the consensus on providing financial help was of varying degree, with Germany showing a high consensus on the matter, while in France there was a higher variety of party attitudes (Conti, 2014).

New member states from Central and Eastern Europe (CEE) were less affected by the crisis, but they are traditionally more reluctant to deeper integration. These countries are members of the EU for a shorter period with a relatively newly acquired national sovereignty after the regime change that they might be reluctant to give up. Nevertheless, as these countries are characterised by a liberal state and a dependent market economy relying on foreign direct investments and foreign firms, and by a technological gap (Hancké, Rhodes, & Thatcher, 2007), they are also called dependent market economies (Nölke & Vliegenthart, 2009). Economic development in these countries after the transition and more importantly after joining the EU was usually based on increased foreign investment and infrastructural development, often financed by EU transfers (Ó Beacháin, Sheridan, & Stan, 2012; Magone, 2011). Economic openness and the high exposure to internationalisation might also be reason why the issue of European integration remains salient (Conti, 2014).

In this way, it is suggested that regional cleavages in the EU became more apparent during the crisis. The distinction between Eurozone and not-Eurozone countries, Eastern and Western member states, Northern and Southern, creditor and debtor countries, increased (Dinan et al., 2017) and traditional patterns of contestation might have been altered:

H2b. Coming from an Eastern member state means less positive attitude towards European integration and less positive attitudes towards the idea of supranational governance.

H2c. Coming from a Southern member state means less positive attitude towards European integration and less positive attitudes towards the idea of supranational governance.

Party or Individual-level Determinants of Supranational Attitudes?

According to the idea of politicisation, the issue of European integration is not only increasingly present in everyday life, but also in party politics as well and recently became an important issue in national party competition. When dealing with the rising Euroscepticism, it has been suggested that public Euroscepticism is primarily absorbed by new or extreme parties (Dalton, 2016; Rohrschneider & Whitefield, 2016), and the rising Euroscepticim is rather due to elite turnover instead of changing attitudes of elite members. These parties have an explicit interest in opposing European integration to differentiate themselves from the others. Mainstream parties, on the other hand, bound by previous reputation are quite stable in their positions on the EU and, this way are less likely to respond to public disillusionment, although differences exist between old and new member states. Mainstream parties in new member states have less reputational investment in this respect owing to their countries' recent membership (Rohrschneider & Whitefield, 2016). The position of a party on European integration issues is, in this way, gaining importance in the domestic party competition. However, it is generally true that the centre parties tend to be more open to international interdependence and to support European integration on an instrumentalist basis, while the extreme parties are more likely to reject the idea of the EU, albeit for different reasons: on the extreme left the EU is criticised as being too much in favour of a liberal free market, while on the right the supranational character of the EU is rejected (Aspinwall, 2002).

It is assumed that a party's position on European integration is associated with their stands on two dimensions that are structuring political competition in the national political arena (Marks, Hooghe, Nelson, & Edwards, 2006). While the ideological position on the economic left–right dimension defines a party's position on questions of redistribution, welfare and government regulation of the economy, another dimension, related to non-economic or communal issues, also structures the political space. The latter, very diverse dimension contrasting liberal and postmaterialist values against traditional, authoritarian and nationalist approaches, might encompass many issues and goes along groups of green/alternative/libertarian (GAL) versus traditionalist/ authoritarian/ nationalist (TAN) parties (Marks et al., 2006). These two dimensions produce very specific patterns of contestation of European integration. Party attitudes are strongly clustered along the left–GAL versus the right–TAN dimension. Taking these dimensions into account parties on the economic left are often socially liberal as well, as in the case of social democrats or green parties. These left–GAL orientations also produce more positive attitudes towards the EU. Parties towards the right–TAN end of the political spectrum, like conservatives and Christian democrats express a more reserved enthusiasm towards European integration. However, the two main sources of opposition to Europe is an extreme leftist attitude of the party, opposing the integration as an elitist capitalist project, or a radical TAN stance of the party in which case European integration is viewed as an elitist supranational project that weakens national autonomy and traditional values. In this way, supposing that MPs attitudes and opinions are well-embedded in party positions:

H3a. MPs in parties with higher TAN scores demonstrate a less positive attitude towards European integration and are more willing to reject the idea of supranational governance.

H3b. Likewise, MPs in parties with higher left scores demonstrate a less positive attitude towards European integration and are more willing to reject the idea of supranational governance.

H3c. MPs in parties with more extreme positions, either on the GAL/ TAN or the economic left–right spectrum, demonstrate a less positive attitude towards European integration, and are more willing to reject the idea of supranational governance.

The second proposition is all the more relevant as the Eurozone crisis is supposed to have increased left-wing Euroscepticism as the opposition should have been triggered by an opposition of the EU conceived as a liberal project (Börzel & Risse, 2018). However, these main drivers of contestation of the integration project, although proved to be valid across EU countries are conditioned by the domestic party structure of a certain country.

As a heritage of the state–socialist regime and the characteristics of the post-transition period, the structure of party competition in Eastern countries is somewhat different. As opposed to the mentioned general tendencies in Western member states, the source of contestation of the European project tends to be unipolar in new member states of Central and Eastern Europe where traditional party structure produces left–TAN and right–GAL parties, of which only the former is opposing the idea of European integration (Marks et al., 2006). This way, as opposed to Western countries where left and TAN criticism appear in the opposite spectrum of the national political space, in Eastern countries these dimensions collapse in the same parties making the source of contestation unipolar. Nevertheless, despite the intensity of the effect of these two dimensions on party attitudes, the main tendency of causality remains similar in Western and Eastern countries (Marks et al., 2006):

H3d. The effect of the party position on the GAL/TAN and economic left–right dimensions has a distinct intensity on attitudes of MPs coming from an Eastern member state.

Besides party ideological orientations, other individual dispositions of national parliamentarians about questions of European integration must also have an effect. Individual attitudes towards the European integration project have been amply discussed with regards to public opinion. Several explanations about the individual drivers of the opinions on the European integration process have been elaborated where instrumental and identity-based explanations got the majority of the attention. According to the utilitarian logic, attitudes towards European integration are defined by a rational evaluation of the EU's advantages and disadvantages at the individual or at the country level (e.g. Anderson, 1998; Brinegar & Jolly, 2005; Eichenberg & Dalton, 1993; Gabel, 1998; McLaren, 2006). On the other hand, identity-based explanations put forward the effect of affective attachment to Europe on the perceptions of the European integration process (e.g. Bruter, 2005; Carey, 2002; Duchesne & Frognier, 1995; Hooghe & Marks, 2005; McLaren, 2006; Opp, 2005; Risse, 2010; Robyn, 2005), where belonging to a group or loyalty is decisive in defining attitudes, especially among the general public owing to lower level of cognitive capacities, knowledge or interest towards the issue (Hooghe & Marks, 2009). Therefore it is assumed that:

H4a. A more positive instrumental evaluation of the benefits of the European integration leads to more positive attitude towards European integration and more positive attitudes towards the idea of supranational governance.

H4b. Likewise, a higher level of attachment to Europe leads to more positive attitude towards European integration and more positive attitudes towards the idea of supranational governance.

It is also important to note that rational evaluation of a country's EU membership might be in line with the idea of specific support to a system, while identity-driven attitudes might provide diffuse support to a system (Fuchs, 2011), being also less prone to change in time. It has also been suggested that instrumental evaluation of the question might have increased over the period of the Eurozone crisis owing to increased politicisation of the issue (Hobolt & Wratil, 2015).

Furthermore, Europeanisation of everyday lives and social contexts, that is, travelling abroad, foreign contacts, etc., also called social transnationalism (e.g. Kuhn, 2011; Mau, 2010), are increasingly shaping everyday experiences of the people. Members of the parliament, however, are in a position even more exposed to that phenomenon than the general public. Exposed to European questions in an everyday basis in their work, members of the national parliament might undergo a socialisation process that lead to changed, more European attitudes with changed expectations and behaviours. In the neo-functionalist theoretical approach, European integration is happening partly through this process: integration occurs if European elites seek supranational solutions for shared problems (Haas, 1961). Constructivist perspectives on the European integration process also stress the importance of social learning in a European environment leading to common meanings and beliefs (Checkel, 2003). These shared rules, shared codes of political conduct and an integrated structure of interactions play a key role in securing cooperation and competition within a regime and contributing to stable functioning of it according to the new elite paradigm as well (Higley & Burton, 1989). This socialisation process has been primarily studied among EU officials and MEPs, but only limited evidence was found for its existence (Beyers, 2005; Hooghe, 2005; Scully, 2005), underscoring that before eventually 'going native', a pre-selection takes place as those who are exposed to this potential Europeanisation are already those who had more European dispositions, and their socialisation is foremost embedded in the national context. Even though socialisation of national civil servants might be even more limited, frequent contacts with EU institutions might nevertheless have an effect on attitudes towards Europe:

> *H5*. Personal international experiences and experiences with European institutions contribute to more positive attitude towards European integration and more positive attitudes towards the idea of supranational governance.

DATA AND METHOD

Individual supranational attitudes of national political elites are dealt with based on survey data collected among MPs in 2007 and 2009 within the INTUNE project as well as in 2014 within the ENEC project. Nine countries are included in the analysis, limited by the available data: Bulgaria, France, Germany, Greece, Hungary, Italy, Lithuania, Portugal and Spain. Although not all EU member states are represented, the list includes new member states from state–socialist past, and both creditor and debtor countries during the crisis. Northern countries are missing from the sample, so the main tendencies found are only valid for the countries included. The country samples (see Appendix 1) consist of members of the national parliaments (MPs) representing their composition in terms of gender, party affiliation and front/back-bencher positions.

The comparative analysis takes into account the effect of the Eurozone / economic crisis through the three years of data collection. Changes in national political elites' attitudes have, however, several sources. Changes might be due to changing attitudes of national political elite members, but can also be owing to elite turnover, that is, changing elite members and the appearance of new, anti-EU parties in national parliaments. Indeed, several elections were held in the countries included in the analysis over the studied period. As seen in Appendix 1, the share of first time MPs, a possible indicator of elite turnover, shows a great variance over the waves and the different countries, the highest shares are found in the Greek (50%) and the Italian (68%) parliaments in 2014. Furthermore, the general trends show that the number of newcomers was significantly higher in 2014 than in the preceding waves. Changes in the national parliaments included in the analysis also meant changes in their party composition. While Socialists/Social democrats and Liberal parties, traditionally in the left–TAN segment being more positive towards the EU, decreased their share in the parliaments over the period, Conservatives and Christian Democrats, rather in the right–TAN segment with more reserved attitudes towards the EU, increased their share (see Table 1). Outside mainstream parties, New left parties that tend to be more critical towards European integration, and Extreme right parties, supposedly the most Eurosceptic party grouping, also increased their presence.

Dimensions of Supranationalism – Dependent Variables

Supranationalism is addressed through two manifestations of the term: general attitudes towards the European integration project and preferences for supranational governance. The latter is conceived as a continuum between intergovernmentalism (primary role of member states) and federalism (primary role of the European Commission; Stone Sweet & Sandholtz, 1997).

General attitudes towards European integration were measured by asking whether one thinks that European unification should be strengthened or if it has already gone too far.[3] Attitudes proved to be quite stable over the period of the crisis, with only Hungarian and Italian national elites changing their opinion significantly (see Table 2). Italian MPs showed a decreasing support for further unification between 2007 and 2009, but by 2014, their positions became the second most positive after the Spanish elite. In contrast, the Hungarian elite became more positive by 2009, followed by a significant drop in positive attitudes by 2014. The Spanish elite proved to be the most positive and the Lithuanian elite the most negative among the countries included in the analysis.

The other, more specific measure of supranational attitudes is related to preferences for supranational governance in the European Union. Usually intergovernmentalist/state–centrist attitudes are opposed to federalist/ supranational preferences, appearing in one continuum. An obvious methodological choice to reproduce such a continuum is through the construction of an index: how one

Table 1. Party Families by Wave.

	2007	2009	2014
$N =$	747	617	595
%	100.0	100.0	100.0
Socialists/social democrats	40.4	35.8	30.6
Conservatives	26.5	29.0	30.4
Liberals	5.9	4.9	2.4
Christian democrats	5.9	7.9	13.9
Right liberals	5.2	6.2	2.7
Left liberals	4.0	6.3	2.4
Communists	2.1	1.1	1.0
Greens	1.7	1.3	1.8
New left	1.1	2.4	6.7
Agrarians	0.9	0.3	0.0
Extreme right	0.0	0.5	2.0
Ethnic minority, regionalist, others	6.2	4.2	6.1

Sources: INTUNE 2007, 2009, ENEC 2014
Cramer's V: 0,183****

Table 2. Attitudes towards European Unification and Supranational Preferences for Governance (Average on a 0–10 Scale).

	European Unification			Supranational Governance		
	2007	2009	2014	2007	2009	2014
Bulgaria	6.67	6.75	7.21	4.19	4.26	3.72
France	6.48	6.84	6.94	5.32	3.66	3.31
Germany	7.41	7.62	7.56	3.65	4.39	4.29
Greece	7.57	7.24	7.03	3.97	4.27	3.72
Hungary	6.43	7.12	5.05	4.83	5.16	3.06
Italy	7.72	7.04	7.88	5.38	5.12	5.56
Lithuania	6.34	6.27	5.97	3.31	3.69	3.09
Portugal	6.74	6.43	6.75	3.40	4.00	3.98
Spain	8.13	8.11	8.02	5.19	5.13	5.37

Sources: INTUNE 2007, 2009 and ENEC 2014.

evaluates the role of (a) the member states and (b) the European Commission (EC) as central actors of the integration project. The former stands for inter-governmental preferences, while the latter for federal solutions. The index was constructed by subtracting the answer given to these two statements from one another. The individual difference between the preferred level of a federalist solu-tion and the preferred level of an intergovernmental solution creates a continuum where on the one end pure intergovernmentalist preferences and on the other end pure federalist preferences are found. This index was then rescaled on a 0–10 scale to help comparison with the previous measure.

The main tendency is that preferences for supranational institutional design increased slightly between 2007 and 2009, but decreased by 2014 (see Table 2). In line with previous tendencies in terms of the general supranational attitudes, Spanish and Italian MPs are the most supranational while the Lithuanian are the most state-centred in their institutional preferences. French parliamentarians had strong supranational preferences in 2007 that turned towards an increasing intergorvernmentalism in 2009 and 2014. Their German counterparts followed an opposing tendency with an increasing supranationalism between 2007 and 2009, while Hungarian parliamentarians became the most state–centred by 2014 from a rather supranationalist position before.

In terms of the link between these two manifestations of supranationalism, it is suggested that the 'integration paradox' (Bickerton et al., 2015) applies, that is, that member states are favourable to more integration but reject any further supranationalism that would involve delegation of competences. The link between the two dimensions (H1) can be explored through bivariate correlation analysis (see Table 3). While the relation between the two dimensions was rather weak at the outset, it evolved during the period and became stronger by 2014. There were important regional differences as well: the two dimensions are the most con-nected in Southern countries, however, CEE countries also perform better than their French or German counterparts. This way, the results did not confirm the 'integration paradox' if individual attitudes of MPs are concerned, and *H1* can be

Table 3. Spearman Correlation between Attitudes towards European Unification and Supranational Preferences for Governance

	Nonparametric Corr.	Sig.	N
Total	0.356	***	1,867
2007	0.256	***	676
2009	0.343	***	580
2014	0.465	***	611
Western	0.231	***	360
Western × 2007	0.037		117
Western × 2009	0.287	***	117
Western × 2014	0.349	***	126
CEE	0.319	***	598
CEE × 2007	0.25	***	224
CEE × 2009	0.316	***	208
CEE × 2014	0.374	***	166
Southern	0.404	***	909
Southern × 2007	0.327	***	335
Southern × 2009	0.397	***	255
Southern × 2014	0.489	***	319

Significance: *** < 0.01, ** < 0.05, * < 0.1.

discarded. The two explored aspects of supranationalism are, even if the relation is not that strong, positively connected.

A Regression Approach – Explanatory Variables

Factors influencing supranational attitudes are analysed through a hierarchical regression approach in which the dependent variables are general supranational attitudes towards further strengthening of the European integration project (Models 1a,b) and preferences for intergovernmental /federalist governance in the EU (Models 2a,b). To see how elite attitudes changed over the studied period (*H2a*), the regression models are run on pooled data including all countries across the three time points of the data collection (2007, 2009 and 2014) where 2009 and 2014 results are compared to 2007. To control for the effect of the country context referring to debtor and creditor countries during the Eurozone crisis, and for initial differences in terms of attitudes towards the European integration process, Southern and CEE member states will be compared to Western member states *H2b* and *H2c*).

Besides countries or country groups, parties also represent an important context for individual attitudes of national parliamentarians. To take this context into account, the individual-level data were combined with party characteristics from the 2007, 2010 and 2014 waves of the Chapel Hill Expert Survey (CHES) trend file (Bakker et al., 2015; Polk et al., 2017). Expert's evaluation on a certain party's position on the economic left–right and the GAL/TAN scale was used matching each MP's party with its respective evaluation in the respective year.

Fig. 1 shows how GAL/TAN and economic left–right positions (taken from the CHES database) combines with party families (taken from the INTUNE/ENEC

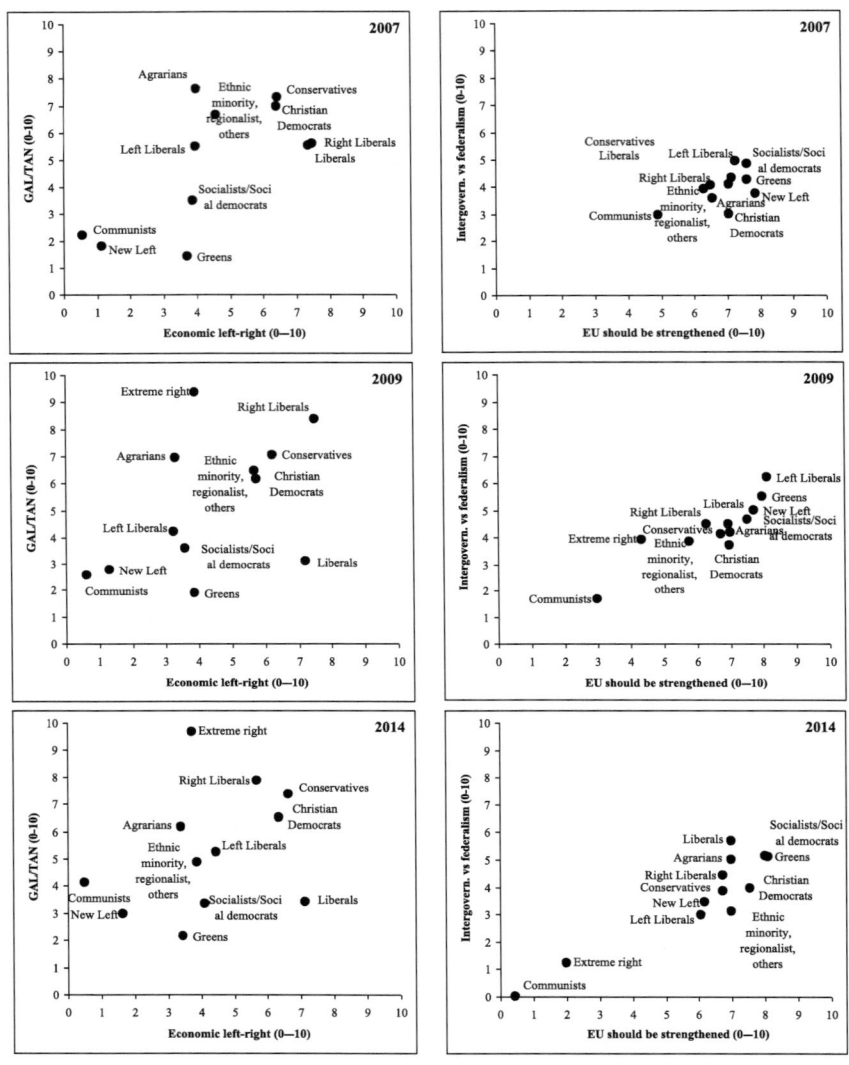

Fig. 1.   Party Families in Terms of Their Positions on the GAL/TAN and Economic
Left–Right Dimensions and Their Members' Individual Attitudes towards the
European Integration Process.

Sources: CHES 2006, 2010, 2014, INTUNE 2007, 2009, ENEC 2014.

database), and how these party families perform in terms of their members' individual attitudes towards the European integration process. Overall, party family positions are quite stable in the space defined by the GAL/TAN and on the
economic left–right dimensions, and more or less follow what has been suggested
by Marks et al. (2006). Conservative, Christian Democratic parties and Right

Liberals can all be found in the right–TAN segment, while Agrarians and Extreme right parties (not included in the 2007 wave yet) are placed in the left/TAN segment. Left/GAL parties include Communists, the New Left, Social Democratic parties, the Greens and Left Liberal parties, while Liberals are the only party family in the right–GAL segment (except for 2007). Ethnic minority and regionalist parties are regrouping various parties with eventually different positions and size; this might be the reason for its changing position across the different waves. Furthermore, some fluctuation might be due to regional specificities, that is, different structure of political contestations in Western and Eastern countries: while positions of Social Democratic, Christian Democratic, Conservative and Liberal parties are quite similar, radical TAN parties show a rather rightist orientation in Western countries and a rather leftist orientation in Eastern countries (Marks et al., 2006), making, interestingly, the Extreme right parties appear rather in the centre, leaning towards the left. Similarly, Agrarian parties have a rightist orientation in the West, while following leftist values in the East.

When exploring how party families/ positions translate into individual attitudes towards the European integration process of their members in national parliaments, results are in line with previous studies. Furthermore, some important tendencies are revealed. MPs of mainstream parties (Social Democrats, Christian Democrats, Conservatives and Liberals) do indeed hold a more positive opinion about supranationalism (Marks et al., 2006), while members of Extreme right and Communist parties take more and more distance from these across the different waves of the analysis.

MPs in mainstream parties with left/GAL orientation (Socialists / Social democrats and Greens) are more Euroenthusiastic, while those coming from a party with more accentuated TAN values (Conservative and Christian Democrats) are somewhat less positive. The overall suggestion that mainstream parties are also more stable in terms of their party position related to the EU seems to be valid for individual attitudes of their members as well. On the other hand, the most noticeable changes, besides the Communists and the Extreme right parties, happened to attitudes of MPs of New Left and Left liberal parties. Interestingly, MPs in Agrarian parties, supposed to hold less favourable party positions towards the EU owing to TAN values, are to be found among the mainstream and with less pronounced Europessimistic attitudes as it could have been expected.

In this way, besides taking into account the effect of parties' positions on the economic left–right (*H3b*) and the GAL/TAN scale (*H3a*), in the regression models the extremeness of these positions is also addressed (*H3c*); furthermore, the latter is decomposed to its effects in 2009 and 2014 and compared to 2007, whereas its effects in Southern and CEE countries are compared to Western countries (*H3d*). Using these interaction terms, the increased presence of extremist parties can be controlled for and the phenomenon can be better understood.

The regression models include several individual level explanatory variables as well. According to previous studies it is supposed that supranational attachment will have a positive effect on supranational preferences (identity-based explanations – *H4b*), just as positive evaluation of a country's EU membership (instrumental explanations – *H4a*). The socialisation hypothesis (*H5*) approaches supranationalism of national elites through personal experiences. Frequent contacts with EU institutions are thus considered as a European socialisation effect on parliamentarians. Indeed, contacts became more frequent by 2014, 55% of the MPs interviewed is in contact with EU institutions at least once a month as opposed to 47% in 2007. This tendency is especially noticeable in Italy, Lithuania and Portugal. Besides professional experiences with the EU, other previous transnational experiences such as having lived abroad are also supposed to be important drivers of supranationalism. Sex and the year of birth are included as socio–demographic control variable. The measurement and expected effects of the different variables are summarised in Appendix 2.

This way, the presented regression models have the objective to reveal the effect of individual-, party- and country-level determinants of supranational attitudes of national political elites. In the regression models, a multilevel approach is used to take into account the 'nested' character of the data: when the clustering of individuals by certain groups such as countries or parties might violate the assumption of independent error terms (Steenbergen & Jones, 2002). This approach has already been applied in several studies dealing with attitudes towards the EU (Brinegar & Jolly, 2005; Hooghe & Marks, 2005; Steenbergen et al., 2007). Individual attitudes of MPs, in this case, are contextualised with respect to three dimensions. The country constitutes the first context that needs to be taken into account. Second, these national characteristics may change over time, especially during a period of crisis such as the Eurozone crisis. To take nation and time appropriately into account as contextual dimensions a two-level linear regression approach is used. Level one is constituted by individual MPs, while level two is a combination of their respective countries and the year in which the three surveys were conducted (country in year). As 9 countries are included in the analysis at three different points in time, the total number of level-two units equals 27. Party characteristics were modelled as level one determinants.[4]

In this way, in the regression models both individual, party- and country-level explanatory variables are included; however, it is worth mentioning that these models do not necessarily represent causal relationships in technical terms. All the presented regression models are random intercept models where the intercept (the average value of the dependent variables) is allowed to vary across countries.[5]

DETERMINANTS OF THE ATTITUDES – THE RESULTS OF THE REGRESSION MODELS

Results of the hierarchical linear regression models show that the included variables explain about 22–24% of the variance of the attitudes towards further strengthening of the European integration while less, 11%, of the variance of preferences towards supranational governance of the EU. In terms of general attitudes towards the EU (Model 1a) no significant change was detected across the different waves, while MPs in Southern countries were slightly more favourable to further strengthening European integration than their counterparts in Germany and France, both creditor countries. This finding is in line

Table 4. Hierarchical Linear Regression on Individual Attitudes towards European Unification.

	Model 1a			Model 1b		
	EU Should Be Strengthened			EU Should Be Strengthened		
	Coef.	P>|z|	Std.Err.	Coef.	P>|z|	Std.Err.
Fixed Effects						
wave2009	−0.096		0.236	0.420	*	0.239
wave2014	−0.061		0.228	0.879	**	0.387
South	0.410	*	0.225	0.424		0.316
CEE	−0.339		0.234	−0.168		0.387
Female	0.051		0.109	0.046		0.106
Year of birth	−0.005		0.006	−0.006		0.006
European attachment	0.630	****	0.091	0.613	****	0.084
Country benefited	2.040	****	0.471	1.890	****	0.446
Contacts	0.030		0.048	0.026		0.048
Lived in another EU country	0.018		0.116	−0.001		0.115
GAL/TAN	−0.210	****	0.038	−0.183	****	0.037
GAL/TAN extr.	0.003		0.020	0.055		0.039
GAL/TAN extr. × CEE				−0.018		0.046
GAL/TAN extr. × South				0.034		0.044
GAL/TAN extr. × 2009				−0.069	***	0.022
GAL/TAN extr. × 2014				−0.126	****	0.038
Left–right	0.046		0.058	0.033		0.054
Left–right extr.	−0.051	*	0.027	−0.015		0.035
Left–right extr. × CEE				0.000		0.041
Left–right extr. × South				−0.038		0.042
Left–right extr. × 2009				−0.046		0.045
Left–right extr. × 2014				−0.059		0.051
Constant	4.161	****	0.502	3.828	****	0.550
Variance Components						
Level 1 (individual)	4.094	(.256)	****	4.028	(.251)	****
Level 2 (country × wave)	0.222	(.072)	****	0.177	(.065)	***
n_{ij} =	1,746			1,746		
n_j =	27			27		
−2 × Log Likelihood (−2LL)	7,451.698			7,419.216		
−2LL difference (to unconditional model)	963.796			996.279		
R_{12}	0.215			0.235		

Notes: Random intercept models. Maximum likelihood estimates with adaptive quadrature. Estimated standard errors in parenthesis/with italics. Significance: **** < 0.001, *** < 0.01, ** < 0.05, * < 0.1.

with previous suggestions (Conti, 2004) that in these countries political elites are more Euroenthusiastic; however, there was no evidence for the expected negative change owing to dissatisfaction caused by the imposed austerity measures. In terms of the effects of party positions, MPs in TAN parties are indeed less favourable towards further strengthening of the EU while the left–right position of the party does not make a difference. Extreme positions do not seem to matter much

Table 5. Hierarchical Linear Regression on Individual Preferences for Supranational Governance.

	Model 2a			Model 2b		
	Supranational Governance			Supranational Governance		
	Coef.	*P>|z|*	Std.Err.	Coef.	*P>|z|*	Std.Err.
Fixed Effects						
wave2009	0.024		*0.371*	0.276		*0.358*
wave2014	−0.319		*0.393*	−0.024		*0.362*
South	0.574		*0.439*	0.744	*	*0.399*
CEE	0.082		*0.405*	0.410		*0.388*
Female	−0.263		*0.170*	−0.244		*0.169*
Year of birth	−0.002		*0.006*	−0.002		*0.006*
European attachment	0.342	****	*0.079*	0.342	****	*0.078*
Country benefited	1.261	**	*0.542*	1.214	**	*0.557*
Contacts	0.037		*0.070*	0.033		*0.069*
Lived in another EU country	0.244	**	*0.118*	0.230	***	*0.117*
GAL/TAN	−0.261	****	*0.045*	−0.278	****	*0.041*
GAL/TAN extr.	−0.015		*0.016*	0.012		*0.027*
GAL/TAN extr. × CEE				−0.001		*0.036*
GAL/TAN extr. × South				−0.037		*0.040*
GAL/TAN extr. × 2009				−0.015		*0.032*
GAL/TAN extr. × 2014				−0.019		*0.050*
Left–right	0.074		*0.062*	0.105		*0.065*
Left–right extr.	−0.034	*	*0.018*	0.005		*0.042*
Left–right extr. × CEE				−0.108	*	*0.060*
Left–right extr. × South				0.002		*0.040*
Left–right extr. × 2009				−0.036		*0.038*
Left–right extr. × 2014				−0.056		*0.036*
Constant	2.937	***	*0.991*	2.651	***	*0.947*
Variance Components						
Level 1 (individual)	4.637	(.334)	****	4.606	(.334)	****
Level 2 (country × wave)	0.496	(.105)	****	0.519	(0.114)	****
$n_{ij} =$	1783			1783		
$n_j =$	27			27		
$-2 × $ Log Likelihood (−2LL)	7,843.382			7,832.643		
−2LL difference (to unconditional model)	766.668			777.407		
R_{12}	0.110			0.112		

Notes: Random intercept models. Maximum likelihood estimates with adaptive quadrature. Estimated standard errors in parenthesis/with italics. Significance: **** < 0.001, *** < 0.01, ** < 0.05, * < 0.1.

either, while in terms of left–right positions it has a slight negative effect, in terms of extreme GAL/TAN positions the main effect is not significant. Nevertheless, if decomposed by waves (Model 1b), it seems that the latter has a significantly increasing effect on individual attitudes, but still, overall it is not yet significant. Nevertheless, if the differentiated effect of extreme GAL/TAN positions through the different waves is controlled for, the main effect of time becomes significant.

This means that if it was not for the impact of the extreme GAL/TAN parties, general support towards European integration might even have increased over the period as opposed to expectations. These results eventually show signs of possible polarisation of elites' attitudes. If standard deviance is considered as a measure for polarisation, it has indeed increased somewhat in the studied period, especially in France, Greece, Portugal and Hungary in 2014 (see Fig. 2).[6]

Beyond the effect of party positions, individual-level predictors also, if not most importantly, play a major role. A higher European attachment and a favourable instrumentalist evaluation of the EU membership both have a significant and positive effect on the attitudes towards further strengthening European integration. The different measures of socialisation, however, did not seem to matter.

Tendencies of preferences about supranational governance show some similarities (Model 2a). Time and country groups do not have a significant impact on individual attitudes, while the GAL/TAN party dimension does, in the expected direction, TAN party positions coexist with lower preference for supranational governance. The left–right dimension, however, makes a difference only when it is considered on its extremes, when it has a negative effect. When decomposing

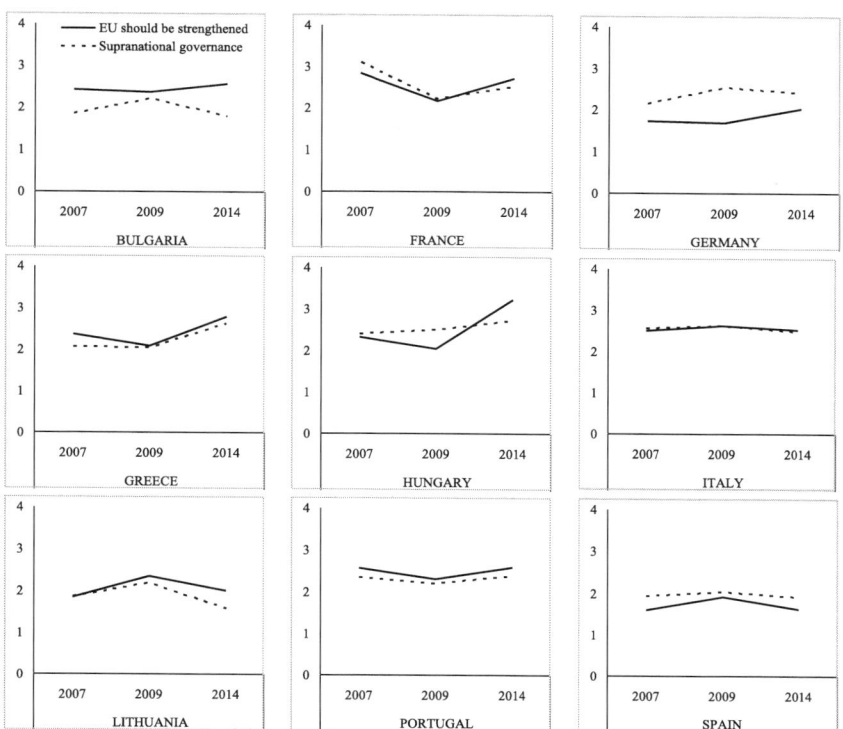

Fig. 2. Polarisation of Attitudes towards European Unification and Preferences for Supranational Governance (Standard Deviation).

this effect it is revealed that this mainly comes from CEE countries (Model 2b). The decomposition of the different dynamics in the different country groups also reveals that MPs in Southern countries are more favourable for supranational governance than their counterparts either in other Western countries or in CEE countries, which stands in contradiction of expected tendencies. In terms of individual level predictors, similarly to general attitudes, preferences for supranational governance are also positively linked to identity-based factors and instrumentalist approaches. Socialisation, however, seems to matter for supranational preferences of governance. Not professional socialisation though, but personal experiences of having lived in another EU countries contribute to being more favourable to a supranational form of governance in the EU as opposed to a state-centrist approach.

Summarising these results in terms of the proposed hypotheses it seems that national elites' attitudes towards supranationalism is rather stable despite initial expectations. There is no evidence that it would have decreased, in fact, some results suggest that it may even become more positive if the slightly increasing effect of extreme GAL/TAN party positions are under control. This way, *H2a* is disproved. There was no significant impact of regional differences either, at least in the expected direction: despite initial expectations about the detrimental effect of imposed austerity measures, MPs in Southern member states managed to preserve their initially more positive attitudes towards the different aspects of supranationalism even if this effect is very weak. This way, *H2b* about MPs in Eastern member states being less favourable towards European integration is rejected, and *H2c* about the same effect in Southern member states is proved to be opposite.

In terms of the effect of party positions, the GAL/TAN positions indeed play an important role in the formation of individual attitudes. The more traditionalist/authoritarian/nationalist a party is, the less favourable are its members towards the European integration process, while green/alternative/libertarian party positions mean more individual Euroenthusiasm as well, meaning that *H3a* is proved to be right. The party position on the economic left–right scale, nevertheless, has no effect at all despite initial expectations. In this sense individual attitude formation differs from party positions on European integration matters and *H3b* is disproved. Extreme positions on these two dimensions, on the other hand, show different dynamics. Extreme GAL/TAN party positions do not play a significant role in individual attitudes; however, there is a slightly increasing but still not statistically significant tendency of its effect over time. Extreme positions on the economic left or right dimension, on the other hand, has indeed a slight negative effect, but it is only true in CEE countries. In this way, results show mixed evidences for *H3c*, which is disproved in the case of extreme GAL/TAN party positions, while the results confirm *H3d* in the sense that indeed there are regional differences, although in different ways than was expected. The GAL/TAN and the economic left–right dimensions in party positions do not have a more or less intense effect on individual attitudes of MPs in Eastern member states, but extreme positions on the economic left–right have a slight, but detectable influence only in these countries.

Besides party positions, individual-level predictors proved to be of key importance to understand MPs supranational attitudes. The two main logics of support, confirmed several times among the general public, are of key importance among members of the national political elites as well. Both attachment to Europe and instrumentalist evaluation of a country's EU membership proved to have a positive effect on both the attitudes towards further strengthening the European integration process in general and preferences for supranational governance in the EU. As a result, both *H4a* and *H4b* are confirmed. It is difficult, however, to compare their effect to the effect of party-level determinants within models or to each other across models owing to different scale and level of measurement. Socialisation to EU institutions, on the other hand, however it may seem relevant as a driver of supranational attitudes of national parliamentarians, did not play a significant role. Nevertheless, if social transnationalism is considered in personal terms instead of the frequency of professional contacts with EU institutions, the experience of having lived abroad contributes to a higher openness towards supranational governance among members of the political elites. In this way, the socialisation hypothesis (*H5*) is just partly confirmed.

DISCUSSION/CONCLUSIONS

The aim of the chapter was to explore national political elites' supranationalism along different dimensions, see how it changed during the period of the Eurozone/economic crisis, increasing public disillusionment with the European integration project, and the rise of extremist/populist/ anti-EU parties. The chapter adopts a novel approach to analyse the question: it combines individual and party-level predictors across countries and different time points.

Supranational attitudes of MPs are dealt with through two dimensions: attitudes towards further strengthening of the European integration process and preferences for supranational governance. It seems that these two dimensions are increasingly and positively connected, and their factors of influence are also very similar. In this way, the suggestion of Bickerton et al. (2015) about the 'integration paradox', that is, growing European integration based on increased intergovernmental coordination instead of increased supranationalism, does not seem to hold when individual attitudes and preferences of national political elites are concerned. Increased support for further integration comes with increased preferences towards supranational governance according to the neo-functionalist logic of integration.

The most important outcome of the chapter is that in the nine countries included in the analysis, involving creditor countries (Germany and France), Southern (debtor) and Eastern member states of the EU, there was no significant change in the different dimensions of supranationalism over the studied period. Attitudes of national political elites seem to be quite stable with no real difference between the different country groups. Expectations that positive attitudes of national political elites would decrease owing to economic hardship or to the intervention/imposed austerity measures, do not hold. Southern countries, most affected by the crisis do not seem to follow this path either, there are even signs of persisting higher Euroenthusiasm. Furthermore, it was supposed that owing to the increasing presence of new, often extremist and populist parties in the national parliaments, change in the overall opinions would follow. Party positions indeed have an effect on individual attitudes; MPs of parties with traditionalist/authoritarian/nationalist values are indeed less inclined towards supranationalism. Extreme party positions, an indicator of the effect of the new, anti-EU parties in national parliaments, have increasing, but still not significant effect in terms of communal values (GAL/TAN) and just a slight effect when it comes to extreme party positions of the economic left–right scale, that is rather characterising Eastern member states. In fact, if it was not for the tendency of growing effects of extreme party positions on the GAL/TAN scale, supranational attitudes would even have increased. Hence, behind the overall stability of national political elites' attitudes there might still be some initial polarisation of attitudes where two different tendencies are levelling each other's effect out.

Besides the effects of party positions, the effects of the attachment to Europe and the instrumental evaluation of their country's EU membership proved to be a key to understanding individual formation of the attitudes. Although the included measures of socialisation did not prove to be decisive determinants, national political elites seem to be very committed to the European integration process. Attachment to Europe can be considered as the manifestation of diffuse support, less prone to change and resistant to bad economic performance of a system. In light of these findings, it is also interesting to note that, in terms of party positions, the left–right economic dimension, standing for redistributive issues, have less impact than the GAL/TAN dimension which is rather connected to communal concerns. This way, the source of eventual erosion of the national elite support to European integration might be due to communal issues and less redistributive ones. It seems that the European integration is less contested because of its capitalist and liberal character (extreme leftist critique), than because it weakens national autonomy and traditional values. Indeed, there are some evidences that left-wing Euroscepticism decreases supranational attitudes; however, this has not increased over the studied period during the Eurozone crisis as opposed to what has been suggested (Börzel & Risse, 2018).

A general concern when it comes to the future of the European integration is how much national elites are integrated and whether they form a consensually unified elite able to ensure stable functioning of the European Union. The results of the analysis indicate that the consensus persisted across the studied period despite economic hardship, increasing public disillusionment and the presence of extremist parties. Nevertheless, there are initial signs of the latter having an increasing effect, which might eventually cause an increasing polarisation of the attitudes in the future. Polarisation, owing to Eurosceptic stances on the other hand might have eroding effect on the elite consensus. Furthermore, previous research has shown that divided elite opinions on European integration matters, under certain circumstances, might lead to even lower support for the EU among the general public (Hooghe & Marks, 2005). Although signs of polarisation of elite attitudes are still weak in the studied period, this is a phenomenon that is worth to be checked how it has evolved after the period covered by this chapter.

ACKNOWLEDGEMENTS

The Hungarian part of the ENEC research received funding from the National Research, Development and Innovation Office (project number: 110917) between 2014 and 2017. The author was supported by the same funding while writing the initial version of this chapter.

NOTES

1. Bulgaria, France, Germany, Greece, Hungary, Italy, Lithuania, Portugal and Spain
2. 'Supranationality in structural terms, therefore, means the existence of governmental authorities closer to the archetype of federation than any past international organisation, but not yet identical with it. While almost all the criteria point positively to federation, the remaining limits on the ability to implement decisions and to expand the scope of the system independently still suggest the characteristics of international organisation.' (Haas, 2004, p. 59) and 'Thus the symbiosis of inter-ministerial and federal procedures has given rise to a highly specific, and certainly corporate, series of techniques whose tendency to advance integration is patent even though it is neither clearly federal nor traditionally inter-governmental. Yet this symbiosis and the codes connected therewith are the essence of supranationality' (Haas, 2004, p. 526).
3. The exact wording of the questions can be found in Appendix 2.
4. Time could not constitute a third level as three waves are insufficient to fulfil the common statistical criteria for the number of units at a third level. Accordingly, time couldn't be modelled as level one determinant, because by doing this all cross-level interactions would become significant. The party context could not, however, constitute a third level either, as there were many parties with very low membership. In this case, it was the small size of the groups that didn't fulfill the common statistical criteria for the size of units at a third level.
5. All models were run in STATA using GLLAMM with maximum likelihood estimation using adaptive quadrature that is considered more adequate and provide better estimates (Rabe-Hesketh & Skrondal, 2008, pp. 124–128.). Significance test for variance components were calculated according to Snijders and Bosker's (1999, p.86) suggestion.
6. The increased level of the standard deviance of the dependent variables is also noticeable in 2014, taking all countries together. Strengthening European integration: 2.32 in 2007, 2.24 in 2009 and 2.59 in 2014. Supranational governance: 2.39 in 2007, 2.36 in 2009 and 2.46 in 2014.

REFERENCES

Anderson, C. (1998). When in doubt, use proxies: Attitudes toward domestic politics and support for European integration. *Comparative Political Studies, 31*(5), 569–601.
Aspinwall, M. (2002). Preferring Europe ideology and national preferences on European integration. *European Union Politics, 3*(1), 81–111.
Bakker, R., de Vries, C., Edwards, E., Hooghe, L. Jolly, S., Marks, G., … Vachudova, M. (2015). Measuring party positions in Europe: The Chapel Hill expert survey trend file, 1999–2010. *Party Politics, 21*(1), 143–152.

Ó Beacháin, D., Sheridan, V., & Stan, S. (Eds.). (2012). *Life in post-communist Eastern Europe after EU membership*. New York, NY: Routledge.

Best, H., Lengyel, G., & Verzichelli, L. (2012). Introduction. In H. Best, G. Lengyel, & L. Verzichelli, (Eds.), *The Europe of elites: A study into the Europeanness of Europe's political and economic elites (Intune)* (pp. 1–13). Oxford: Oxford University Press.

Beyers, J. (2005). Multiple embeddedness and socialization in Europe: The case of council officials. *International Organization, 59*(4), 899–936.

Bickerton, C., Hodson, D., & Puetter, U. (2015). The new intergovernmentalism: European integration in the post-Maastricht era. *Journal of Common Market Studies, 53*(4), 703–722.

Börzel, T. A., & Risse, T. (2018). From the euro to the Schengen crises: European integration theories, politicization, and identity politics. *Journal of European Public Policy, 25*(1), 83–108.

Brinegar, A. P., & Jolly, S. K. (2005). Location, location, location. National contextual factors and public support for European integration. *European Union Politics, 6*(2), 155–180.

Bruter, M. (2005). *Citizens of Europe? The emergence of a mass European identity*. Basingstoke: Palgrave Macmillan.

Carey, S. (2002). Undivided loyalties. Is national identity obstacle to European integration? *European Union Politics, 3*(4), 388–413.

Carrubba, C. J. (2001). The electoral connection in European Union politics. *The Journal of Politics, 63*(1), 141–158.

Checkel, J. T. (2003). "Going native" in Europe? Theorizing social interaction in European institutions. *Comparative Political Studies, 36*(1–2), 209–231.

Conti, N. (2014). Introduction. In N. Conti (Ed.), *Party attitudes towards the EU in the member states. Parties for Europe, parties against Europe* (pp. 1–18). London: Routledge.

Cotta, M., & Russo, F. (2012). Europe à la carte? European citizenship and its dimensions from the perspective of national elites. In H. Best, G. Lengyel, & L. Verzichelli (Eds.), *The Europe of elites. A study into the Europeanness of Europe's political and economic elites* (pp. 14–42). Oxford: Oxford University Press.

Dalton, R. J. (2016). Stability and change in party issue positions: The 2009 and 2014 European elections. *Electoral Studies, 44*(4), 525–534.

Dinan, D., Nugent, N., & Paterson, W. E. (2017). A multi-dimensional crisis. In D. Dinan, N. Nugent, W. E. Paterson (Eds.), *The European Union in crisis* (pp. 1–15). London: Palgrave Macmillan.

Duchesne, S., & Frognier, A-P. (1995). Is there a European identity? In O. Niedermayer & R. Sinnott (Eds.), *Public opinion and internationalized governance* (pp. 193–226). Oxford: Oxford University Press.

Easton, D. (1965). *A systems analysis of political life*. London: John Wiley & Sons.

Eichenberg, R., & Dalton R. (1993). Europeans and the European community: The dynamics of public support for European integration. *International Organization, 47*(4), 507–534.

Fuchs, D. (2011). European identity and support for European integration. In S. Lucarelli, F. Cerutti, & V. A. Schmidt (Eds.), *Debating political identity and legitimacy in the European Union* (pp. 55–75). London: Routledge.

Gabel, M. (1998). Public support for European integration: An empirical test of five theories. *The Journal of Politics, 60*(2), 333–354.

Gerhards, J., & Lengfeld, H. (2015). *European citizenship and social integration in the European Union* (pp. 55–75). London: Routledge.

Haas, E. B. (2004). *The uniting of Europe: Political, social and economic forces, 1950–1957*. Notre Dame, Indiana: University of Notre Dame Press.

Haas, E. B. (1961). International integration: The European and the universal process. *International Organization, 15*(3), 366–392.

Hancké, B., Rhodes, M., & Thatcher, M. (Eds.). (2007). *Beyond varieties of capitalism: Conflict, contradictions, and complementarities in the European economy*. New York, NY: Oxford University Press.

Harteveld, E., van der Meer, T., & De Vries, C. E. (2013). In Europe we trust? Exploring three logics of trust in the European Union. *European Union Politics, 14*(4), 1–24.

Higley, J., & Burton, M. (1989). The Elite variable in democratic transitions and breakdowns. *American Sociological Review, 54*(1), 17–32.

Higley, J., & Burton, M. (2006). *Elite foundations of liberal democracy.* Lanham, MD: Rowman & Littlefield.

Hobolt, S. B., & Wratil, C. (2015). Public opinion and the crisis: The dynamics of support for the euro. *Journal of European Public Policy, 22*(2), 238–256.

Hooghe, L. (2005). Several roads lead to international norms, but few via international socialization: A case study of the European Commission. *International Organization, 59*(4), 861–898.

Hooghe, L. (2012). Images of Europe: How commission officials conceive their institution's role. *Journal of Common Market Studies, 50*(1), 87–111.

Hooghe, L., & Marks, G. (2005). Calculation, community and cues. Public opinion on European integration. *European Union Politics, 6*(4), 419–443.

Hooghe, L., & Marks, G. (2009). A Postfunctionalist Theory of European Integration: From Permissive Consensus to Constraining Dissensus. *British Journal of Political Science, 39*(1), 1–23.

Hooghe, L., & Marks, G. (2019). Grand theories of European integration in the twenty-first century. *Journal of European Public Policy, 26*(8), 1113–1133. doi:10.1080/13501763.2019.1569711

Kuhn, T. (2011). Individual transnationalism, globalisation and Euroscepticism: An empirical test of Deutsch's transactionalist theory. *European Journal of Political Research, 50*(6), 811–837.

Magone, J. M. (2011). Centre-periphery conflict in the European Union? Europe 2020, the Southern European model and the euro-crisis. In A. Ágh (Ed.), *European Union at the crossroads: The European perspectives after the global crisis* (pp. 71–122). Budapest, Hungary: Budapest College of Communication, Business and Arts.

Marks, G., Hooghe, L., Nelson, M., & Edwards, E. (2006) Party competition and European integration in the East and West. Different structure, same causality. *Comparative Political Studies, 39*(2), 155–175.

Mau, S. (2010). *Social transnationalism. Lifeworlds beyond the Nation State.* London: Routledge.

McLaren, L. M. (2006). *Identity, interests and attitudes to European integration.* Basingstoke: Palgrave Macmillan.

Moravcsik, A. (1998). *The choice for Europe: Social purpose and state power from Messina to Maastricht.* Ithaca, NY: Cornell University Press.

Nölke, A., & Vliegenthart, A. (2009). Enlarging the varieties of capitalism. The emergence of dependent market economies in East Central Europe. *World Politics, 61*(4), 670–702.

Nugent, N. (2003). *Government and politics of the European Union.* Basingstoke: Palgrave Macmillan.

Opp, K.-D. (2005). The EU and national identifications. *Social Forces, 84*(2), 653–680.

Polk, J., Rovny, J., Bakker, R., Edwards, E., Hooghe, L., Jolly, S., … Zilovic, M. (2017). Explaining the salience of anti-elitism and reducing political corruption for political parties in Europe with the 2014 Chapel Hill Expert Survey data. *Research & Politics, 4*(1), 1–9.

Rabe-Hesketh, S., & Skrondal, A. (2008). *Multilevel and longitudinal modeling using Stata* (2nd ed.). College Station, TX: Stata Press.

Ringlerova, Z. (2015). Weathering the crisis: Evidence of diffuse support for the EU from a six-wave Dutch panel. *European Union Politics, 16*(4), 558–576.

Risse, T. (2010). *A community of Europeans? Transnational identities and public spheres.* Ithaca, NY: Cornell University.

Robyn, R. (Ed.). (2005). *Changing face of European identity.* London: Routledge.

Rohrschneider, R., & Whitefield, S. (2016). Responding to growing European Union-skepticism? The stances of political parties toward European integration in Western and Eastern Europe following the financial crisis. *European Union Politics, 17*(1), 138–161.

Rosamond, B. (2017). The political economy context of EU crises. In D. Desmond, N. Nugent, & W. E. Paterson (Eds.), *The European Union in crisis* (pp. 33–53). London: Palgrave Macmillan.

Scully, R. (2005). *Becoming Europeans? Attitudes, behaviour, and socialization in the European parliament.* Oxford: Oxford University Press.

Sandholtz, W., & Stone Sweet, A. (2012). Neo-functionalism and supranational governance. In E. Jones, A. Menon, & S. Weatherill (Eds.), *The Oxford handbook of the European Union* (pp. 18–33). Oxford: Oxford University Press.

Schimmelfennig, F. (2015a). Theorising crisis in European integration. In D. Desmond, N. Nugent, & W. E. Paterson (Eds.), *The European Union in crisis* (pp. 316–335). London: Palgrave Macmillan.

Schimmelfennig, F. (2015b). What's the news in 'new intergovernmentalism'? A critique of Bickerton, Hodson and Puetter. *Journal of Common Market Studies, 53*(4), 723–730.

Snijders, T., & Bosker, R. (1999). *Multilevel analysis: An introduction to basic and advanced multilevel modeling*. London: Sage.

Steenbergen, M., Edwards, W., & De Vries, C. (2007). Who is cueing whom? Mass-elite linkages and the future of European integration. *European Union Politics, 8*(1), 13–35.

Steenbergen, M. R., & Jones, B. S. (2002). Modeling multilevel data structures. *American Journal of Political Science, 46*(1), 218–237.

Stone Sweet, A., & Sandholtz, W. (1997). European integration and supranational governance, *Journal of European Public Policy, 4*(3), 297–317.

APPENDIX 1. SAMPLE SIZE AND SHARE OF FIRST TERM MPs BY COUNTRY AND WAVE

	Sample Size				First Term MPs (%)			
	2007	2009	2014	Total	2007	2009	2014	Total
Bulgaria	83	76	53	212	62.7	0.0	42.6	35.2
France	81	68	46	195	35.8	29.4	37.0	33.8
Germany	80	79	70	229	10.0	38.0	31.4	26.2
Greece	90	41	74	205	0.0	12.2	50.0	20.5
Hungary	80	72	57	209	27.5	30.6	12.3	24.4
Italy	84	70	82	236	47.6	51.4	68.3	55.9
Lithuania	80	70	54	204	0.0	37.1	37.0	22.5
Portugal	80	68	81	229	45.0	44.1	38.3	42.4
Spain	94	81	81	256	51.1	35.8	49.4	45.7
Total	752	625	598	1975	31.3	31.7	42.2	34.7

Sources: INTUNE 2007, 2009 and ENEC 2014.

APPENDIX 2. INDICATORS, THEIR MEASUREMENT AND EXPECTED DIRECTION OF INFLUENCE

Dependent Variables	Effect	Survey Question Used
General supranational attitudes		Some say European unification should be strengthened. Others say it already has gone too far. What is your opinion? Please indicate your views using a 10-point-scale. On this scale, '0' means unification 'has already gone too far' and '10' means it 'should be strengthened'. What number on this scale best describes your position?
Preferences for supranational governance: intergovernmentalism (0) versus federalism (10)		How much do you agree with the following statements: (a) The member states ought to remain the central actors of the European Union, (b) The European Commission ought to become the true government of the European Union *Agree strongly (4)/ Agree somewhat (3)/ Disagree somewhat (2)/ Disagree strongly (1)* Statement (b) – Statement (c), variable on a −3–3 scale rescaled to 0–10 scale.
Explaining variables – individual level (level 1)		
Affective aspect of supranationalism	+	People feel different degrees of attachment to their region, to their country and to Europe. What about you? Are you very attached, somewhat attached, not very attached or not at all attached? *Very attached (4)/ Somewhat attached (3)/ Not very attached (2)/Not at all attached (1)*
Instrumental evaluation	+	Taking everything into consideration, would you say that (YOUR COUNTRY) has on balance benefited or not from being a member of the European Union? *1. Has benefited/ 2. Has not benefited/ 3. Don't know (volunteered) 4. Refused (volunteered)*
Personal professional experiences – socialisation effect	+	How frequently in your political activity were you in contact with actors and institutions of the EU in the last year? *At least once a week (4)/ At least once a month (3)/ At least once every three months (2)/ At least once last year (1)/ No contacts last year (0)*
Personal transnational experiences – socialisation effect	+	Have you ever lived in another European country (at least for three months (holidays do not account)?
Explaining variables – party level (level 1)		
GAL/TAN position	−	Position of the party in the respective year in terms of their views on democratic freedoms and rights. 'Libertarian' or 'postmaterialist' parties favour expanded personal freedoms, for example, access to abortion, active euthanasia, same-sex marriage, or greater democratic participation. 'Traditional' or 'authoritarian' parties often reject these ideas; they value order, tradition and stability, and believe that the government should be a firm moral authority on social and cultural issues. (0–10 scale) *0 = Libertarian/Postmaterialist/ 10 = Traditional/ Authoritarian*
Squared GAL/TAN position	−	Previous variable recoded on a −5–5 scale and squared – to measure extremist positions.

(*Continued*)

Dependent Variables	Effect	Survey Question Used
Economic left–right position	–	Position of the party in the respective year in terms of its ideological stance on economic issues. Parties can be classified in terms of their stance on economic issues. Parties on the economic left want government to play an active role in the economy. Parties on the economic right emphasise a reduced economic role for government: privatisation, lower taxes, less regulation, less government spending and a leaner welfare state. (0–10 scale)
		0 = extreme left/ 10 = extreme right
Squared economic left–right position	–	Previous variable recoded on a −5–5 scale and squared – to measure extremist positions.
Explaining variables – country level (level 2)		
Effect of time	–	2009, 2014 compared to 2007
CEE and Southern countries	–	CEE countries: Bulgaria, Hungary and Lithuania
		Southern (debtor) countries: Spain, Portugal, Italy and Greece
		Western (creditor) countries: Germany and France (reference category)

THE POLITICAL ELITE AND TRUST IN EU INSTITUTIONS AFTER THE CRISIS. A COMPARATIVE ANALYSIS OF THE HUNGARIAN CASE

György Lengyel and Laura Szabó

ABSTRACT

Around 2006, dissensus became predominant in the Hungarian elite concerning internal affairs. Regarding evaluations of the European integration, however, there were no considerable differences between elite groups at that time. The Hungarian political elite supported the integration process and trusted in EU institutions. The present chapter addresses the issue to what extent the elite attitudes regarding European integration prevailed following the economic crisis of 2008. After a brief overview of the Hungarian context, the authors discuss political elites' (national MPs') trust in supranational institutions in 2007 and 2014 in the European countries. Our analyses find that the Hungarian political elite became one of the most sceptical elites towards the EU.

Next, the supranational trust of political elite and other (economic, administrative and media) elite groups within Hungary is compared. Results reveal that among Hungarian elite segments there is a hidden tension: political elites are critical towards the EU, while economic and media elites are not.

Finally, turning to the international stage again, the elite–population opinion gap is investigated. It is usually the case that elites are more pro-European than the public. Recently, however, in some respects the Hungarian political elite has shown less trust in EU institutions than the population.

Keywords: Trust of elite; EU; Hungary; illiberal democracy; comparative analysis; elite-population gap

Elites and People: Challenges to Democracy
Comparative Social Research, Volume 34, 91–111
ISSN: 0195-6310/doi:10.1108/S0195-631020190000034005

INTRODUCTION: THE PROBLEM AND
ITS THEORETICAL BACKGROUND

The current Hungarian governing elite criticises federalism and the central institutions of the EU, yet envisions its position as within the European Union. It is, therefore, relevant to examine in a comparative perspective to what extent the Hungarian political elite trusts the institutions of the EU, and how this trust changed following the impact of the crisis and subsequent political transformation.

Trust is defined as expectations concerning the predictable and fair working of institutions and behaviour of people. It is a powerful indicator of well-being (i.e. quality of public services, democracy; control of corruption, income and equality) and a fundamental condition of collective action and cooperation (Eurofound, 2018). Studies of social capital have warned us, too, that trust is important for the adequate functioning of political and economic institutions (Coleman, 1990; Cook, 2001, 2009; Gambetta, 1988; Granovetter, 2017; Inglehart, 1999; Putnam, 2001). Investigation of attitudes towards European integration has been mostly done by analysing support for EU membership rather than trust in European institutions. However, as trust in EU institutions has become a central indicator of the legitimacy of the EU, we assume that low trust may indicate perceived lack of legitimacy of the integration process (Arnold, Eliyahu, & Galina, 2012; Bakonyi, 2008; Eurofound, 2018; Hooghe, 2003; Magalhães, 2012; Medgyesi & Boda, 2019).

Several studies have tried to identify factors that may lead to support for EU integration, and many theoretical foundations were built to explain these empirical findings. The *utilitarian theory* states that the citizens' support for European integration is positively related to their welfare gains from integrative policy as citizens with different socioeconomic situations experience different cost and benefits from it (Gabel, 1998). Approaching this theory from the elite perspective, we may hypothesise that the political elites of those countries which benefit from the integration process and membership – for example, the Hungarians – to a greater extent support the European Union and its institutions than those whose benefit is lower. The *cognitive mobilization theory* refers to the cognitive skills and interest of people concerning public issues (Inglehart, 1970). However, when it comes to cognitive skills of the elite groups and especially of the political elites, one may suppose that they are unanimously characterised by high level of political awareness and well-developed skills. Thus, we use proxies in our elite analysis concerning the political elites' international experiences: whether they lived in a foreign country for at least three months and the frequency of interaction with European organisations. *Partisanship* offers another explanation for the support for integration (Gabel, 1998). The citizens adopt attitudes towards integration that reflect the position of the party they support. Applying it to our context, we may assume that the political elites' trust in European institutions is shaped by the attitude towards the integration of the political party they belong to.

If elites are defined as minorities with the excessive capability to influence social reproduction owing to their position or reputation (Best, Lengyel, & Verzichelli, 2012; Higley & Lengyel, 2000) – and we accept this working definition – then, the institutional trust of elites is of exceptional importance in revealing the legitimacy of the EU as a supranational polity. When we come to the interplay between *elites* and *institutions* (Lengyel & Ilonszki, 2012; Lengyel, 2014; Martin, 2017), we follow the arguments of the new elite paradigm (Higley & Pakulski, 2012). We consider the elites as actors who have primary effects on how the institutions work instead of considering them as the passive executors of the institutional will. How the elites relate to each other, how they cooperate, if they are unified or not in relevant questions, is prior to the institutional arrangements.

Not only is the elite-institutions' interplay significant for understanding the support for EU integration so is the *elite–population interference* as well. Carrubba (2001) concluded that until 1992, both elites and the general population held the same attitudes towards the EU integration. This point leads to theories about the EU integration as an elite driven project which assures legitimacy for the elite (Best et al., 2012). Zaller (1992) has noted that the elite and mass population attitudes were closely related because the public opinion was heavily influenced by the elite discourse on political matters. The referendums held in France and the Netherlands in 2005 to ratify the European Constitution, and in Ireland in 2008 to ratify the treaty of Lisbon, were however rejected by the majority of citizens, rejecting in this way the elites' arguments to move towards further EU integration[1]. The general population became in general more sceptical about the benefits of EU membership for their countries than the elite groups; and the elites have a more positive opinion about the success of European governance for their countries than the general population.

Although there is a connection between trust and political order, as argued by Sztompka (1999), the relationship is far from straightforward. In an autocratic regime, citizens are presumed to have trust in a charismatic leader or in the ideological framing of the polity itself. However, this kind of trust may be undermined owing to the arbitrariness of leaders' actions and indirectly by the fact that the autocratic regime–citizen trust relation is asymmetrical. Such rulers do not trust citizens, and utilise harsh surveillance measures that perpetuate a vicious circle of distrust throughout society. A paradoxical feature of the trust–polity relationship is that democracy institutionalises distrust towards those who are in power. Among other factors, accountability and the separation of powers, elections, the rule of law, constitutionalism, judicial review, due process, civil rights, civil society activity, a pluralistic media and open communication are the institutional and procedural guarantees whose hindrance indicates a potential breach of trust. Democracy can work if partners accept the rules of the game and are able to reach consensus about basic issues, instead of engaging in permanent struggles. Among other factors, avoiding *ad hominem* accusations in public debates is important, according to Sztompka. A consolidated democracy presupposes citizen participation, which is built on trust in the conditions that regulate the fairness of institutions. We share these theoretical considerations, and rely upon this approach.

In the following, we investigate the trust of the Hungarian political elite in European Union institutions in three different comparative perspectives: first, in international comparison with other European political elites (members of national parliaments); second, in comparison with economic and other elite groups within Hungary; and third, with the trust of the population, again in an international context. Before doing this, it might be useful to highlight some of the political events and structural conditions of the near past to frame the situation of the current Hungarian elites' institutional trust.

THE HUNGARIAN CASE – A RETROSPECTION

During the cold war years, hard authoritarian repression and attempts at ideological indoctrination led to a revolutionary uprising in 1956, still alive in the collective memory. Although this was stamped out within weeks, with hundreds of participants sentenced to death and hundreds of thousands leaving the country, something changed afterwards. Everyday life became depoliticised and the need for blind trust in leadership was no longer stressed. The principle of 'those who are not against us are with us' was declared and applied. Consolidation then relied upon soft authoritarian methods, leading to the establishment of the image of 'Goulash Communism'. This led to moderate material gains while perpetuating the principles of political control and collective property, as well as full employment and general access to social and health services.

The fading of ideological indoctrination and the down-to-earth pragmatism of elites implied that the regime was awarded legitimacy owing to the promise of security and welfare. It also presupposed growing economic efficiency, which lead to the spread of quasi-market transactions, especially in the co-operative sector.

The economic reform that started in 1968 aimed at enhancing the efficiency and independence of enterprises. The major social impact, however, was that it created a shadow economy based on the household plots of members of agricultural cooperatives, helping mitigate chronic shortages (Kornai, 1992) and making livelihoods easier. However, the oil crisis of the 1970s hit the open Hungarian economy and increased the budget deficit. In parallel with this, after the Helsinki Declaration about security and co-operation in Europe in 1975, democratic opposition groups appeared on the margins of the Hungarian political landscape, spreading 'samizdat' publications and thematising mostly human rights, Hungarian minority issues and environmental problems. These groups became mobilising forces of later events and crystallising points for parties. The Young Democrats, a latecomer group, started their activity at the end of the 1980s as liberal human-rights activists. The core of this group consisted of law students from the countryside who were familiar with the entrepreneurial spirit of the shadow economy and were socialised partly through fraternity house debates. They formed a closed, tough, self-indulgent group with good advocacy skills and a competitive inclination.

The round table talks of 1989–1990 fit the type of transformation which is described in elite theory as 'elite settlement' (Burton & Higley, 1987). The newly emerging democratic parties and the socialist successor party representatives agreed upon the rules of the game and accepted each other's legitimacy. A multiparty representative parliamentary democracy, human rights, property rights, judicial review and a Euro–Atlantic foreign orientation were the pillars of the tacit agreement. The peaceful transformation and the accompanying market opportunities proved to be attractive to foreign investors and observers. Hungary became a member of NATO in 1999 and an EU member state in 2004 following referendums (albeit with only moderate participation). Inherited and accumulating economic difficulties due to a budget deficit and foreign indebtedness were not eased, however. Public dissatisfaction grew in the midst of electoral cycles, and was moderated by irresponsible promises made before elections.

When in 2006, the Young Democrats (FIDESZ) lost the elections, their leader, Viktor Orbán, denied the legitimacy of the governing coalition of socialists (MSZP) and old democratic opposition-based Free Democrats (SZDSZ). The pretext of this was a leaked speech by the Socialist PM Ferenc Gyurcsány, who confessed to fellow party members that leaders had misled the public during the election campaign concerning real economic conditions. There were clear signs that instead of consolidation, elites were simulating democracy, breaching norms and starting to disagree about the rules of the game (Lengyel & Ilonszki, 2012). When FIDESZ won the elections in 2010 with a two-thirds majority, it gave up the idea of consensual democracy and moved not towards a majoritarian, but – as the PM called it, following Zakaria's (1997) terminology – an illiberal model. They introduced a new constitution, media and electoral law, recentralised public administration and downsized the role of judicial review and civil society. They gained a firm hold over the media and repeated their electoral results in 2014 and 2018. In the economy multinational companies gained excessive influence, while among national companies the governing elite built strong networks (Lengyel & Bank, 2014).

DATA AND COMPARATIVE FRAME

Data come from a series of international empirical investigations carried out in 2007, 2009 and 2014, which explored how the meaning of the notion of citizenship changed with the deepening of integration and enlargement of the EU. Through the *Integrated and United: A quest for Citizenship in an ever-closer Europe (IntUne)*, European elite and general population research took place in 18 countries in 2007–2009. The *European National Elites and the Crisis (ENEC) survey* examined the attitudes of political elites to European identity and the scope of governance and representation in 11 EU countries – in 2014. Nine of the countries that were studied, Bulgaria, France, Germany, Greece, Hungary, Italy, Lithuania, Portugal and Spain, overlapped with those from previous waves. Thus we rely upon on these cases.[2] Sample sizes ranged from 46 in France to 81 in Italy, Portugal and Spain (Table 1). National MPs were selected according to a quota for party, gender and repeated mandates. We inquired about the trust of the MPs in three European institutions (the European Parliament, the European Commission and the European Council of Ministers) in all nine countries. Trust in institutions was measured on an eleven-point scale.[3]

Table 1. Distribution of National Political Elites by Party Affiliation and Left–Right Ideological Position (%) (2014).

	BG	FR	DE	EL	HU	IT	LT	PT	ES
Party family affiliation[a]									
Communist-New Left	8.0	2.9	10.1	24.7		4.2		9.5	4.7
Greens		3.4	10.0		2.5			1.0	
Socialist – Social Democrats	2.2	56.3	30.6	9.7	14.6	51.6	27.9	32.2	31.4
Liberals	6.2			3.5	4.5	15.3	41.9		1.4
Conservatives – Christian Democrats	47.6	37.4	49.3	48.6	66.7	7.4	24.3	57.4	59.7
Right – Ethnic	16.0			13.5	11.6	21.5	5.9		2.7
Left-right ideological position									
Left	20.0	40.0	32.8	32.3	19.7	42.4	15.4	32.3	24.2
Centre	21.5	33.8	42.2	30.8	18.2	22.7	52.3	49.2	51.5
Right	58.5	18.5	25.0	33.8	57.6	15.2	32.3	18.5	24.2
No answer	0.0	7.7	0.0	3.1	4.5	19.7	0.0	0.0	0.0
N	53	46	70	74	57	81	54	81	81

Source: ENEC 2014 (weighted percentages). Authors' calculations.
[a]Quota sample of MPs according to party, gender and new/repeated mandates.

In Hungary, in the 2014 elite survey, 58% of the political elite self-reported being on the right on a left–right scale, 18% in the centre, and 20% on the left.[4] The majority of the political elite were members of the party of Young Democrats (FIDESZ; 59%) or its ally the Christian Democrats (KDNP; 8%), as opposed to the Socialist Party (MSZP; 15%) or extreme-right Jobbik (12%), with the rest (greens and independents) reporting as being somewhere in between.[5]

The Hungarian political elite is not unique in these characteristics compared to other national elites but more similar to the Bulgarian elite in terms of their ideological left–right self-positioning. Regarding their distribution by party family affiliation, the Socialist–Social Democrats account for a relatively lower share and the Conservative–Christian Democrats a higher share among Hungarians than among other national political elites.

THE TRUST OF NATIONAL POLITICAL ELITES IN EUROPEAN INSTITUTIONS BEFORE AND AFTER THE 2008 ECONOMIC CRISIS

One of the main conclusions of the 2007 elite survey was that the evaluation of EU institutions by the elite could not be simply derived from the divergence of opinions between those who opposed and those who supported European integration (Best et al., 2012). Several shades of federalist, sovereigntist and unionist attitudes to the Union could be differentiated. Attitudes to the EU institutions also depended on what the different elite groups regarded as the main aim of European integration. Those who self-reported belonging to the centre ideologically had a positive attitude to integration, although the divergence in views among them was also considerable. Rightists and extreme rightists were critical of the EU. In other words, rifts in the evaluation of the EU institutions were governed by diverse *ideological differences*.

Next to ideological differences, the other main factor determining positive attitudes to integration and EU institutions was elites' *national affiliation* and the given country's *historical experience*. In general, there was no significant difference between West- and East-European elites concerning trust in EU institutions, although some elites – the French and German, among others – were rather divided on this issue (Best et al., 2012). The Hungarian elite – our main focus of analysis – was among those who supported integration and evaluated EU institutions positively at that time. When it comes to trust in the European Parliament, the Hungarian political elite differed significantly from the German elite (similarly to elites from other countries), while the trust of the former in the European Commission differed statistically from the trust of their French counterparts (similarly, again, to the elites of other countries).[6] Moreover, the Hungarian political elite did not differ significantly from other elites in their trust in the European Council of Ministers (2007, Fig. 1).

National attachment and ideological views influenced opinions about integration and EU institutions independently, but the ideological orientation had a geographical component: East Europeans were on the right and West Europeans on the left in 2007. Yet, irrespective of their right/left attachment, elite members from pro-EU countries were more supportive to the EU than elite members from EU-critical countries. Also, independently of the geographical position of the country, the proportion of those with a positive attitude to the EU grew as the ideological stance moved from right to left.

We wondered if all these factors still had an effect in 2014. Based on data from the 2014 elite survey, we first present some general features of trust in European institutions at the aggregate level. A statistical comparison of means on the trust scales shows that while there is no significant difference between 2007 and 2014 in trust in European Parliament, the national elites had less trust in the European Commission and the European Council of Ministers in 2014 than in 2007. After splitting the national elites in terms of an East–West sample, we found that only the trust of Western elites had decreased in these institutions, while the attitudes of Eastern elites had not changed significantly. As a consequence, the East–West divide had become significant (Fig. 1). We also found that in 2014, Eastern elites had significantly more trust in the European Commission and the European Council of Ministers than their Western counterparts. In 2007, this was the case only regarding trust in the European Commission.[7] One should note, however, that behind this general picture exist far greater within-region differences, as well as changes in country position.

In 2014, in general, French, Greek, Hungarian and Portuguese elites trusted least in EU institutions, while German and Italian elites had close to average trust and Bulgarian, Lithuanian and Spanish elites had above-average trust.[8] The Hungarian political elite trusted significantly less in the European Parliament than all other elites, except the French; they also showed significantly less trust

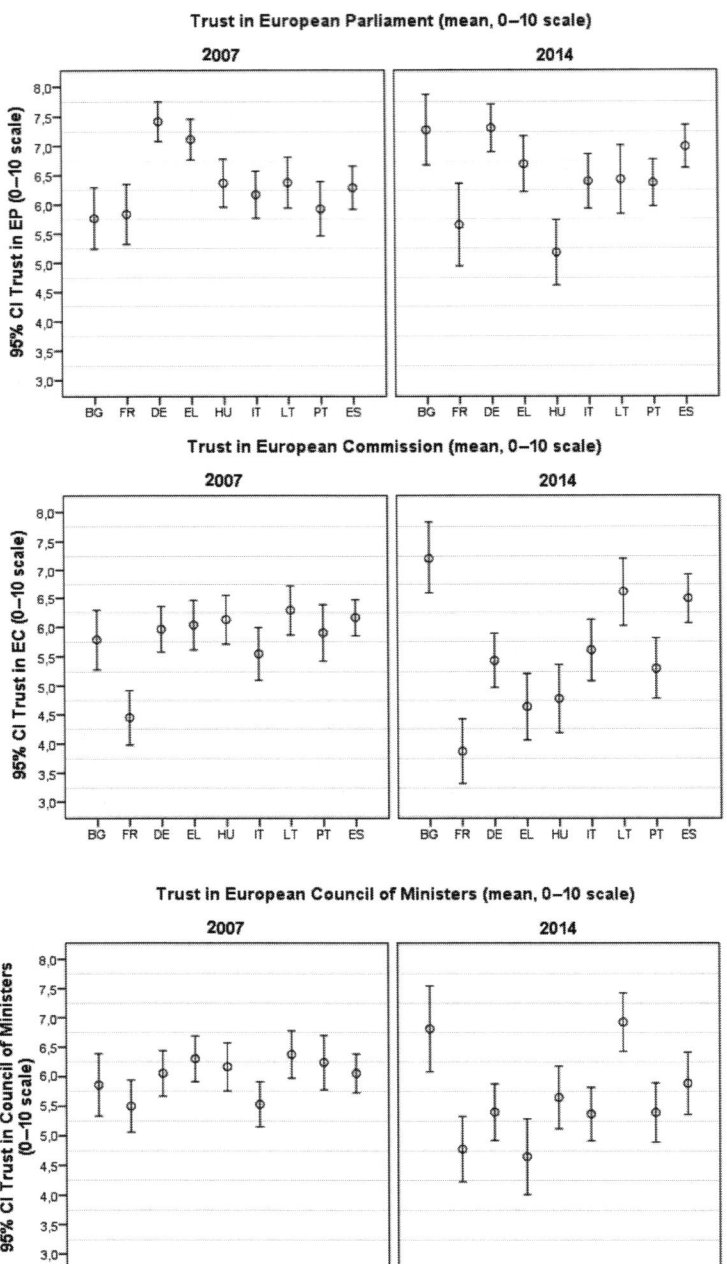

Fig. 1. National Political Elites' Trust in European Institutions in 2007 and 2014 by Country (Mean, 0–10-point scale, 95% Confidence Intervals for Mean).
Source: Intune 2007 and ENEC 2014 databases (unweighted). Authors' calculation.

in the European Commission than their counterparts from Bulgaria, Lithuania and Spain. They did not differ from the elites of other countries in terms of their perceptions of the European Council of Ministers.

The fact that the Hungarian political elite was among the most sceptical elites in terms of its attitude towards the European Parliament in 2014 was partly owing to the relatively significant far-right presence in the Hungarian Parliament (the share of Right–Ethnic members among the political elite was 12%). The other reason was that the governing coalition – Conservatives and Christian Democrats – belonged to the EU-sceptical camp. This is a relatively rare constellation because on average governing party MPs trust significantly more in European institutions than opposition party MPs.

Considering the change in trust between 2007 and 2014, we found that the Hungarian political elite trusted significantly less the European Parliament and the Commission in 2014 than in 2007, while there was no change in their trust of the Council of Ministers in this period (Fig. 1). However, not only in Hungary but also in Greece was a significant decrease in trust identified in two out of the three supranational institutions. In France, Germany and Portugal the political elite trusted only the Council of Ministers significantly less in 2014 than in 2007. In comparison, in Italy and Lithuania, there was no significant change at all. Bulgaria stands out in this respect as its political elite trusted significantly more all three European institutions in 2014 than in 2007.

In 2007, there was no significant difference between Hungary and the other countries in terms of institutional trust (Table 2). However, it turns out that in the case of the EU Parliament and the Commission, the Hungarian elite's trust decreased, while elites in the rest of the countries slightly increased their trust in Parliament on average and did not change their position significantly towards the Commission. The result is that the attitude of the Hungarian elite became significantly different from the other elites. There was no difference concerning trust towards the Council of Ministers: this decreased both in Hungary and in the other countries.

As our discussion above describes, there are important country-level variations in trust in European institutions, and the national affiliation of elites

Table 2. Trust of National Political Elites in EU Institutions in Hungary and in Other Eight Countries (2007 and 2014; 0–10 Scale, Mean and Standard Deviation).

		2007			2014		
		European Parliament	European Commission	Council of Ministers	European Parliament	European Commission	Council of Ministers
Hungary	Mean	6.37	6.13	6.16	5.18	4.77	5.65
	Std. Dev.	1.83	1.89	1.81	2.11	2.22	1.99
Other countries+	Mean	6.36	5.78	6.00	6.63	5.64	5.65
	Std. Dev.	2.01	2.03	1.90	2.06	2.39	2.37
N (sign.)		737(ns)	740(ns)	735(ns)	602(****)	603(***)	602(ns)

Source: Intune 2007, ENEC 2014 (weighted). Authors' calculation.

Notes: + Bulgaria, France, Germany, Greece, Italy, Lithuania, Portugal and Spain; Significance: ****<0.001; ***<0.01.

still played a significant role in 2014 in attitudes towards these institutions. But how did the ideological commitment of elites play a role in terms of trust in European institutions? Recent data show that at the aggregate level of the nine selected countries, ideological *left–right self-positioning* was significantly connected to trust in EU institutions in 2014 as well. Those positioning themselves on the left (0–3 on a 0–10-point scale) had above-average trust in the European Parliament and below average in the other two institutions. In contrast, those positioning themselves on the right (7–10 on the scale) trusted at above-average levels in the Commission and in the Council of Ministers, and close to average in the Parliament. Those who positioned themselves at the centre had average trust in all three European institutions. The connection between ideological position and trust in European institutions proved to be significant in all cases excluding trust in the Parliament. The impact of the *political elite's party family* concerning trust in EU-institutions was also significant in 2014. Extreme-left (including communists and the new left) and extreme-right party members had less than average trust in EU institutions. Liberals in general were more trustful than average, but within this group right–liberals were sceptical about the European Parliament. Greens, in contrast, had above-average trust in Parliament, but distrusted the Commission and the Council. Socialists, social democrats – members of the largest party family – trusted around or slightly above average, while Christian Democrats' level of trust was significantly above average in all respects. Conservatives – the second most numerous party family – trusted the Commission and the Council of Ministers above average, but the European Parliament slightly below average. Finally, regionalists and ethnic minority party members – who, just like liberals, are mostly centrists, but among whom left and right ideological orientations exist – trusted below average in all of the European institutions.

How do these general correlations between supranational trust and ideological left–right self-positioning or party affiliation vary when individual countries are involved in the analysis? The question is whether the relationship between supranational trust and ideological affiliation shows the same pattern in all countries of analysis, or varies by the national affiliation of elites. To address this, we built two two-way Hierarchical ANOVA models, the dependent variable in this analysis being a constructed index of supranational trust.[9]

The results of both hierarchical ANOVA models show that it is not only the main effects of individual variables (national affiliation and left–right ideological self-positioning in Model 1, and national- and party-family affiliation in Model 2) that are significant, but the two-way interaction effects as well (Table 3). The interaction effect in Model 1 is higher than in Model 2 (29% versus 20%). Thus, how the ideological affiliation of political elites (left–right self-positioning and the party family affiliation) affects trust in European institutions differs according to nationality of political elites.

Looking at the country-level analysis, results show that while the Bulgarian, German, Greek, Portuguese and Spanish self-positioned right-wing political elites trust EU institutions, in Hungary, Italy and Lithuania left-wing political elites do (Fig. 2a). And while in Bulgaria, Greece, Portugal and Spain the right-wing

Table 3. Main Effects and Two-way Interactions of National Affiliation and Ideological Left–Right Self-Positioning (Model 1), and Party Family Affiliation (Model 2) of Political Elite on Trust in EU Institutions, Nine Countries (2014; Two-Way Hierarchical ANOVA, Model Goodness of Fit, R^2.

	Dependent Var.	Explanatory Var.	F Sign.	R^2 (%)	Partial Effect (partial η^2) (%)
Model 1	Trust in EU institutions (supranational trust index)	Country	****	43.9	18.6
		Left–right scale	****		13.1
		Country* left–right scale	****		28.7
Model 2	Trust in EU institutions (supranational trust index)	Country	****	47.1	19.2
		Party family	****		29.1
		Country*party family	****		19.5

Source: ENEC 2014 (weighted). Authors' calculations.
Note: Significance: **** < 0.001, Left–right scale: original 0–10-point scale.

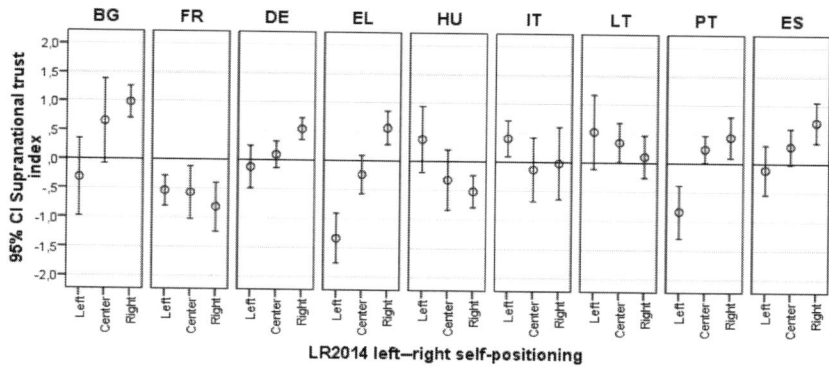

Fig. 2a. Cross Effects of Country and Ideological Left–Right Self-Positioning on Trust in Supranational Institutions, Means and 95% Confidence Intervals for Means on the Supranational Trust Index, 2014. *Source*: ENEC 2014 (weighted data). Authors' calculations.

Conservatives–Christian Democrat parties trusted more in the European institutions, in Hungary and France the left-wing Socialist–Social Democrat party families did (Fig. 2b).[10]

Highlighting the attitudes of the Hungarian political elite, we can summarise first that the *right-wing* self-positioned Hungarian political elite trusted significantly less in European institutions than the Bulgarian, German, Greece and Spanish right-wing elites, but they did not differ from the French, Italian, Lithuanian right-wing elites in this respect. The *left-wing Hungarians* differed significantly only from the Greek left-wing elites. Second, the Hungarian *Conservative–Christian Democrats* trusted significantly less in the European institutions than the Conservatives from Bulgaria, Germany, Greece, Portugal and Spain, but they did not differ from their French, Italian

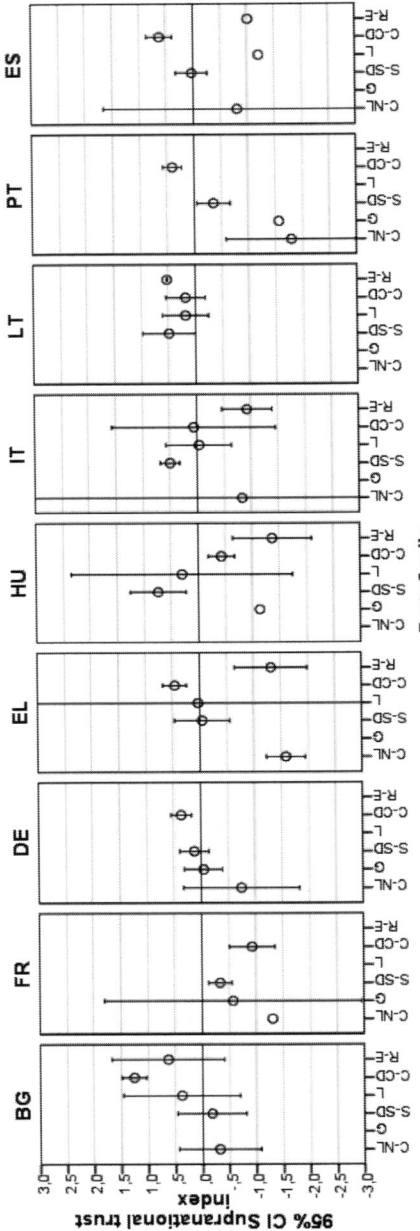

Fig. 2b. Two-way Interaction Effects of National and Party Family Affiliation towards Trust in European Institutions, Means and 95% Confidence Intervals for Means on the Supranational Trust Index (2014). *Source:* ENEC 2014 (weighted data). Authors' calculations. C-NL: Communist-New left; G: Greens; S–SD: Socialist–Social Democrats; L: Liberals; C—CD: Conservatives–Christian Democrats; R-E: Right-Ethnic.

and Lithuanian counterparts. The Hungarian *Socialist–Social Democrats* differed only from the French and Portuguese socialists in their attitude towards the European institutions.

TRUST IN EUROPEAN INSTITUTIONS: THE INTERNAL DIVIDE OF HUNGARIAN ELITE GROUPS

Until now, the attitudes of political elites from different European countries have been compared. We found that the Hungarian political elite were among the most sceptical regarding trust in European institutions in 2014 (compared to the selected eight European countries). We also recall that this was not the case in 2007: the Hungarian elite was more confident in EU institutions at that time (Bakonyi, 2008; Gaxie & Hube, 2012; Lengyel, 2008; Lengyel & Ilonszki, 2012). Was this critical attitude of the political elite towards European institutions characteristic of all elite groups in Hungary? The 2014 elite survey from Hungary explored the attitudes not only of the political but also the economic, media and administrative elites. In this way, we are able to compare the attitudes of the political elite to the attitudes of other elite segments from Hungary and can check to what extent these elite segments are unified in terms of their confidence in supranational institutions.

Our analyses from the 2014 elite survey confirmed that pro-EU members of the economic, media and administrative elite from Hungary outnumbered those who were against it. Looking at the share of those who trust the European institutions (who awarded a positive value on the supranational trust index, see Note 9), we found that 69% of the economic elite, 56% of the media elite and 61% of the administrative elite trusted the supranational institutions. The exception is the political elite, among whom the proportion of those who are sceptical about the European institutions is greater than the proportion of supporters: 58% versus 42%.

Table 4 shows the average trust in different European institutions of the surveyed elite groups from Hungary in 2014. The differences are noteworthy: comparison of the mean values shows that the *political elite* has less trust in these

Table 4. Trust in EU Institutions by Hungarian Elite Group (2014; Mean on 0–10 scale, Standard Deviation in Parentheses).

	European Parliament	European Commission	Council of Ministers
Political elite ($n = 57$)	5.2 (2.1)	4.8 (2.2)	5.6 (2.0)
Economic elite ($n = 34$)	5.4 (1.7)	5.9 (1.5)	6.0 (1.3)
Media elite ($n = 34$)	5.3 (1.9)	6.0 (1.8)	6.0 (1.8)
Administrative ($n = 28$)	5.5 (1.5)	5.9 (1.6)	6.7 (1.4)
F	ns	4.524**	2.374*
η^2		8.4%	4.7%

Source: ENEC 2014. Authors' calculations.
Note: Significance: **<0.05 and *<0.10.

institutions than the other groups of elites. They have the least trust in the
European Commission and in the European Council; additionally, together with
the media elite, they trust the European Parliament least as well. However, our
data were able to depict significant differences between political elites and other
elite groups only when it comes to the trust in the European Commission. Trust in
the European Parliament is similarly low in all elite groups from Hungary, while
in terms of trust in the Council of Ministers the political elite differs only from
the administrative elite.

Importantly, statistically significant differences were found in trust in EU
institutions according to *self-rated left–right ideological affiliation*. The highest
trust was found among those who reported belonging to the left, and the lowest
rate among the rightists, in all elite groups (Fig. 3). The average level of trust of
the political centre is located around the middle of the scale. These findings are
in accordance with the tendencies discerned by Gaxie and Hube (2012) in the
comparative European elite study from 2007, namely, members of the elite with
commitment to the left have more trust in the integration process and EU institutions than those attached to the right. However, it is worth mentioning that the
supranational trust of those from the left and those from right differs significantly
only among the political elite. The right-positioned economic elite does not trust
supranational institutions less than the left-positioned economic elite; the same
was true in the case of the media elite as well (none of the administrative elites
positioned themselves on the left).

For 2014, we found no statistically significant correlation between the frequency of contact with EU institutions and the trust in them. On the other hand,
those Hungarians who had foreign experience (used to live abroad) have more
trust in EU institutions than those who had not (Table 5). This is especially true
of the political elite group: those who had lived abroad trusted the supranational
institutions significantly more than those who had not. Thus, the 2014 findings

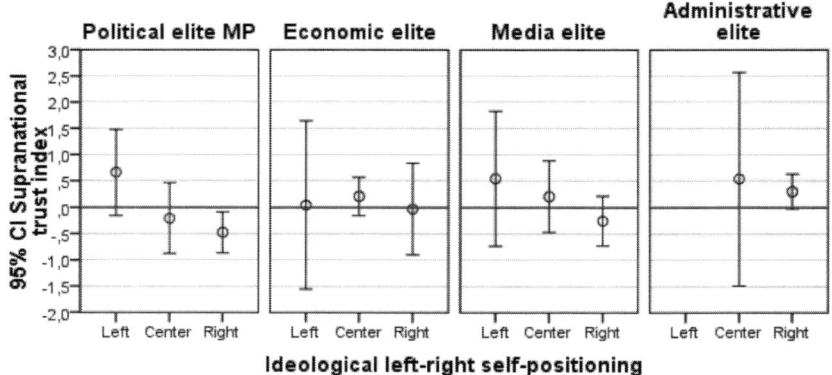

Fig. 3.   Trust in Supranational Institutions According to Self-Reporting on the
Ideological Left–Right Scale and Type of Elite, Hungary, 2014 (Mean, 95%
Confidence Interval of Means). *Source*: ENEC 2014. Authors' calculations.

Table 5. Trust in Supranational Institutions by Type of Elite and Foreign Experience (2014, Hungary, Means of Supranational Trust Index and Standard Deviation).

Elites:	Political	Economic	Media	Administrative
Yes	0.28 (0.94)	0.19 (0.95)	−0.06 (1.14)	0.50 (0.75)
No	−0.43 (1.23)	0.05 (0.65)	0.19 (0.85)	0.13 (0.69)
Total	−0.27 (1.20)	0.12 (0.80)	0.08 (0.98)	0.29 (0.73)
F	3.696*	ns	ns	ns
η^2	6.4%			

Significance: *<0.10. *Source*: ENEC 2014. Authors' calculations.

accord with the previous European research results: openness and foreign experience are associated with greater trust in EU institutions and can even differentiate within the attitudes of the most critical political elite.

THE ELITE–POPULATION GAP CONCERNING SUPRANATIONAL TRUST

In the *general population*, there was a significant difference between trust in European and national institutions on a Europe-wide basis: EU institutions were trusted 15–20% more than national ones in 2007. There was no exception in this respect concerning countries. As a likely effect of the crisis, one can see that trust in political institutions dropped significantly. This drop was greater in the case of EU institutions (12–13% points on average) than in the case of national ones (5–6 %). In some countries such as the Mediterranean ones, especially Spain and Greece, the drop was enormous. In Germany there was a drop in the trust of European institutions and an increase in trust towards national parliament and government. In Lithuania, both trust in EU and national institutions increased. The gap between trust in EU and national institutions declined but still exists (Krekó, Molnár, Félix, Barna, & Boneva, 2015), favouring EU-institutions in all of the nine investigated countries, except Germany.

On average, *elites* trusted more in the European Parliament and European Commission than the respective publics in 2007, including Hungary. The general picture remained the same in all countries but Hungary in 2014. In spite of the decrease, the absolute majority of the population still trusted in EU institutions, but this was no longer the case in the national political elite (Fig. 4).

As regards the population, the economic crisis alone does not explain sufficiently the decrease in supranational institutional trust. The proportion of EU supporters in Hungary was already constantly decreasing between 2004 and 2008. Trust in EU institutions had also gone down following Hungary's accession to the European Union in 2004. By contrast, the proportion of those who professed a European identity in Hungary rose after the country's accession, from 35% in 2004 to 67% in the autumn of 2015 (Standard Eurobarometer Survey, pp. 68, 84). If the thesis that suggests that the spread of European identity has a positive

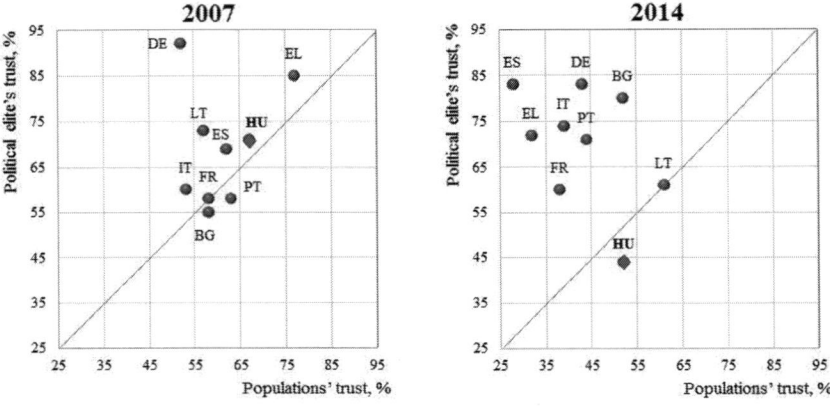

Fig. 4. The Elite–Population Gap: Trust in the European Parliament (%; 2007 and 2014). *Source*: Intune 2007–2009, ENEC 2014, Standard Eurobarometer Survey 68, 82. Authors' calculations.

impact on evaluation of EU integration (Hooghe & Marks, 2005) were true, trust in the European Union should have increased in Hungary.

Nor do utilitarian-instrumentalist considerations – which claim that the greater the gains, the greater the support given to the EU by the population (Gabel, 1998) – play a decisive role in Hungary. In fact, Hungary is one of the major net per capita beneficiaries of the EU budgetary period lasting until 2020, and the decisive majority of Hungarian state investment is financed from EU resources.

It, therefore, appears plausible that underlying the growing Euroscepticism of the Hungarian population is a shift in the attitude of the political elite to the European Union, a change in public discourse and an alternative evaluation of the Hungarian economic situation (Martin, 2017).

The Hungarian case is interesting not only because there was a huge drop in the supranational trust of the political elite, but also because owing to this development the political elite's supranational trust became lower than that of the Hungarian population. This situation is not without antecedents: it happened with the French and Greek elites in the case of the European Commission, while Bulgarian and Portuguese elites trusted slightly less in the European Parliament than their population. By 2014, the elite–population gap in terms of supranational trust had grown in all countries under investigation except Hungary (where the reverse occurred). More exactly, the absolute value of the trust gap grew in Hungary as well, but while previously – as with everywhere else – an elite–population gap was observable, now a population–elite trust gap prevails.

The fact that elite and public opinion come closer to each other might be interpreted in terms of adaptation and responsiveness. Even among the circumstances of mutual trust and elite responsiveness, responsibility, to use Sartori's (2005) terms (see also Ilonszki & Lengyel, 2018), may dictate and legitimate moves in the opposite direction, leading to growth in the elite–mass gap. But if the rare case occurs that the elite–population opinion gap flips (typically, elites were more supportive and the public less so, while now it is the other way around), it suggests an extremely sharp political turn. In principle, there may be political reasons for this, but there may also be unforeseen consequences. Besides the more predictable international consequences, such a situation may confuse and divide the public, contributing to their turning away from public affairs, and undermining civic morale.

CONCLUSION

The comparative European elite surveys based on data collected in 2007, 2009 and 2014 revealed that political elites' trust in European institutions did not change significantly between these years on average, although behind this general picture great changes occurred according to regions and nations. While previously the West–East divide did not exist in this respect, it had become significant by 2014 when the investigated East-European political elites trusted more in the EU institutions than their Western counterparts. This is remarkable because, at the same time, one of the political elites from the East, the formerly EU-enthusiastic Hungary, had become completely distrustful. This is related to the break-up of the former elite consensus and the establishment of an illiberal regime by the governing Young Democrat FIDESZ party after it won a two-thirds majority in the 2010 elections. In other words, the Hungarian political elite's slightly above-average trust in EU institutions evaporated between 2007 and 2014 as a result of the economic crisis and the accompanying populist turn in national politics. The Hungarian political elite became one of the most sceptical of European institutions, trusting significantly less in the European Parliament than the elites of all other countries except the French; they also trust significantly less in the European Commission than their counterparts from Bulgaria, Lithuania and Spain.

The fact that the Hungarian political elite was among the most sceptical ones towards the European Parliament in 2014 is partly owing to the relatively significant far-right presence in the Hungarian Parliament. The other reason is that the governing coalition – the Conservatives–Christian Democrats – belongs to the EU-sceptical camp. This is a relatively rare constellation because governing party MPs, typically, have significantly more trust in European institutions than opposition party MPs. The distrust in EU institutions found in the governing political elite and the criticisms they voice about the European Union in accord with or fed by their distrust are clear indications of a strengthening Euroscepticism.

These data show that there are important country-level variations in trust in European institutions and the national affiliation of elites still played a significant role in 2014. But how does the ideological commitment of elites play a role when it comes to trust in European institutions? Highlighting the attitudes of the Hungarian political elite, we summarise first that the *right-wing* self-positioned Hungarian political elite trusts significantly less the main European institutions than the Bulgarian, German, Greek and Spanish right-wing elites; but they do not differ from their French, Italian, Lithuanian and Portuguese peers in this respect. The *left-wing* Hungarian elites differ significantly only from the Greek left-wing elites. Second, the Hungarian *Conservative elites* trust significantly less the European institutions than Conservatives from Bulgaria, Germany, Greece, Portugal and Spain; but they do not differ from their French, Italian and Lithuanian counterparts. The Hungarian *Socialist–Social Democrats* differ only from the French and Portuguese socialists in their attitude towards the European institutions.

In an international comparison it has been proven that both the main effects and two-way interaction effects of national and ideological affiliation on supranational trust are significant. The effect of the political elite's party family remains significant even when their national affiliation is controlled for; i.e. according to nationality, which party family has more trust in the supranational institutions differs. The main effect of the left–right ideological position on supranational trust is relatively low, but the interaction effect with the elites' national background proves to be strong. These results lead to the conclusion that besides the party family affiliation of elite groups, ideological left–right self-positioning is also important regarding trust in EU institutions, and these effects are significantly modified by the elites' nationality.

Is this critical attitude of the political elite towards European institutions characteristic of all Hungarian elite groups? Our analyses from 2014 confirmed that this is not the case. The pro-EU economic, media and administrative elite from Hungary outnumber those who are against integration. The political elite is the only elite among whom the proportion of sceptics about the European institutions is greater than that of supporters. It should be mentioned that those who used to live abroad have more trust in EU institutions than the rest, and this is especially true of the political elite group. These findings stress again that openness and foreign experience foster greater trust in EU institutions and can even differentiate the attitudes of the most critical political elite.

The EU is considered by critics to be an elite project (Haller, 2008) because elites are more pro-European than the public opinion. The general tendency is for national political elites to trust more in supranational solutions than their respective publics. The Hungarian specificity, however, is that the political elite in 2014 has less trust in the European Parliament than the population. This situation raises questions about the content of responsiveness and the responsibility of elite behaviour. Critics argue that clientelism, arbitrariness and conflict-seeking dominate the political actions of the governing elite. This description coincides with Sztompka's characterisation of the autocratic regime, in which trust in charismatic leadership is stressed and trust relations are asymmetrical due to the distrust of leaders.

ACKNOWLEDGEMENTS

György Lengyel acknowledges receipt of a grant from EFOP 3.6.3 when finalising this chapter. Laura Szabó was supported by OTKA NN 110917 while working on a project related to this chapter.

NOTES

1. ... and encouraging the elites (or at least the East and Central European elites), to concentrate more on national developments and questions of national self-identification and thus on the 'negative' side of Europeanisation, paving the way for 'Negative Europeanisation' (Gallina, 2007).

2. Regarding the different waves, see Best et al. (2012), http://www.uni-corvinus.hu/index.php?id=23241; Lengyel (2008), http://portal.uni-corvinus.hu/index.php?id=23242; Ilonszki (2010); Vogel and Teruel (2016); Conti, Göncz, and Real-Dato (2018); and Vogel, Gebauer, and Salheiser (2018).

3. The wording was the following: 'Please tell me using a score of 0–10 how much you personally trust each of the following EU institutions to usually take the right decisions. 0 means that you do not trust an institution at all, and 10 means you have complete trust.'

4. About 4% refused to expose their ideological stance. The question wording was: 'On a left–right scale where 0 means the left and 10 means the right, where would you place yourself?' We encoded this variable for the descriptive analysis as follows: left: 0–3; centre: 4–6; right: 7–10.

5. The political elite was weighted according to the parties' proportions in parliament; where the findings are presented by party affiliation, the weighted figures are used; where totals or averages of countries are presented, countries were equally weighted.

6. All means on the 0–10-point trust scales were compared with F statistics when equal variance was assumed and with Welch as well as the Brown–Forsythe robust test of equality of means analysis when equal variance was not assumed—this holds throughout the research described in this paper. The multiple comparison of means was performed with Scheffe when equal variance was found, and with Games–Howell and Dunnett C post hoc tests when equal variance was not assumed. The mean differences are considered significant when they exist at the 0.05 level.

7. Results and data not presented here in table or graph format are available from the authors on request.

8. When we compare the individual country percentages to the average of the nine selected countries, we check the statistical differences by calculating the adjusted residuals of the cross-tabulation statistics.

9. We are not alone among scholars who have considered the uni-dimensionality of trust in EU institutions (Arnold et al., 2012). For the sake of our multivariate analysis we constructed the dependent *supranational trust index variable* with principal factor analysis, regressing the three trust variables: trust in EP, EC and Council of Europe. Results indicate all three trust variables scale uni-dimensionally across the same latent structure with factor loadings 0.92, 0.88 and 0.81. This scale had an eigenvalue of 2.3 and accounted for 75% of variance, with a Kaiser–Meyer–Olkin measure of sampling adequacy of 0.68. The descriptive statistics for the supranational trust index variable are: $N=584$; Mean=0.000; Std. Deviation=1.000; Minimum= -3.109; Maximum=2.072.

10. Our data show no significant differences in supranational trust between the Conservatives–Christian Democrats and Socialist–Social Democrats in Italy and Lithuania.

REFERENCES

Arnold, C., Eliyahu, V. S., & Galina, Z. (2012). Trust in the institutions of the European Union: A cross-country examination. In L. Beaudonnet & Mauro, D. D. (Eds.) *Beyond Euro-skepticism: Understanding attitudes towards the EU.* European Integration online Papers (EIoP). Special Mini-Issue, 2(16), Article 8. Retrieved from http://eiop.or.at/eiop/texte/2012-008a.htm

Bakonyi, E. (2008). Az európai intézmények iránti bizalom. [Trust in European institutions.] In Gy. Lengyel (Ed.). *A magyar politikai és gazdasági elit EU-képe. [The attitudes of Hungarian political and economic elite towards the European Union.]* (pp. 51–69). Budapest, Hungary: Új Mandátum Kiadó.

Best, H., Lengyel, Gy., & Verzichelli, L. (2012). *The Europe of elites: A study into the Europeanness of Europe's political and economic elites*. Oxford: Oxford University Press.

Burton, M. G., & Higley, J. (1987). Elite settlements. *American Sociological Review*, *52*(3), 295–317.

Carrubba, C. (2001). The electorate connection in European Union politics. *Journal of Politics*, *63*, 141–158.

Coleman, J. (1990). *Foundations of social theory*. Cambridge, MA.: Harvard University Press.

Conti, N., Göncz, B., & Real-Dato, J. (Eds.). (2018). *National political elites, European integration and the Eurozone crisis*. London: Routledge.

Cook, K. (Ed.). (2001). *Trust in society*. New York, NY: Russell Sage Foundation.

Cook, K. (Ed.). (2009). *Whom can we trust? How groups, networks and institutions make trust possible*. New York, NY: Russel Sage Foundation.

Eurofound. (2018). *Societal change and trust in institutions*. Luxembourg: Publications Office of the European Union.

Gabel, M. (1998). Public support for European integration: An empirical test of five theories. *Journal of Politics*, *60*(2), 333–354.

Gallina, N. (2007). Political elites in Eastern Central Europe: Paving the way for 'negative Europeanisation? *Contemporary European Studies*, *2*(2), 75–91.

Gambetta, D. (Ed.). (1988). *Trust. Making and breaking cooperative relations*. Oxford: Basil Blackwell.

Gaxie, D., & Hube, N. (2012). Elites' positions on European institutions. In H. Best, Gy. Lengyel, & L. Verzichelli (Eds.), *The Europe of elites: a study into the Europeanness of Europe's political and economic elites* (pp. 122–146). Oxford: Oxford University Press.

Granovetter, M. (2017). *Society and economy. Framework and principles*. Cambridge. MA: Belknap Press.

Haller, M. (2008). *European integration as an elite process: The failure of a dream?* New York, NY: Routledge.

Higley, J., & Lengyel, Gy. (Eds.). (2000). *Elites after state socialism: Theory and analysis*. Lanham, MD: Rowman and Littlefield.

Higley, J., & Pakulski, J. (2012, July 10). *Elites, elitism and elite theory: Unending confusion?* Paper prepared for Research Committee on Political Elites (RC02) panel "Elite Dilemmas and Democracy's Future", World Congress of the International Political Science Association, Madrid.

Hooghe, L. (2003). Europe divided? Elites vs. public opinion on European Integration. *European Union Politics*, *4*(3), 281–304.

Hooghe, L., & Marks, G. (2005). Calculation, community, and cues: Public opinion on European integration. *European Union Politics*, *6*(4), 419–443.

Ilonszki, G. (Ed.). (2010). *Perceptions of the European Union in new member states. A comparative perspective*. London: Routledge.

Ilonszki, G., & Lengyel, Gy. (2018). Irresponsible elites in opposition and government: The Hungarian case. In L. Vogel, R. Gebauer, & A. Salheiser (Eds.), *The contested status of political elites. At the crossroads* (pp. 185–202). New York, NY: Routledge.

Inglehart, R. (1970). Cognitive mobilization and European identity. *Comparative Politics*, *3*, 45–70. Retrieved from https://www.jstor.org/stable/pdf/421501.pdf?refreqid=excelsior%3Ad0f0f360f6 ed948dfb6f814d5e71dde3

Inglehart, R. (1999). Trust, well-being and democracy. In M. E. Warren (Ed.), *Democracy and trust* (pp. 85–120). Cambridge: Cambridge University Press.

Kornai, J. (1992). *The socialist system: The political economy of communism*. Princeton, NJ: Princeton University Press.

Krekó, P., Molnár, Cs., Félix, A., Barna, I., & Boneva, M. (2015). *Trust within Europe*. Budapest, Hungary: Political Capital.

Lengyel, Gy. (Ed.). (2008). *A magyar politikai és gazdasági elit EU-képe*. [The EU-image of the Hungarian political and economic elite.] Budapest, Hungary: Új Mandátum Kiadó.

Lengyel, Gy. (2014). Elites in hard times: The Hungarian case in comparative conceptual framework. *Comparative Sociology*, *13*(1), 78–93.

Lengyel, Gy., & Bank, D. (2014). The 'small transformation' in Hungary: Institutional changes and economic actors. In K. Blum-B. Martens & V. Trapman (Eds.), *Business leaders and new varieties of capitalism in post-communist Europe* (pp. 58–78). London: Routledge.

Lengyel, Gy., & Ilonszki, G. (2012). Simulated democracy and pseudo-transformational leadership in Hungary. *Historical Social Research/Historische Sozialforschung, 37*(1)(139), Elite Foundations of Social Theory and Politics, 107–126.

Magalhães, P. C. (2012). Europe à la carte? Public support for policy integration in an enlarged European Union. In D. Sanders, P. C. Magalhães, & G. Tóka (Eds.), *Citizens and the European polity. Mass attitudes towards the European and national polities.* Oxford: Oxford University Press (Published in Oxford Scholarship Online, January 2013).

Martin, J. P. (2017). Continuity or disruption? Changing elites and the emergence of cronyism after the Great Recession – The case of Hungary. *Corvinus Journal of Sociology and Social Policy, 8*(3), 255–281). doi:10.14267/CJSSP.2017.3S.11

Medgyesi, M., & Boda, Zs. (2019). Institutional trust in Hungary and the countries of the EU. In I. Gy. Tóth (Ed.), *Social Report 2019* (pp. 341–356). TÁRKI Social Research Institute Inc. Budapest,

Putnam, R. (2001). *Bowling alone: The collapse and revival of American community.* New York, NY: Simon and Schuster.

Sartori, G. (2005 [1976]). *Parties and party systems. A framework for analysis.* Cambridge: Cambridge University Press.

Standard Eurobarometer Survey 68 (2007), 82 (2014), 4 (2015). TNS, Brussels.

Sztompka, P. (1999). *Trust. A sociological theory.* Cambridge: Cambridge University Press.

Vogel, L., & Teruel, J. R. (Eds.). (2016). *National political elites and the crisis of European integration. Country studies 2007–2014. Historical Social Research, 41*(4).

Vogel,, L., Gebauer, R. & Salheiser, A. (Eds.). (2018). *The contested status of political elites. At the crossroads,* London: Routledge.

Zakaria, F. (1997). The rise of illiberal democracy. *Foreign Affairs, 76*(6), 22–43.

Zaller, J. (1992). *The nature and origin of mass opinion.* Cambridge: Cambridge University Press.

PART II

ELITE RECRUITMENT AND MOBILITY

THE (RE-)PRODUCTION OF ELITES IN PRIVATE AND PUBLIC BOARDING SCHOOLS: COMPARATIVE PERSPECTIVES ON ELITE EDUCATION IN GERMANY

Anja Gibson

ABSTRACT

Recently, the public and academic discussion on elite education and the selection of top performers in Germany has led to a renewed controversy about social exclusion and inequality. Consequently, the use of terms such as 'elite', 'excellence' and 'intellectual giftedness' have provoked a debate about the necessity, opportunities, and rejection of educational distinctions. This chapter takes a comparative perspective to examine a private boarding school with a rich tradition, and a relatively new state-run public boarding school, examining their status as exclusive educational institutions, including their selection processes, elite aspirations and educational philosophies. The analysis focusses on how the schools construe themselves as elite and how exclusive membership is created and negotiated within the boarding school context. Using a multilevel qualitative approach and empirical data, this chapter offers findings on mechanisms of elite formation in boarding schools between two poles: the reproduction of an existing elite status and the production of elites from scratch. The analyses show the establishment of a distinct composition of students – either selected by milieu affiliation or by cognitive abilities – resulting in specific processes of coherence and distinction within the school communities. Thus, this chapter makes a contribution to a differentiated observation of new educational hierarchies in Germany.

Keywords: Boarding school; elite; educational hierarchies; Germany; private school; public school

Elites and People: Challenges to Democracy
Comparative Social Research, Volume 34, 115–135
Copyright © 2019 by Emerald Publishing Limited
All rights of reproduction in any form reserved
ISSN: 0195-6310/doi:10.1108/S0195-631020190000034006

INTRODUCTION

Exclusive educational institutions have been a particular focus of recent debates on education in Germany – not least because of new developments and new differentiations in the educational system that indicate the emergence of new paths to elite education in Germany. Such vertical processes of differentiation are by no means novel, but there are tendencies to new differentiations and educational hierarchies (cf. Ullrich 2014; overview: Deppe, Helsper, Kreckel, Krueger, & Stock, 2015; Helsper & Krueger, 2019).

Current developments in the upper secondary education, for example, are, first, owing to the expansion of secondary school education: almost half of the students attend schools that provide them with the highest secondary qualifications possible and access to higher education (cf. Autorengruppe Bildungsberichterstattung, 2018). Second, they are owing to developments regarding the formation of educational quasi-markets and increasing school autonomy (cf. Bagley, 2006; Bellmann, 2008; Bradley & Taylor, 2002; Walford, 1996; West & Hind, 2007). These changes lead to new, exclusive separations and competitive situations between individual institutions (cf. Helsper, 2012; Helsper & Krueger, 2014; overview: Deppe, Luedemann, & Kastner, 2018).

Against the backdrop of these developments, recent discussions are simultaneously taking place: first, on the promotion of excellence (*Exzellenzfoerderung*) and elite education (*Elitebildung*) and second, about the *necessity, opportunities* and *rejection* of educational distinctions (cf. Deppe et al., 2018; Ecarius & Wigger, 2006; Hartmann, 2002, 2013). The ambivalence both of these discussions and of these recent developments in educational policy is currently reflected in the concurrent trends towards inclusion and exclusion in the German educational system. These trends are evident in attempts to ensure equality on the one hand and an increase in selectivity and stratification on the other (cf. Bröckling & Peter, 2014; Krueger & Helsper, 2014; Krueger et al., 2012).

The comprehensive international research on elite education and elite schools (cf. Angod, 2015; Cookson, 2009; Cookson & Persell, 1985, 2010; Howard & Gaztambide-Fernández, 2010; Howard, Polimeno, & Wheeler, 2014; Kenway et al., 2017; Kingston & Lewis, 1990; Koh & Kenway, 2012, 2016; Mangset, 2017; Maxwell & Aggleton, 2013, 2015; Maxwell, Deppe, Krueger, & Helsper, 2018; Toernqvist, 2018; van Zanten, 2010; Wakeford, 1969; Weinberg, 1967), underlines the role education plays in maintaining existing distinctions and educational hierarchies and also creating new ones. In this regard, the studies on elite schools indicate new dialectic requirements in the educational system: the recognition and gratification of achievements as a precondition for social mobility and high social status – and therefore trends of meritocracy – alongside demands and expectations of elite groups which seek to secure and advance their social and economic position (cf. Maxwell & Aggleton, 2015, p. 1).

In contrast to international debates and research, elite education was long absent from scientific discussions in Germany – not least because of the negative connotations since its use by the Nazi Regime. Compared to other countries, there is hardly any sociological concept in Germany that is as hotly disputed as the elite concept (cf. Ecarius & Wigger, 2006; Krueger & Helsper, 2014). Historically, the term 'elite' has undergone several phases in Germany in which the taboo surrounding it was removed and then re-established (cf. Bluhm & Strassenberger, 2006; Deppe et al., 2015; Hoffmann-Lange, 2001; Hradil & Imbusch, 2003). Even though the term is increasingly being used in a positive sense, there is still some uncertainty regarding its usage within public debate. The ideological weight of the term during the Nazi era and its proximity to terms such as 'the ruling class', 'authoritarian leadership' and 'economic privilege' is still relevant today, at least in German-speaking countries (cf. Krueger & Helsper, 2014). As a result, there is a gap in research on elite education and elite educational institutions. I, therefore, initiated a study on elite boarding schools and their role in the German educational system (cf. Gibson, 2017).

This chapter takes a comparative perspective to examine processes of differentiation within the educational system and show how *elites* and *excellence* are constructed in exclusive educational institutions. Using a qualitative multilevel approach, the first step of analysis focusses on a comparison between the micro- and meso-levels (institution, interaction and individual). In a second step, it takes the following aspects of each of the schools into consideration: different forms of funding (private resp. public), the historical background (rich in tradition resp. relatively new), the contrasting clientele (upper class children resp. gifted children from non-privileged milieus) and different concepts of elite (elite by origin resp. performance elite), which have particular significance for elite education in Germany.

Based on this approach, I will demonstrate mechanisms of elite formation in state-run and private boarding schools and show that internal selection procedures are essential factors for quality and allow schools to establish a distinct composition of students, resulting in specific processes of coherence within the schools, elitist attitudes and acts of distinction by the clientele. Furthermore, this leads to a discussion of educational justice: exclusive boarding schools in Germany are seen as an opportunity to select the best and promote excellence, but they also reinforce social exclusion and educational inequality.

EDUCATING A RESPONSIBLE ELITE ON EXCLUSIVE BOARDING SCHOOLS – EMPIRICAL INSIGHTS

Research Design and Methodological Approach

There are approximately 34,000 schools[1] in the general educational system in Germany. Only 263 of these schools are boarding schools. Most of them are private schools – run by the church, an association or private individuals or groups. A large number of private schools are co-funded by the government. State-run boarding schools are generally tuition free and receive public funding from the federal state or the municipality. Around 150 boarding schools are *Gymnasien*[2] – the highest secondary school track in Germany (for an overview of German boarding schools see Zuechner, Peyerl, & Siegfried, 2018).

Although they have a marginal status within the school system, upper second-ary boarding schools (*Internatsgymnasien*) are among the few elite educational institutions[3] in Germany (cf. Helsper, 2006, p. 169; Kalthoff, 1997) owing to their specific educational programmes and objectives as well as the institutional exclu-sivity of the schools: With their isolated or even secluded atmosphere, and their select clientele, these schools satisfy the two most important criteria of eliteness: *selection* and *separation* (Paris, 2003, p. 61, own translation).

While boarding schools in general have been the topic of much debate in the German media – generally in terms of polarisations such as 'breeding grounds for the elite', 'ghettos for the rich', 'schools for eggheads' and 'child prisons' – they have scarcely been mentioned in scholarly discussions. I, therefore, selected two German boarding schools which style themselves as exclusive educational institutions for elite formation and which I analysed from micro- and meso-level perspectives using a qualitative multilevel approach.[4] The following aspects were taken into consideration:

First, how do the schools construe themselves as exclusive and how are the schools' aspirations – forming elites – reflected in the educational philosophies of the schools? Another objective was to assess what kind of parents and students the schools attract and how students are selected.

Second, I examined processes of distinction – ways in which social groups mark their differences to others (cf. Bourdieu, 1996a) – as well as processes of coherence, that is, practices of homogenisation, communitisation and collective identity formation within the schools and therefore to what extent excellence, sin-gularity and exclusive membership of a select boarding school community are created and negotiated.

And third, I examined the habitus of students[5] within the context of educa-tional processes as well as the match (*Passungsverhaeltnis*) between the individual and institutional concepts of the habitus of the students. However, this chapter will not go into this in more detail.

The study takes three theoretical approaches: First, I refer to different concepts and understandings of 'elite' and 'excellence' (cf. Hartmann, 2008; Krueger & Helsper, 2014; Ricken, 2009) to describe and categorise elite and excellence semantics used by the schools. As a second theoretical framework, I refer to Pierre Bourdieu and the key terms of his sociological work, 'habitus', 'capital' and 'field', and reconstruct the student's habitus (cf. Bourdieu, 1996a, 1996b, 1998; Bourdieu & Passeron, 1990). A third approach is the reference to the theory of school culture (cf. Helsper, Boehme, Kramer, & Lingkost, 2001; Boehme, Hummrich, & Kramer, 2015; Kessler, 2017) to identify the specific culture of the school in its complexity. In this context, school cul-tures are understood as symbolic, meaning-based constellations, shaped and transformed by the school actors – that is, the symbolic order of discourses, interactions, practices and artefacts.

The first step of this study was to examine the self-presentations (e.g. mission statements, school websites and brochures) of all existing German upper second-ary boarding schools at the time.[6]

The schools were required to explicitly use notions of elite education and/or academic excellence such as references to educating future elites, promoting excellence and educating top-performance students in their mission statements and to have implemented additional selection procedures for admission (e.g. achievement or intelligence tests and interviews). The schools were not allowed to be solely sports boarding schools. The reason for this was that the term 'elite' has its own connotations in the field of sports, where the emphasis is on physical performance, and thus differs from other elite semantics. Profile specialisations, special education services and curricula, school partnerships, trusteeships, etc. were noted before making the initial selection. These factors were weighed in order to achieve a contrasting selection of schools. From a narrowed list of 23 upper secondary boarding schools, I selected two schools for maximum possible contrast within the field of elite education: a traditional private boarding school with a focus on progressive education and a comparatively 'young' public boarding school for gifted students. As exclusive schools for select students, they are particularly associated with elite education and the promotion of excellence. At the same time, they are schools that style themselves as elite educational institutions (in detail see Gibson, 2017, pp. 85-114).

It was exceedingly difficult to gain access to the selected boarding schools. Reasons for refusing research access were recent changes in the school (school management, profile, etc.) and that school management showed critical attitudes towards their everyday school life being researched. This was owing to prior negative experiences with scientific researchers and therefore the fear of defamation (for access barriers to exclusive educational institutions and entanglements of field researchers see Gibson, 2019 and the contributions in Howard & Kenway, 2015). In the end, the relationship was established via a process of assessment: over the course of several interviews with the head teachers, school committees and teaching staff, the schools tested my integrity as a researcher and, in particular, sought to establish whether I was a 'good habitual fit' for the school. Once I received a positive response from the school committee, I was admitted as a 'temporary full-fledged member' of the school community and was given unrestricted access to the school. I spent a total of two months at the schools, participating in all school and extra-curricular activities (cf. Gibson, 2017, 2019).

The data for this study are based on school mission statements, expert interviews with head teachers, 27 biographical interviews with students in senior classes and more than 800 hours of ethnographical observations of everyday school life (e.g. in class, during leisure time activities, meal times, meetings and school events). Selected data were reconstructed using Ralf Bohnsack's documentary method, which is both a methodological epistemic approach and a research practice based on the sociology of knowledge, the ethnomethodological tradition of research, iconology and cultural sociology (cf. Bohnsack, 1983, 1989, 2014; Bohnsack, Loos, Schaeffer, Staedtler, & Wild, 1995; Bohnsack, Nentwig-Gesemann, & Nohl, 2013; Bohnsack, Pfaff, & Weller, 2010a; Mannheim, 1952).

The framework of the documentary method can be described as a praxeological cal sociology of knowledge and allows the reconstruction of 'implicit knowledge that underlies everyday practice and gives an orientation to habitualised actions independent of individual intentions and motives' (Bohnsack, Pfaff, & Weller, 2010b, p. 20). For this reason, the documentary method provides access to pre-reflexive or tacit knowledge, which is implied in the practice of action. Therefore, to analyse the documentary meaning, one must ask about the modus operandi of practical action, that is, 'how' practice is produced or accomplished (cf. Bohnsack, 2010, p. 103). The modus operandi, or the habitus, to use Pierre Bourdieu's term (cf. Bourdieu, 1996a, 1996b, 1998, Bourdieu & Passeron, 1990), can thus be identified (cf. Bohnsack, 2010, p. 106). This approach enquires into the immanent or literal meaning. Within this context, the documentary method differentiates between two forms of understanding: the immanent and the non-immanent. The former works on a matter-of-fact or explicit level; the latter, the genetic interpretation, is based on implicit shared experiences of social actors (cf. Bohnsack et al., 2010b, p. 21):

> By reconstructing social structure and the patterns of orientation in everyday practice from data material, such as interviews, group discussions, pictures, or films, this method contributes to overcoming a classical dilemma of qualitative research, which either remains on the level of common sense knowledge or claims to offer a privileged access to information on social structure beyond the knowledge of the actors themselves. (Bohnsack et al., 2010b, p. 20)

Taking this into consideration, the analytic stance shifts from asking 'what' to 'how', that is, from the 'question of truth and normativity in the construction of social reality to the question concerning its development and social production' (Bohnsack et al., 2010b, p. 21). It is, therefore, 'possible to reach the level of the so-called "atheoretical" knowledge, that is seen as an [sic.] not directly explicable knowledge of actors, and as underlying every social (inter)action' (Bohnsack et al., 2010b, p. 21).

For my study, I evaluated all the collected data using the documentary method. I chose this method because the material collected focussed on different fields and thus required a 'methodology that comprised and integrated different methods and the corresponding metatheory' (Bohnsack et al., 1995, p. 430). As the documentary method was used on all data, it was possible to analyse how the various survey methods interacted with one another and to coherently triangulate them. At the same time, this method enabled systematic comparisons of individual cases, which were carried out on both an intrascholastic (within a single school) and interscholastic level (between schools) using a multilevel comparison. This process involves a qualitative multilevel analysis (cf. Helsper, Hummrich & Kramer, 2013; Hummrich & Kramer, 2011), which uses multi-method triangulation to connect different qualitative survey methods, thereby making it possible to systematically integrate and contrast various levels of social aggregation and meaning (cf. e.g. Bohnsack et al., 1995; Gibson & Helsper, 2018; Helsper, Dreier, Gibson, Kotzyba, & Niemann, 2018a; Helsper et al., 2001) and comprehensively compare and classify them.

I will present the results of these multilevel comparisons based on case studies (cf. Gibson, 2017, pp. 115–332) in the following sections.[7]

Introduction of the Private and State-run School – Educational Philosophies and Concepts of Elite

In the following, I would like to introduce the two exclusive schools that were examined, placing a particular emphasis on the educational philosophies, selection procedures and processes for constructing elites.

Boarding School I is a private upper secondary school with a rich tradition that focusses on progressive education. A special feature of this school is that teachers and their families live in residence with students on school grounds. This allows relationships to develop that can be described as family-like. The school recruits students from across Germany and some from other countries. School tuition is – compared to other boarding schools in Germany – quite high at about €33,000 a year.[8] However, families who do not have the required financial means may receive support from a small contingent of scholarships reserved for students with excellent academic performance.

With its distinctive profile, the school primarily attracts educated middle- and upper-class families – the majority of the parents are freelancers, academics, doctors and lawyers. Students are selected according to academic performance, as well as their habitus, which must be compatible with the school. This is determined through an intuitive assessment of their attitude during an interview with the head teacher and involves aspects such as manner, values and habits, which must meet the requirements of the school and is connected to the specific school culture. In this school, ideal students are conceptualised as follows: they come from conservative milieus that value education and learning and appreciate the school traditions and values of solidarity and community. At the same time, they distinguish themselves through cultured, disciplined attitudes and possess a broad general knowledge.

The clientele consists of students who are already expected to assume positions in management and become members of the societal elite later in life. This assumption by teachers, parents and the head teacher is primarily based on the students' status as children of the current elite who will follow in their parents' footsteps. For example, in many cases they will later take over their parents' and grandparents' companies. Thus, the 'elite' is not created within the boarding school but 'refined' by developing the individual excellence of the students and combining it with a sense of responsibility. Essentially, this school sees itself responsible for comprehensive academic education and character formation (e.g. virtues and moral values, self-regulation, social skills and sense of responsibility for the community), that is, for holistic personal development.

The teachers assume an important role in this process: their task is to form certain facets of their students' personalities, to shape their knowledge, behaviour, values and skills and to, thereby, prepare them for their predetermined professional status. The head teacher elaborates in an interview:[9]

> The majority of students will most certainly assume positions in management (…). As a teacher, I must therefore ask myself: will what I am doing put me into a moral or ideological conflict? I always say: it does just as much good to work in schools in a socially disadvantaged area as it does to work here. But with one difference: here I have a completely different clientele. The

fact is that most of the students here will later have a high status in society. And as a teacher I have to ask myself: am I making my own small contribution to this by giving them a certain attitude or ethos?

Boarding School II, on the other hand, is a state-run boarding school for the gifted that is still very new. Parents only pay for room and board (about €4,500 Euro a year). Some of the students receive state support as well as grants to cover these costs. In contrast to the private boarding school, only a few teachers live on the school grounds and those that do so do not live in residence with the students.

Students come from all over Germany, as well as from other countries. It is mainly children from middle-class families who attend the school – the majority of parents are university graduates or have attained intermediate school certificates and completed training in commercial professions or skilled trades. The selection of students is based on standardised intelligence tests and a group examination in which a school committee assesses academic and social skills. The selection procedure emphasises cognitive abilities and – as the analyses show – focus on ideal students with the following characteristics: a strong work and performance ethos that is associated with a lifestyle based on fulfilling their personal potential as well as on academic learning, acquiring knowledge, and acting responsibly.

The state-run boarding school construes itself as an educational institution that allows exceptionally gifted students[10] to develop their inner potential. By connecting individual achievement with a sense of responsibility, the school wishes to help create responsible elite. The school focusses on elite status as the result of a process: it is only possible for its students to become a member of the elite through a developmental process that is the result of effort and personal investment and that may not always be successful. The head teacher elaborates in an interview:

> That does not mean that each of our students later becomes a member of the elite. But this is what is expected of us. So we must remember: these children were specially selected. They are in the top three percent in terms of intellectual potential. And we must ask ourselves: how can we turn this potential into achievement so that these students become valuable and responsible members of society? That's what the term 'responsible elite' means. It's not just about powerful elites or economic elites or about the world of the rich and beautiful. It's about education! And our fundamental educational principles are: a willingness to achieve and a sense of responsibility.

As this comparison illustrates, both boarding schools see themselves as exceptional educational institutions that set themselves apart from other schools, but they draw distinctions very differently:

The private boarding school distinguishes itself by upholding tradition while at the same time seeking educational innovation. It also emphasises its higher degree of autonomy as a private school and distances itself from current social trends, such as the focus on efficiency and the importance of certificates. In contrast, the state-run boarding school specialises in offering specific concepts for gifted students and emphasising its role as an affordable public school, presenting itself as an educational institution that encourages excellent achievements above and beyond societal demands.

The private boarding school succeeds in distinguishing itself through its long history, maintaining 'old' lines of distinction as well as integrating modern trends without reforming its basic profile. In doing so, the school ensures that it continues to appeal to wealthy, well-educated and upper- and middle-class families who are interested in upholding conventional values. The success of this concept is reflected in the fact that 'family dynasties' have established themselves at this school: families whose members have attended this boarding school for several generations continue to choose this school. Newly founded schools like the state-run boarding school for the gifted, however, cannot rely on traditional concepts or historical 'roots'. For this reason, in many cases these schools focus on innovative profiles, which give them a special status.[11] Especially families from the wider middle-classes, who strive to promote their children's talents as much as possible, and thus give them the opportunity for social advancement through education, are attracted to these schools.

In terms of selection procedure, these schools are also opposed to one another. The private boarding school emphasises a student's background, community values and family conduct. The head teacher assesses intuitively whether students are a suitable fit for the school in an interview with the family. In contrast, a student's giftedness is the central admission criteria for the state-run boarding school. This is determined in a standardised IQ test. These are also crucial for defining the ideal students for each of the schools: both schools only admit students who show a willingness to achieve, are self-disciplined and have a deep wish to acquire knowledge and assume responsibility. However, each school gives different weight to these characteristics: the private boarding school places a great deal more emphasis on a sense of community, strong character and refinement than cognitive abilities and academic achievement, both of which are more important for the state-run boarding school.[12]

Although both schools aim to educate responsible elite that serves society, the private boarding school favours the formation of a specific character over strong academic achievements, while this aspect is emphasised at the state-run boarding school. This preference is also directly related to the elite concepts at each of the schools: the private boarding school sees its students as future managers who are expected to have a high status in society and therefore relates to an elite concept based on social origin and the 'ruling elite'. This concept is diametrically opposed to that of the state-run boarding school: whether students come from privileged social origins is not relevant for this school, as it believes that a legitimate elite status can be achieved through combining personal achievement and responsibility. According to the analyses, this school emphasises achievement elites.

To present a more detailed impression of the schools, and especially to better investigate the negotiation of exclusive membership and belonging in exclusive educational institutions, this chapter will also focus on the level of interaction.

Interaction in Class: Acts of Distinction and Processes of Coherence

One of the central starting points for the study was the hypothesis that a specific concept of excellence and elites exists in exclusive educational institutions and that this is reflected in the interpretations and practices of the teachers and students. This assumption was confirmed by the observations made in each of the field studies: acts of distinction and processes of collective identity formation were evident.

In the following, I will present some of the central results regarding these acts of distinction, that is, the ways in which the students at each of the schools distance themselves from other people or groups, attitudes and ideas and how they demonstrate this sense of difference in everyday school life.

In the *private boarding school*, ties to both a particular milieu and to the school community were particularly strong. Students at the school distance themselves from other social milieus through their social origin, conservative upbringing and their position as students at a distinguished school. This leads to a strong sense of distinction from outsiders and an internal coherence based on forming an exclusive community with one another. Furthermore, the analyses of the classroom observations demonstrate that these distinctive acts can also lead to a kind of oppositional behaviour: This can be seen, for example, in situations where expectations are not met, such as when a subject matter is considered below the students' 'level', for example, a discussion of teenage slang that does not correspond to the eloquent formal language used by the students. Teachers who deprecatingly call the students 'outsiders' for distancing themselves in this way are confronted with the fact that the students consciously embrace this exclusive outsider status. Based on the analysis, the students style themselves already as elite, that is, a privileged group attending a boarding school that corresponds to their privileged status.

In contrast, strong internal divisions were apparent at the *state-run boarding school*: students are mainly concerned with displaying their own excellent achievements, in some cases with the aim of degrading the achievements of others and thereby discrediting both teachers and peers. The strong focus on individual performance is especially reflected in the rejection of teaching methods that require cooperation, such as group work. The analyses of classroom observations and interviews with students illustrate that students openly reject such methods – on the one hand because they indicate their distrust in the abilities of their peers and therefore do not want to cooperate with them and on the other hand because group work does not allow individual achievement to be appreciated in its own right by the teachers. The common ground shared by these students – this is a key finding – are individualist and non-cooperative attitudes,[13] that is, a collectively divided internal distinction where every student wants to be special and the very best. Nevertheless, coherence is established through the students' shared sense of difference: students see themselves as particularly intelligent children from a distinguished school that is very different from other schools.

The two boarding schools show opposing approaches to forming a community: while the private boarding school emphasises the importance of milieu and communitisation when building a school community and the students strongly differentiate between the 'inside' (the school community) and the 'outside', the state-run boarding school shows more internal trends towards exclusion and the establishment of competitive situations that advocate very individualist attitudes.

EMPIRICAL RESULTS AND THEORETICAL REFLECTIONS

I will now present seven of the central findings of this study, focussing on the construction of elites in German boarding schools in a comparative perspective:

First, exclusive boarding schools construe themselves as places that (re-)produce elites. The results of this study regarding profiling strategies and methods of marking distinctions used by boarding schools supports the theory that processes of hierarchisation take place in the German educational system (see also Helsper & Krueger, 2019). Both of the schools in this study secure their exclusive status by means such as their distinct profiles, their reputation and their special curriculum. More centrally, however, exclusivity is established by the school's social mandate to contribute to the formation of elites – either by securing the *re*production of an existing elite status or by *producing* the elite from scratch.[14] In this manner, the boarding schools define themselves as elite educational institutions – a fact that Gaztambide-Fernández (2009a, 2009b) also confirms in his ethnographic studies on objectives, selection strategies, and the increasing diversity of the boarding school clientele of an US-boarding school.

However, it is also important to note that both schools are aware of the problematic and negative implications of the term 'elite' in Germany (see introduction). For this reason, the schools I examined have developed various means that enable them to use the term 'elite' within their context without being suspicious or breaking a taboo – a conclusion that Helsper et al. (2018a) and Helsper, Niemann, Gibson, and Dreier (2018b) also came to in their studies of exclusive German secondary schools. Both schools have worked to redefine the concept of 'elite' within a specific contextual logic: The private boarding school uses the term 'excellence', while the public boarding school distinguishes between different types of elite, such as responsible elites or performance elites, in order to refer to the 'positive sides' of the term and not the 'negative' (social and economic privilege, authoritarian leadership and power elite). My research thus corresponds with the findings of other studies in Germany that the term 'elite' is used more readily by schools when it refers to performance and responsibility, that is, an elite that serves society (cf. Helsper et al., 2018a, 2018b; Krueger & Helsper, 2014; Krueger, Kessler, Otto, & Schippling, 2018; Krueger, Kessler, & Winter, 2015).

Second, internal selection procedures allow schools to establish a distinct composition of students as well as to distinguish their students from those at other schools. Boarding schools have recruitment rituals that range from standardised procedures such as intelligence tests to unstructured interviews. The profile of the school and its educational programme are directly linked to who is admitted: the central role of achievement at the state-run boarding school makes talent a relevant factor. By contrast, the importance of values and traditions related to a particular milieu at the private boarding school mean that a pupil's compatibility with the school community carries much more weight in the selection procedure. The latter procedure gives the school a great deal of freedom in selecting students because intuitive and even strategic decisions can be made when selecting students for admission. In general, boarding schools legitimise their selection procedures by referring to the necessity of maintaining their profile and protecting the school community by choosing suitable students. Another finding was the circular, social and institutional intertwining of choice and selection that enables a 'cream skimming' (Bellmann, 2008, p. 257; and Helsper et al., 2018b) for these schools and leads to a 'consecration' (*Weihe*; Bourdieu & Passeron, 1990) of the clientele, that is, the title of 'elite' is bestowed upon the students who are associated with excellence (see also Hernandez, 1997; Karabel, 2005; Khan, 2010; Stevens, 2007).

Third, the choice of an exclusive boarding school is often the result of strategic considerations: either to gain or to maintain a certain exclusive status. Students whose families are less familiar with exclusive institutions are especially likely to regard boarding schools as a way of gaining privilege as well as securing their future status. This is especially the case for scholarship holders at the private boarding school, where tuition is very high and for the students at the public boarding school. However, students who are already familiar with exclusive educational institutions do not speak of being granted privileges. Instead, they believe they are entitled to attend a distinguished school.

These results highlight different concepts of privilege, as Howard (2008, 2010) points out in his studies on privilege in public and private schools: The students I examined from non-privileged families understand privilege as 'something individuals experience' (Howard, 2010, p. 81), while the socioeconomic privileged students construct their own privilege as a dimension of their identity, 'as a particular sense of self-understanding' (Howard, 2010) and justify their advantages in life.[15] In his study on an elite US-boarding school which cultivates privilege of a 'new' elite, Khan (2011, pp. 39–40) concludes that students 'explain their successes as a result of hard work and talents and reject the trappings of entitlement'. Nevertheless, the concept of meritocracy regarding elite education can also obscure inequalities.

One important finding with regard to selection is the connection between family and milieu: boarding schools are involved in family reproduction processes in a number of different ways (cf. Bourdieu, 1996b; Bourdieu, Boltanski, & de Saint Martin, 1981, p. 44ff.): either as an institutional continuation of the family mode of reproduction, as is the case at the private school where children frequently take over their parents' companies, or as a reinforcement of inherited dispositions and a source of motivation to rise above the family 'legacy' and strive for better career opportunities, as is the case at the school for the gifted.

Fourth, the exclusive socialisation at the boarding schools leads to elitist attitudes and acts of distinction. My research findings concur with other studies on elite (boarding) schools, which clearly demonstrated that participation in everyday life at exclusive educational institutions and the distinct constructions that exist in such institutions directly affect the teachers and students at those schools (cf. Gaztambide-Fernández, 2009a, 2009b; Khan, 2011). One of these is a study on cultural practices of knowledge acquisition and the creation of well-educated and well-behaved students in different German boarding schools, carried out by Kalthoff (1997), who also concludes that membership in an exclusive and select community encourages students to develop specific ways of thinking that are characteristic of the elite and to identify with the educational institution.

Peshkin (2001) has similar findings: in his study of a private, prestigious high school he comes to the conclusion that elite education has an impact on identity and moral decision-making processes.

Observations of everyday school life and interviews with the students have shown that students see themselves as a select group that must distinguish itself from other groups of students, thereby expressing that they belong to a 'higher class'. At the private boarding school, the students primarily justify their elite status by reference to their social origin, exclusive education and personality traits. The elite status is referred to less often in everyday life at this school: the fact that it is not the subject of discussion is owing to a sense of security in the possession of this status so that it is no longer necessary to communicate it – something that has already been established by Daloz (2012a, 2012b, pp. 215ff.). It is especially important to students at the public boarding school that responsible elite exists that serves society and distinguishes itself through exceptional achievements.

A central result is that the students are convinced of their own elite status not just because they are members of an exclusive group. Instead, a combination of social origin, the distinction of admission to an exclusive educational institution and the experience of attending that school foster an elitist way of thinking and contribute to conferring the privileged status (cf. also Gaztambide-Fernández, 2009a; Howard, 2008; Peshkin, 2001). In this connection, I also found that processes of distinction often continue after graduation as students take courses and attend institutions that are just as distinguished (cf. Hartmann, 2002; how the rising professional elite are shaping careers and private life, see Katchadourian & Boli, 1994).

Fifth, the construction of distinction by the school and its students is the foundation for community formation in exclusive boarding schools. If ties to a specific milieu are the basis for the formation of a community – as is the case with the private boarding school – an 'inside' is established at the school that strongly differentiates itself from the 'outside'. It was particularly interesting that no exceptions were made at this school: once students succeed in being admitted, they become part of the community and are accepted by all students. This applies equally to scholarship holders from families with more modest means and students from financially privileged families and different milieus. This finding is contrary to results of other studies on elite boarding schools (cf. e.g. Gaztambide-Fernández, 2009a; Khan, 2011) and might be explained by the admission criteria of this specific private school which promotes within-school-community solidarity and selects its students accordingly (see also Howard & Nguyen, 2017 for the development of bonds and sense of belonging in elite schools). This also applied to me as a researcher at the school: once I passed the admission process for my field research I was a 'temporary full-fledged member' of the school (in detail: Gibson, 2019).

If, however, achievement is emphasised – as at the boarding school for the gifted – a number of internal trends towards exclusion and differentiation can be detected and individualist and non-cooperative attitudes tend to develop.

Sixth, peers at boarding schools are an important source of influence on educational developmental processes. Peers can have either an emotional, stabilising and at times even normative effect within a group or they can be a motivating benchmark for students to compare themselves against (see also Fuchs, 2016; Krueger, Kessler, & Winter, 2016). In both schools, recognition from peers helps to guarantee successful school performance. This is particularly relevant for students with weak school performance: peers are motivational figures who encourage even weaker students to improve their achievement.

Seventh, exclusive boarding schools are caught within the apparently unresolvable tension at the heart of elite education: they are an opportunity to select the best and promote excellence, but they also encourage social exclusion and educational inequality. Elite schools such as the boarding schools examined in this study play an important role in processes of stratification. People not only speak of 'granting privileges to those who are already privileged', but also recognise that equality in education is not always equivalent to fairness. Within this context, one of the things that became clear was that it is not only marginalised students or children from less-educated families who face labelling processes by teachers or peers and institutional discrimination in the educational system; they also occur for students with strong economic or cultural privilege. Students were interviewed who had experienced discrimination at prior schools owing to the financial privileges of their parents and their educational background or due to their above-average abilities. This could be called 'exclusive discrimination' (Gibson, 2017, p. 427) and becomes a question of educational justice, too, which must be investigated in further studies.

DISCUSSION: IMPLICATIONS AND PERSPECTIVES

While there has been a strong interest in elite education in Germany over the past two decades, very few studies have been conducted on elite educational institutions. This is quite surprising as new lines of segregation appear to be developing in the educational system such as the expansion of the private school sector, trends to internationalisation and university excellence initiatives. This also leads to the promotion of competition and distinction among educational institutions (cf. i.e. Bloch, Mitterle, Paradeise, & Peter 2017; Helsper & Krueger, 2019; Helsper et al., 2018a; Krueger et al., 2016; Maxwell et al., 2018).

These developments were the basis for conducting my own study on the establishment of educational hierarchies in the German educational system in conjunction with an examination of the special position held by boarding schools within these developments and within the context of elite education. There were two reasons to focus on exclusive German boarding schools: First, owing to their selection process, they embody the image of a self-contained educational institution. Second, the special constellation of relationships and the general conditions at these schools – such as opportunities for connecting academic education with character building – create a special field in which elite education is implementable. For this reason, select boarding schools have frequently been considered to be elite institutions or places for the creation of excellence in Germany (cf. Gibson, 2017; Helsper et al., 2018a).

Additional research questions can be drawn from these observations, which I would like to touch on here:

First, education policy, as it relates to elite education and its educational and organisational consequences, must be further examined. The results make clear that changes in the German educational system are taking place: like Norway and Sweden, Germany in general is characterised as an egalitarian educational system (for an overview see Maxwell & Aggleton, 2015). Until recently, Germany's higher education institutions and secondary schools showed no difference in rank. But this fiction of equality has been called into question, not least owing to the fact that Germany's educational institutions are now seen in a globalised competition in an educational quasi-market (cf. e.g. Bagley, 2006; Bradley & Taylor, 2002; Walford, 1996). This has led to a noticeable increase in the hierarchisation of educational institutions and vertical stratifications in Germany resulting in the establishment of high-performance educational elite institutions (cf. Deppe et al., 2015). There is now a great deal of competition for the best schools and the best references to give children a chance to have the widest possible range of professional freedom to acquire socially relevant positions in their future careers (cf. e.g. Labaree, 1997). Additional studies are needed to examine how school culture is being transformed (or not) by these developments in educational policy and new trends in the field of education (see also Cookson & Persell, 2010).

Second, comparative international research is needed to analyse transformations of elite semantics and constructions. From the perspective of elite theory, the use of topoi for achievement, excellence and responsibility at the exclusive schools in this study was evidence for a democratic understanding of elitism based on meritocratic principles. Different points of reference in the use of terms such as 'elite' and 'excellence' in schools have shown that an analysis of current debates in educational policy regarding elite education and the promotion of excellence is one important starting point for additional, in particular comparative and international research – not least because of evidences for a shifting of elite constructions in other countries (for an overview see Howard & Gaztambide-Fernández, 2010; Maxwell & Aggleton, 2015; van Zanten & Ball, 2015; also Toernqvist, 2018).

Third, in-depth, comparative studies of elite and non-elite boarding schools and the habitus formations of their students are needed. In reference to school culture theory (cf. Boehme et al., 2015; Helsper et al., 2001; Kessler, 2017), the analyses of the boarding school settings indicate specific cultural concepts and practices and therefore different school cultures. These can be understood as symbolic, meaning-structuring constellations in individual schools and shaped and transformed by school actors in interaction, which corresponds with certain milieus and habitus (cf. Helsper, 2006). The results confirm that the selection of students with certain social backgrounds, abilities and attitudes depend on how they fit in this specific educational context (see also Bourdieu & Passeron, 1990), and that this as well affects the possibilities of their success within the school. This also supports the thesis of an existence of an interrelation of individual primary habitus formations by the students and secondary habitus formations requested by the schools. The differences in the school cultures and concepts of elite education that were observed in this study could be examined in more depth in further studies by contrasting these differences with other select elite boarding schools with different profiles as well as non-exclusive schools (cf. i.e. Helsper et al., 2018a).

Fourth, research is also needed on how secondary boarding schools' meritocratic visions, ideals, and mechanisms of educational inequality are changing. The developments regarding elite education raises the question of the establishment and reinforcement of social inequality, which needs further examination (cf. e.g. Howard & Gaztambide-Fernández, 2010; Kenway et al., 2017; Koh & Kenway 2016; Maxwell et al., 2018): The unequal distribution of resources – especially cultural and economic capital – has an impact on the educational participation of school actors and their educational success (cf. Bourdieu, 1996b; Bourdieu & Passeron, 1990). Despite higher educational opportunities due to the educational expansion, there is less equal opportunity on account of the fact of legitimising social inequality based on principles of meritocracy (cf. Becker & Lauterbach, 2010; Hadjar, 2008). Although studies of elite educational institutions show that they are operating with increasingly open and meritocratic legitimation horizons, they are still becoming less exclusive and install 'democratic inequality' (cf. Karabel, 2005; Khan, 2011, pp. 196–197). It even becomes obvious in studies of admission policies of exclusive educational institutions (cf. Helsper & Krueger, 2015; Karabel, 2005; Stevens, 2007): their findings indicate the systematic exclusion of specific students from certain exclusive educational programmes or schools and therefore trends to a reproduction of social inequality.

NOTES

1. Not including vocational schools.

2. German secondary education includes different types of schools, among them *Gymnasien* which are designed to prepare students for university and grant the *Abitur* as their final certificate, after year 12. The transition process of students to secondary school is usually after grade four and varies between the federal states (cf. e.g. Maaz, Baumert, Gresch, & McElvany, 2010). Recently, almost 50 percent of the fourth graders attend a *Gymnasium* (cf. Autorengruppe Bildungsberichterstattung 2018, p. 94). Because of the large amount of applications for some of the schools, access must be limited owing to availability. Most state schools do not have other options for selecting students, but some *Gymnasien* are free to select students according to their own criteria, a practice known as 'cream skimming' (Bellmann, 2008, p. 257), which establishes further opportunities for segregation (cf. West & Hind, 2007).

3. There are diverse types of elite schools (for an overview on the global scale, see Kenway et al., 2017; for Germany see Deppe & Kastner, 2014). For a definition of elite boarding schools, see Gaztambide-Fernández (2009b).

4. The project was funded by the German Academic Scholarship Foundation (*Studienstiftung des Deutschen Volkes*).

5. I refer to several meanings of the term: first, to the individual habitus of adolescents—their attitudes, practices and orientations in general (individual primary habitus, cf. Bourdieu, 1998). Second, to school-related practices and orientations as an aspect of the individual habitus, the student habitus (Schuelerhabitus; cf. Helsper, Kramer, & Thiersch, 2014), that is, the incorporated dispositions of an adolescent with whom he or she relates to school requirements (the secondary habitus, cf. Bourdieu & Passeron, 1990).

6. The data were collected in 2009 and 2010. The sample only included schools with more boarders than day students.

7. The results presented here are based on analyses of the mission statements, interviews with head teachers, interviews with students in senior classes and observations of everyday school life. The presentations follow the qualitative approach using case studies. Owing to limited space, I cannot provide a detailed description of the data interpretation process (cf. Gibson, 2017, pp. 109–114).

8. Most of the private boarding schools charge fees under €20.000 a year (cf. Zuechner et al., 2018, pp. 434–435).

9. The translations give the sense of the interview statements but are not a verbatim reproduction of the oral transcriptions in the German. All data have been anonymised.

10. This category refers to students with an intelligence quotient score above 130.

11. These findings are confirmed by other studies (cf. Helsper et al., 2018a; Kotzyba, Dreier, Niemann, & Helsper, 2018; Ullrich, 2014). To remain competitive on the education 'market', newly established *Gymnasien* emphasise new and innovative profiles such as international concepts and diploma as well as specific pedagogical objectives (e.g. education for the gifted).

12. For similar strategies in two elite secondary institutions in Buenos Aires, see Ziegler (2017).

13. This internal distinction surprises as these students live together and have a strong sense of togetherness as gifted children of this special school. But this closeness does not apply when it comes to academic performance and assessment. Nonetheless, the analyses show that peers are an essential reference: they encourage weaker students to improve their achievements.

14. This contrast does not imply that there is no reproduction of the social status in the state-run boarding school as well. It is obvious that top-performances in school often correlate with the socioeconomic status of the family. The main difference lies in the school's educational programs: one focusses on already existing elites, which must be 'refined' and the other one on the meritocratic selection through achievement of a future elite. Nonetheless both schools want to educate a responsible elite that serves society.

15. See Howard (2008, 2010) for ways in which affluent students resist their privilege.

REFERENCES

Angod, L. (2015). *Behind and beyond the ivy: How schools produce elites through the bodies of racial others*. Doctoral dissertation, University of Toronto, Ontario.

Autorengruppe Bildungsberichterstattung. (Eds.). (2018). *Bildung in Deutschland 2018*. Bielefeld, Germany: wbv Media.

Bagley, C. (2006). School choice and competition: A public market in education revisited. *Oxford Review of Education*, *32*(3), 347–362.

Becker, R., & Lauterbach, W. (Eds.). (2010). *Bildung als Privileg*. Wiesbaden, Germany: Verlag fuer Sozialwissenschaften.

Bellmann, J. (2008). Choice policies. In H. Ullrich & S. Strunck (Eds.), *Begabtenförderung an Gymnasien* (pp. 249–271). Wiesbaden, Germany: Verlag fuer Sozialwissenschaften.

Bloch, R., Mitterle, A., Paradeise, C., & Peter, T. (Eds.). (2017). *Universities and the production of elites. Discourses, policies, and strategies of excellence and stratification in higher education*. London: Palgrave Macmillan.

Bluhm, H., & Strassenberger, G. (2006). Elitedebatten in der Bundesrepublik. In H. Muenkler, G. Strassenberger, & M. Bohlender (Eds.), *Deutschlands Eliten im Wandel* (pp. 125–145). Frankfurt, Germany: Campus.

Boehme, J., Hummrich, M., & Kramer, R. (Eds.). (2015). *Schulkultur*. Wiesbaden, Germany: Springer VS.

Bohnsack, R. (1983). *Alltagsinterpretation und soziologische Rekonstruktion*. Opladen, Germany: Westdeutscher Verlag.

Bohnsack, R. (1989). *Generation, Milieu und Geschlecht*. Opladen, Germany: Leske + Budrich.

Bohnsack, R. (2010). Documentary method and group discussions. In R. Bohnsack, N. Pfaff, & W. Weller (Eds.), *Qualitative analysis and documentary method in international educational research* (pp. 99–124). Opladen, Germany: Barbara Budrich.

Bohnsack, R. (2014). *Rekonstruktive Sozialforschung*. Opladen u. Barbara Budrich, UTB.

Bohnsack, R., Loos, P., Schaeffer, B., Staedtler, K., & Wild, B. (1995). *Die Suche nach Gemeinsamkeit und die Gewalt der Gruppe*. Opladen, Germany: Leske + Budrich.

Bohnsack, R., Nentwig-Gesemann, I., & Nohl, A.-M. (Eds.). (2013). *Die dokumentarische Methode und ihre Forschungspraxis*. Wiesbaden, Germany: Springer VS.

Bohnsack, R., Pfaff, N., & Weller, W. (Eds.). (2010a). *Qualitative analysis and documentary method in international educational research*. Opladen & Farmington Hills: Barbara Budrich.

Bohnsack, R., Pfaff, N., & Weller, W. (2010b). Reconstructive research and documentary method in Brazilian and German educational science – An introduction. In R. Bohnsack, N. Pfaff, & W. Weller (Eds.), *Qualitative analysis and documentary method in international educational research* (pp. 7–38). Opladen, Germany: Barbara Budrich.

Bourdieu, P. (1996a). *Distinction: A social critique of the judgement of taste* (8th ed.). Cambridge, MA: Harvard University Press.

Bourdieu, P. (1996b). *State nobility: Elite schools in the field of power*. Stanford, CA: University Press.

Bourdieu, P. (1998). *Practical reason: On the theory of action*. Stanford, CA: University Press.

Bourdieu, P., Boltanski, L., & de Saint Martin, M. (1981). Kapital und Bildungskapital. Reproduktionsmechanismen im sozialen Wandel. In P. Bourdieu, L. Boltanski, M. de Saint Martin, M. & P. Maldidier (Eds.), *Titel und Stelle* (pp. 23–87). Frankfurt, M., Germany: Europaeische Verlagsanstalt.

Bourdieu, P., & Passeron, C. (1990): *Reproduction in education, society and culture*. London: Sage Publications.

Bradley, S., & Taylor J. (2002). The effect of the quasi-market on the efficiency-equity trade-off in the secondary school sector. *Bulletin of Economic Research, 54*(3), 295–314.

Broeckling, U., & Peter, T. (2014). Mobilisieren und Optimieren. Exzellenz und Egalitaet als hegemoniale Diskurse im Erziehungssystem [On mobilizing and optimizing - Equality and excellence as hegemonic discourses of the German educational system]. In H.-H. Krueger & W. Helsper (Eds.), *Elite und Exzellenz im Bildungssystem: Nationale und internationale Perspektiven [Elite and excellence in the education system: National and international perspectives]* (pp. 129–147). Wiesbaden, Germany: Springer VS.

Cookson, P. W., Jr. (2009). Perspectives on elite boarding schools. In M. Berends, M. G. Springer, D. Ballou, & H. J. Walberg (Eds.), *Handbook of research on school choice* (pp. 461–478). New York, NY: Routledge.

Cookson, P. W., Jr, & Persell, C. H. (1985). *Preparing for power. America's elite boarding schools*. New York, NY: Basic Books.

Cookson, P. W., Jr, & Persell, C. H. (2010). Preparing for power: Twenty-five-years later. In A. Howard & R. A. Gaztambide-Fernández (Eds.), *Educating elites. Class privilege and educational advantage* (pp. 13–29). Lanham, MD: Rowman & Littlefield Publishers.

Daloz, J.-P. (2012a). *The sociology of elite distinction*. New York, NY: Palgrave Macmillan.

Daloz, J.-P. (2012b). Elite (un)conspicuousness. *Historical Social Research, 37*(1), 209–222.

Deppe, U., Helsper, W., Kreckel, R., Krueger, H.-H., & Stock, M. (2015). Germany's hesitant approach to elite education. In A. van Zanten, S. J. Ball, & B. Darchy-Koechlin (Eds.), *World yearbook of education 2015. Elites, privilege and excellence: The National and global definition of educational advantage* (pp. 82–95). London: Routledge.

Deppe, U., & Kastner, H. (2014). Exklusive Bildungseinrichtungen in Deutschland [Exclusive education institutions in Germany]. In H.-H. Krueger & W. Helsper (Eds.), *Elite und Exzellenz im Bildungssystem [Elite and excellence in the education system]* (pp. 263–283). Wiesbaden, Germany: Springer VS.

Deppe, U., Luedemann, J., & Kastner, H. (2018). Processes of internationalisation, stratification and elite formation in the German education system. A general view. In C. Maxwell, U. Deppe, H.-H. Krueger, & W. Helsper (Eds.), *Elite education and internationalisation. From the early years to higher education* (pp. 309–330). New York, NY: Palgrave Macmillan.

Ecarius, J., & Wigger, L. (Eds.). (2006). *Elitebildung – Bildungselite*. Opladen, Germany: Barbara Budrich.

Fuchs, J. (2016). Peerbeziehungen im Internat und ihre biografische Relevanz. In H.-H. Krueger, C. Kessler, & D. Winter (Eds.), *Bildungskarrieren von Jugendlichen und ihre Peers an exklusiven Schulen* (pp. 119–140). Wiesbaden, Germany: Verlag fuer Sozialwissenschaften.

Gaztambide-Fernández, R. A. (2009a). *The best of the best: Becoming elite at an American boarding school*. Cambridge, MA: Harvard University Press.

Gaztambide-Fernández, R. A. (2009b). What is an elite boarding school? *Review of Educational Research, 79*(3), 1090–1128.

Gibson, A. (2017). *Klassenziel Verantwortungselite. Eine Studie zu exklusiven, deutschen Internatsgymnasien und ihrer Schuelerschaft.* [Required standard: A responsible elite. A study on exclusive boarding schools in Germany] Wiesbaden, Germany: Springer VS.

Gibson, A. (2019): Geladene 'Zaungaeste' im Elitekontext - Zugangshuerden und Verwicklungen beim qualitativen Forschen in exklusiven Internatsschulen. [Invited 'onlookers' in elite settings - Access barriers and entaglements during ethnographic field research] In H.-H. Krueger, W. Helsper & J. Luedemann (Eds.), Methodische Herausforderungen in der Elitebildungsforschung. *Zeitschrift für Qualitative Forschung, 20*(1), 9-25.

Gibson, A., & Helsper, W. (2018). Passungstypologie von individuellen und institutionellen Schuelerhabitus – eine mehrebenenanalytische relationale Typenbildung. In R. Bohnsack, N. F. Hoffmann, & I. Nentwig-Gesemann (Hrsg.), *Typenbildung und Dokumentarische Methode* (pp. 151–169). Opladen, Germany: Barbara Budrich.

Hadjar, A. (2008). *Meritokratie als Legitimationsprinzip.* Wiesbaden, Germany: Verlag fuer Sozialwissenschaften.

Hartmann, M. (2002). *Der Mythos von den Leistungseliten.* Frankfurt, M., Germany: Campus.

Hartmann, M. (2008). *Elitesoziologie.* Frankfurt, M. u.a., Germany: Campus.

Hartmann, M. (2013). *Soziale Ungleichheit – Kein Thema fuer die Eliten?* Frankfurt, M., Germany: Campus.

Helsper, W. (2006). Elite und Bildung im Schulsystem – Schulen als Institutionen-Milieu-Komplexe in der ausdifferenzierten höheren Bildungslandschaft. In J. Ecarius & L. Wigger (Eds.), *Elitebildung – Bildungselite* (pp. 162–187). Opladen, Germany: Barbara Budrich.

Helsper, W. (2012). Distinktion in der gymnasialen Schullandschaft. In S. Lin-Klitzing, D. Di Fuccia, & G. Mueller-Frerich (Eds.), *Aspekte gymnasialer Bildung* (pp. 116–134). Bad Heilbrunn, Germany: Klinkhardt.

Helsper, W., Boehme, J., Kramer, R.-T., & Lingkost, A. (2001). S*chulkultur und Schulmythos.* Opladen, Germany: Leske + Budrich.

Helsper, W., Dreier, L., Gibson, A., Kotzyba, K., & Niemann, M. (2018a). *Exklusive Gymnasien und ihre Schueler. Passungsverhaeltnisse zwischen institutionellem und individuellem Schuelerhabitus.* Wiesbaden, Germany: Springer VS.

Helsper, W., Hummrich, M., & Kramer, R.-T. (2013). Qualitative Mehrebenenanalyse. In H. Boller, B. Friebertshaeuser, A. Langer, A. Prengel, & S. Richter (Eds.), *Handbuch qualitative Forschungsmethoden in der Erziehungswissenschaft* (pp. 119–135). Weinheim, Germany: Juventa.

Helsper, W., Kramer, R.-T., & Thiersch, S. (Eds.). (2014). *Schuelerhabitus.* Wiesbaden, Germany: Springer VS.

Helsper, W., & Krueger, H.-H. (Eds.). (2015). *Auswahl der Bildungsklientel.* Wiesbaden, Germany: Springer VS.

Helsper, W., Krueger, H.-H., & Luedemann, J. (Eds.). (2019). *Exklusive Bildung und neue Ungleichheit. Ergebnisse der DFG-Forschergruppe "Mechanismen der Elitebildung im deutschen Bildungssystem". [Exclusive education and new inequality. Findings of the DFG-research group "Mechanisms of elite formation in the german education system", own translation]. Zeitschrift fuer Paedagogik,* special issue 65.

Helsper, W., Niemann, M., Gibson, A., & Dreier, L. (2018b). 'Elite' and 'excellence'. A delicate matter for head teachers of exclusive secondary schools in Germany. In A. van Zanten (Ed.), *Elites in education,* Vol. *3.* The Fabrication of Elite Identities in Families and Schools (chapter no. 51). New York, NY: Routledge.

Hernandez, M. A. (1997). *A is for Admission: An insiders guide to getting into the Ivy League and other top colleges.* New York, NY: Warner Books.

Hoffmann-Lange, U. (2001). Elite research in Germany. *International Review of Sociology, 11,* 201–216.

Howard, A. (2008). *Learning privilege: Lessons of power and identity in affluent schooling.* New York, NY: Routledge.

Howard, A. (2010). Stepping outside class: Affluent students resisting privilege. In A. Howard & R. A. Gaztambide-Fernández (Eds.), *Educating elites. Class privilege and educational advantage* (pp. 79–95). Lanham, MD: Rowman & Littlefield Publishers.

Howard, A., & Gaztambide-Fernández, R. A. (Eds.). (2010). *Educating elites. Class privilege and educational advantage*. Lanham, MD: Rowman & Littlefield Publishers.

Howard, A., & Kenway, J. (Eds.) (2015). New directions for research on elites and elite education: Methodological challenges and possibilities. *International Journal of Qualitative Studies in Education*. special issue *28*(9).

Howard, A., & Nguyen, H. (2017). Privileged bonds: Lessons of belonging at an elite boarding school. In C. Halse (Ed.), *Interrogating belonging for young people in schools* (pp. 41–164). Hampshire: Palgrave Macmillan.

Howard, A., Polimeno, A., & Wheeler, B. (Eds.). (2014). *Negotiating privilege and identity in educational contexts*. New York, NY: Routledge.

Hradil, S., & Imbusch, P. (Eds.). (2003). *Oberschichten – Eliten – Herrschende Klassen*. Opladen, Germany: Leske + Budrich.

Hummrich, M., & Kramer, R.-T. (2011). Qualitative Mehrebenenanalyse als triangulierendes Verfahren – Zur Methodologie von Mehrebenendesigns in der qualitativen Sozialforschung. In J. Ecarius & I. Miethe (Eds.), *Methodentriangulation in der qualitativen Bildungsforschung* (pp. 109–134). Opladen, Germany: Barbara Budrich.

Kalthoff, H. (1997). *Wohlerzogenheit. Eine Ethnographie deutscher Internatsschulen*. Frankfurt, M., Germany: Campus.

Karabel, J. (2005). *The chosen*. Boston, MA: Houghton Mifflin.

Katchadourian, H., & Boli, J. (1994). *Cream of the crop: The impact of elite education in the decade after college*. New York, NY: Basic Books.

Kenway, J., Fahey, J., Epstein, D., Koh, A., McCarthy, C., & Rizvi, F. (2017): *Class choreographies elite schools and globalization*. London: Palgrave Macmillan

Kessler, C. (2017). *Doing School. Ein ethnographischer Beitrag zur Schulkulturforschung*. Wiesbaden, Germany: Springer VS.

Khan, S. R. (2010). Getting in: How elite schools play the college game. In A. Howard & R. A. Gaztambide-Fernández (Eds.), *Educating elites* (pp. 97–112). Lanham MD: Rowman & Littlefield Publishers.

Khan, S. R. (2011). *Privilege: The making of an adolescent elite at St. Paul's School*. Princeton, NJ: Princeton University Press.

Kingston, P. W., & Lewis, L. S. (Eds.). (1990). *The high-status track: Studies of elite schools and stratification*. Albany, NY: State University of New York Press.

Koh, A., & Kenway, J. (2012). Cultivating national leaders in an elite school: Deploying the transnational in the national interest. *International Studies in Sociology of Education*, *22*(4), 333–351.

Koh, A., & Kenway, J. (2016). *Elite schools. Multiple geographies of privilege*. New York, NY: Routledge.

Kotzyba, K., Dreier, L., Niemann, M., & Helsper, W. (2018): Processes of internationalisation in Germany's secondary education system. In C. Maxwell, U. Deppe, H.-H. Krueger, & W. Helsper (Eds.), *Elite education and internationalisation. From the early years to higher education* (pp. 191–208). New York, NY: Palgrave Macmillan.

Krueger, H.-H., & Helsper, W. (Eds.). (2014). Elite und Exzellenz im Bildungssystem. Nationale und Internationale Perspektiven [Elite and excellence in the education system: National and international perspectives]. *Zeitschrift fuer Erziehungswissenschaft*, special issue *17*(19). Wiesbaden, Germany: Springer VS.

Krueger, H.-H., Helsper, W., Sackmann, R., Breidenstein, G., Böckling, U., Kreckel R., ... Stock, M. (2012). Mechanismen der Elitebildung im deutschen Bildungssystem [Mechanisms of elite education in the German education system]. *Zeitschrift fuer Erziehungswissenschaft*, *15*(2), 327–343.

Krueger, H.-H., Kessler, C. I., Otto, A., & Schippling, A. (2018). 'Elite' and 'excellence' from the perspective of young people and their peers at exclusive schools. In A. van Zanten (Ed.), *Elites in education*, Vol. *3*. The Fabrication of Elite Identities in Families and Schools (chapter no. 55). New York, NY: Routledge.

Krueger, H.-H., Kessler, C., & Winter, D. (2015). Schulkultur und soziale Ungleichheit. Perspektiven von Schulleitungen an exklusiven Gymnasien auf den Elite- und Exzellenzdiskurs. In J. Boehme, M. Hummrich, & R.-T. Kramer (Eds.), *Schulkultur. Theoriebildung im Diskurs* (pp. 183–210). Wiesbaden, Germany: Springer VS.

Krueger, H.-H., Kessler, C. I., & Winter, D. (2016). *Bildungskarrieren von Jugendlichen und ihre Peers an exklusiven Schulen*. Wiesbaden, Germany: Springer VS.

Labaree, D. F. (1997). *How to succeed in school without really learning: The credentials race in American education*. New Haven, CT: Yale University Press.

Maaz, K., Baumert, J., Gresch, C., & McElvany, N. (Eds.). (2010). *Der Uebergang von der Grundschule in die weiterfuehrende Schule*. Bonn, Germany: BMBF.

Mangset, M. (2017). Elite circulation and the convertibility of knowledge: Comparing different types and forms of knowledge and degrees of elite circulation in Europe. *Journal of Education and Work, 30*(2), 129–144.

Mannheim, K. (1952). *Essays on the sociology of knowledge*. London: Routledge & Kegan Paul.

Maxwell, C., & Aggleton, P. (Eds.). (2013). *Privilege, agency and affect*. Basingstoke: Palgrave Macmillan.

Maxwell, C., & Aggleton, P. (Eds.). (2015). *Elite education: International perspectives*. New York, NY: Routledge.

Maxwell, C., Deppe, U., Krueger, H.-H., & Helsper, W. (Eds.). (2018). *Elite education and Internationalisation. From the early years to higher education*. New York, NY: Palgrave Macmillan.

Paris, R. (2003). Autoritaet – Fuehrung – Elite. In S. Hradil & P. Imbusch (Eds.), *Oberschichten – Eliten – Herrschende Klassen* (pp. 55–72). Opladen, Germany: Leske + Budrich.

Peshkin, A. (2001). *Permissible advantage? The moral consequences of elite schooling*. Mahwah/NJ: Lawrence Erlbaum Associates Publishers.

Ricken, N. (2009). Elite und Exzellenz – Machttheoretische Analysen zum neueren Wissenschaftsdiskurs. *Zeitschrift fuer Paedagogik, 55*(2), 194–210.

Stevens, M. L. (2007). *Creating class. College admissions and the education of elites*. Harvard: Harvard University Press.

Toernqvist, M. (2018). The making of an egalitarian elite: School ethos and the production of privilege. *The British Journal of Sociology, 70*(2), 551–568.

Ullrich, H. (2014). Exzellenz und Elitenbildung in Gymnasien. Traditionen und Innovationen. In H.-H. Krueger & W. Helsper (Eds.), *Elite und Exzellenz im Bildungssystem* (pp. 181–201). Wiesbaden, Germany: Springer VS.

van Zanten, A. (2010). The sociology of elite education. In M. W. Apple, S. J. Ball, & L. A. Gandin (Eds.), *The Routledge international handbook of the sociology of education* (pp. 329–339). New York, NY: Routledge.

van Zanten, A., & Ball, S. J. (with Darchy-Koechlin, B.) (Eds.). (2015). *Elites, privilege and excellence: The national and global redefinition of educational advantage*. In World Yearbook of Education 2015. New York, NY: Routledge.

Wakeford, J. (1969). *The Cloistered Élite. A sociological analysis of the English public boarding school*. London: Praeger.

Walford, G. (Ed.). (1996). *School choice and the quasi-market*. Wallingford: Triangle Books.

Weinberg, I. (1967). *The English public schools*. New York, NY: Atherton Press.

West, A., & Hind, A. (2007). School choice in London, England: Characteristics of students in different types of secondary schools. *Peabody Journal of Education, 82*(2/3), 498–529.

Ziegler, S. (2017). Personalization and competition in elite schools in Buenos Aires: School strategies for the production and legitimization of dominant groups. *Journal of Education and Work, 30*(2), 145–155.

Zuechner, I., Peyerl, K., & Siegfried, L.-M. (2018). Internate in Deutschland [Boarding schools in Germany]. *Zeitschrift fuer Paedagogik, 64*(4), 417–440.

THE CLASS IDENTITY NEGOTIATIONS OF UPWARDLY MOBILE INDIVIDUALS AMONG WHITES AND THE RACIAL OTHER: A USA-FRANCE COMPARISON

Jules Naudet and Shirin Shahrokni

ABSTRACT

This chapter explores the class identities of upwardly mobile and middle-class members of racial minorities in France and the United States. Through in-depth interviewing with African Americans and descendants of North African immigrants in, respectively, the United States and France, and comparing these with their counterparts of the racially dominant group, the chapter shows that racial processes significantly shape the mobility experiences and the range of dilemmas, challenges and identity negotiations faced by our minority respondents. Drawing on the Critical Race Theory and on the minority culture of mobility theory (Neckerman, Carter, & Lee., 1999), it suggests that the ongoing salience of racial discrimination coupled with the maintenance of ties with socially disadvantaged members of their groups significantly shape the ways in which our respondents make sense of their class location. The chapter further points to under-researched nation-specific ideological repertoires in shaping our respondents' mobility experiences and class identities.

Keywords: Class; mobility; race; international comparison; minorities; socialisation

INTRODUCTION

This chapter explores the class identities of upwardly mobile and first-generation middle-class African-Americans and descendants of North African immigrants,

Elites and People: Challenges to Democracy
Comparative Social Research, Volume 34, 137–158
Copyright © 2019 by Emerald Publishing Limited
All rights of reproduction in any form reserved
ISSN: 0195-6310/doi:10.1108/S0195-631020190000034007

respectively, in France and the United States. Drawing on in-depth, open-ended interviews with members of minoritised groups and with individuals pertaining to the racially dominant population embarked on paths of extreme upward mobility, we examine how perceptions about class location are informed by the respondents' position in the racially stratified social order (Naudet, 2018; Rollock, 2014). We, therefore, draw on a conception of race[1] and class[2] as matrices of socialisation that function along autonomous yet intersecting modes. We further draw upon Ball's definition of 'social class as a 'relational [...], contextual, dynamic [...]' process' (Ball, 2003, p. 175; quoted in Rollock et al., 2013, p. 259) and set out to explore the possible continuities and discontinuities between individuals' objective class position and the perceptions they draw about their location in the socio-economic order (Daye, 1994; Moore, 2008; Neckerman, Carter, & Lee, 1999; Rollock et al., 2013).

In particular, our analysis reveals that despite national and group-specific variations in the ways in which mobility is experienced, the narratives of our minority respondents point to a set of feelings, dispositions and experiences specific to what (Neckerman et al., 1999) have called a 'minority culture of mobility'. Indeed, the maintenance, for many, of strong connections with their working class families and childhood friends coupled with the experience of ongoing everyday racism despite 'having made it' strongly shape the ways in which our minority respondents make sense of their mobility experiences and their class location in both contexts.

While a growing literature has unveiled the complexities of class identification processes among middle-class racial minorities in various national contexts,[3] in France, studies looking into the experiences of mobility have largely carried the principle of colour-blindness inscribed in the Republic-based 'fiction of universalism' (Amiraux & Simon, 2006). In particular, these have generally conceptualised mobility as a movement between two internally homogeneous classes and investigated the experiences of members of the racially dominant group. The knowledge hitherto produced has therefore invisibilised the privileges associated with Whiteness and presented the experiences and identities of a fragment of the upwardly mobile as the *normal*, the universal characteristics of the mobility experience. As Rollock (2012b, p. 518) writes, 'Much of the power of Whiteness lies in the fact that it is often disguised and *mis*recognized [...] as the morally acceptable, as normal, as natural'. Studies have thereby failed to examine the possible injuries, dilemmas and rewards associated with mobility from the standpoint of members of racially minoritised groups. This omission has further been reinforced by the fact that the bulk of research on the descendants of minority immigrants have centred on the lives of those situated at the bottom of the social hierarchy, contributing to downplaying the heterogeneity of their class experiences. Building on the insights of Critical Race Theory, this chapter departs from the widely unquestioned focus on White people as normative foci of analysis and debunks unspoken dimensions of mobility-associated challenges and dilemmas tied to being a successful member of a population over-represented in lower social strata *and* targeted by racism. Through a close analysis of the narratives elaborated by our racially minoritised respondents, it reveals that the challenges they face are not reducible to continued class disadvantages in socially privileged settings; second, it suggests that some of the strategies they mobilise to forge a sense of place in their educational and professional environments are rooted in racially shaped dispositions and resources.

We discuss these issues by focussing on two countries where the members of minority groups have been the chief victims of ethno-racial discriminatory practices. If indeed, in the United States, the Civil Rights movements opened significant opportunities for African-Americans, the racial divide between Blacks and Whites still reveals the 'cumulative and 'sedimentary' impact of a long history of racial oppression' (Bobo, 2011, p. 140). In fact, discriminatory practices make it particularly difficult for African-Americans to achieve upward mobility: they are far less likely than their white counterparts to experience 'rags-to-riches' trajectories (Hertz, 2005) and overall they possess about ten to eleven times less wealth than their white, upper-middle class counterparts (Oliver & Shapiro, 1995). Discrimination persists even at the highest levels of the class structure and leads to the racial isolation of the African-American bourgeoisie (Benjamin, 1991). In France, while descendants of North African immigrants have experienced some socio-economic gains in comparison with the former, migrant generation, a systematic gap prevails between their educational qualifications and their professional, financial and residential resources (Beauchemin, Hamel, Lesné, Simon, & TeO Team, 2010; Lepinard & Simon, 2008; Meurs, Pailhe, & Simon, 2006; Silberman & Fournier, 2006; Simon, 2003). Increasingly, research points to their being the prime targets of discrimination in the opportunity structure. In the realm of education, in particular, as Lepinard and Simon (2008, p. 23) write, children of North African immigrants have systematically been relegated to the 'worst schools, the less prestigious courses and universities'. As is increasingly revealed in public opinion polls, governmental discourses and media representations, anti-Muslim and anti-Arab sentiments have been on the rise and primarily targeted North African immigrants and their children (Dubet et al., 2013; Hajjat & Mohammed, 2013).

If an emergent scholarship has begun to intersectionally explore mobility experiences and class formations, it has rarely been done so comparatively, across majority and minority racial groups. Furthermore, this scholarship has not examined the role of nationally specific processes in shaping both the specific mobility injuries that minorities may face and the strategies they elaborate to respond to these. Yet, as Lamont and Thévenot (2000, pp. 8–9) explain 'each nation makes more readily available to its members' specific sets of tools through historical and institutional channels, which means that members of different national communities are not equally likely to draw on the same cultural tools to construct and assess the world that surrounds them'. The range of 'national repertoires of evaluation' (Lamont & Thévenot, 2000) at the disposal of upwardly mobile minorities may, therefore, significantly structure their mobility experiences, and particularly, these may restrain the strategies groups deploy to respond to the challenges they encounter.

For obvious space reasons, we have deliberately chosen to ignore important intra-group differences[4] to focus instead on the less explored comparison between members of majority groups and members of minority groups as well as on the comparison between France and the United States. Our chapter starts with a discussion of the literature on upward mobility, followed by a presentation of the methodology employed throughout our research. The subsequent section of the chapter briefly presents the experiences of mobility by the members of majority groups in both countries. Next, we discuss the narratives collected among members of minority groups, drawing attention to the interplay between nation-specific ideological contexts and minority-based experiences of mobility.

THEORISING THE EXPERIENCE OF UPWARD INTERGENERATIONAL MOBILITY: CLASS, RACE AND NATIONAL PROCESSES

A vast literature exploring individuals' experiences of social ascension has shed light on the 'symbolic violence' that accompanies the movement between classes (Bourdieu, 1989; Granfield, 1991; Lehmann, 2009; Naudet, 2018; Reay, Crozier, & Clayton, 2009; Shahrokni, 2018, 2015). As is revealed, upwardly mobile individuals generally experience a sense of 'culture shock' (Torres, 2009) upon entry into their new social settings. Dominant members of these groups indeed display habits, tastes and styles that are emblematic of the privileged classes. 'The dialect in which they converse; the brands of their clothing and the cars they drive' (Torres, 2009, p. 888), these distinctive social markers contribute to generating firm cultural boundaries and lead to feelings of isolation, shame and intimidation among the upwardly mobile. Moreover, fears of 'class betrayal' often shape the mobility experience as moving up a highly unequal opportunity structure may be lived as a painful 'rupture' from people and places tied to one's home environment (Bourdieu, 1989; Shahrokni, 2018, 2015). Additionally, the upwardly mobile may have to maintain class-heterogeneous family, neighbourhood and friendship ties and deploy strategies aimed at negotiating a wide range of class-based problems and be committed to financially and materially 'giving back' to family and friend members. Aside from these class-related costs, a growing scholarship has showed how race-based forms of inequality, independent of, or jointly with, class, may inform the injuries of social ascension (Bettie, 2002; Neckerman et al., 1999; Torres, 2009). In particular, Neckerman et al. (1999) suggest the persistent salience of discrimination in their middle-class educational, professional and residential settings together with the weight of inter-class relations with co-ethnic members 'left behind' create unique mobility dilemmas in the lives of upwardly mobile and middle-class minorities. Notably, they may have to cope with such discriminatory practices as the 'glass-ceiling effect'.[5] Being one of the few minorities in their middle-class settings may also create a psychological toll largely unknown to their counterparts of majority background. In capturing these, the 'minority culture of mobility' elaborated by Neckerman et al. (1999) represents an innovative theoretical advancement. Our chapter further identifies the extent to which the narratives of success laid out by our minority respondents are shaped by nationally specific 'cultural tool kits' (Lamont & Thévenot, 2000;

Lamont et al., 2002). It may notably be hypothesised that in France, the strategies deployed by upwardly mobile minorities may be restrained by the Republic-based, colour-blind rhetoric of universalism, a discourse that remains dominant despite the emergence of competing ideological repertoires promoting minority empowerment (Amiraux & Simon, 2006; Juteau, 2006). In the United States, on the other hand, successful members of racially disadvantaged groups may build on more readily available resources grounded in community-based networks (Neckerman et al., 1999; Vallejo, 2012).

Our analysis thus contributes to enriching the theoretical model proposed by Neckerman et al. (1999) in two ways. Our first contribution is empirical. While in elaborating this theory the authors have brought a major advancement to the scholarship on the links between mobility, assimilation and acculturation in the lives of successful minority groups, their propositions have lacked a rigorous empirical basis. Here, we apply the minority culture of mobility theory to two distinct empirical cases. Next, our cross-national comparative framework enables us to refine the model by shedding light on the interplay between nation-specific ideological contexts and minority-based experiences of mobility.

METHODOLOGY

Our analysis draws on in-depth, semi-structured interviews conducted with upwardly mobile members of the white, majority population and, respectively, with successful African Americans in the United States and descendants of North African immigrants in France.

In total 42 and 69 interviews were conducted, respectively, in the United States and in France. Respondents, aged between 18 and 65 years of age, had all achieved extreme educational mobility. Those who entered the job market occupied prominent positions in the private sector, public service and academia (researchers and faculty members). Their parents had occupied professions ranging from menial work to low clerical positions. Interviews were conducted between 2008 and 2010 in the United States and France.

In France, our respondents were all alumni of *grandes écoles*[6] or recipients of PhD diploma from French universities. In particular, the upwardly mobile and middle-class descendants of North African immigrants being a relatively new and small population, we decided to include individuals currently embarked on strong educational mobility paths; our recruits for this group were, therefore, principally students and young graduates of France's *grandes écoles*. In the United States, the top civil servants were members of the *Senior Executive Service* (SES), one of the highest ranks that can be attained in Federal public service. People working in the private sector held a degree equivalent to a Master or a MBA.

Respondents were recruited by running announcements on the mailing lists of alumni networks and of professional associations as well as by using snow-ball sampling. Such a selection process necessarily entails a bias for only those who considered it worthwhile to narrate their trajectory and who were ready to volunteer for it have been interviewed. We, nonetheless, made sure that our

Table 1.   Interviews Conducted in the United States between
April 2007 and September 2007.

	Number of Interviewees
Academia	16
	Minorities: 5
Top civil service	16
	Minorities: 2
Private sector	10
	Minorities : 5
Total interviews	42
	Minorities: 12

Table 2.   Interviews Conducted in France from 2008 and 2010.

	Number of Interviewees
Academia	11 (3 minorities)
Top civil service	18 (1 minority)
Students of *grandes écoles*	20 (20 minorities)
Private sector	20 (10 minorities)
Total interviews	69

announcements were run among diverse networks and the narratives we collected are actually so varied that the suspicion of a sample composed of individuals sharing a common experience of mobility can safely be ruled out.[7] Tables 1 and 2 provide the details of the socio-demographic features of our interviewees.

In the interviews, respondents were asked to provide us with colourful descriptions of their educational and professional experiences. Because entry into a selective higher education establishment was reconstructed as a major turning point in their lives, even, a 'life changing' event, respondents extensively described their experiences in these institutional sites before moving to detailed descriptions of their work environments, social relationships, etc. The enactment of not only family-related and extra-school friendship commitments, but also social, and for some, political engagements was further outlined and extensive descriptions about the respondents' circles of friends, about the people they consider to be 'like them' and those who they did not identify with were provided.

THE MOBILITY EXPERIENCE FROM A MAJORITY PERSPECTIVE

White-Americans' Narratives and the American Dream

The narratives of our White Americans are characterised by recurrent references to the American Dream. If this ideology is multifaceted and encompasses competing principles (Hochschild, 1995, McNamee & Miller, 2004), two of its salient dimensions, in particular, structure our White-Americans' mobility narratives. The first is the 'transgenerational' aspect of the American Dream, that is, as Sennett and Cobb (1993) argue, the notion, highly influential among many American working class families, that offspring's should surpass one's socio-economic achievements. Echoing this deep-seated principle, many of our White respondents highlight an acute sense of awareness of their parents' sacrifices and pay tributes to their abnegation. They further point out that the standards of success they have reached closely reflect the aspirations the former generation held. Their mobility trajectories, therefore, constitute a *validation* of their parents' values. As such, the narratives make the statement that strong principles inherited from their family environment have been preserved, in fact, celebrated, through their achievements.

The second aspect of the American dream ideology that informs White-American interviewees' narratives is expressed in the valorisation of competition and an ethos of hard work. Americans are indeed much more likely than their French counterparts to highlight the personal attributes that have been conducive to their achievements. They further express a strong belief in the meritocratic norm and most assert that meritocracy is one of the emblematic features of their country. Moreover, this widely shared representation among our White-Americans certainly largely explains the fact that mobility, among them, is rarely reconstructed as causing moral dilemmas as, the argument goes, it simply mirrors the hardships and the struggles one was ready to experience in order to climb the social ladder. The idea that there is a difference in nature between the elite and the masses is actually challenged by the belief that one can always succeed if one really wants to. These narratives thus reveal a tendency to downplay socio-cultural differences between members of their home environment and their new group. Surely, the interviews evoke identity adjustments and phases of tension, but they remain framed by the conviction that no radical differences exist between the different groups that compose the American society.

France's Majority Respondents' Narratives and the Double Absence Rhetoric

Contrary to most White Americans, respondents from the majority group in France largely consider that their group of origin is significantly different from their group of arrival. Their interviews are consequently constructed around the idea that they belong neither to one nor to the other. Questions of social distinction are in fact at the core of their narratives, some of them suggesting that their mobility path represents nothing but a quest towards the mastery of 'social codes', as they put it, in reference to the dispositions of the dominant classes. This quest is often described to be accompanied by a 'labor of deculturation, correction and retraining that is needed to undo the effects of inappropriate learning' (Bourdieu, 1984, p. 71). The emphasis on social distinction among our French respondents corroborates Lamont's (1992) analysis of the French upper-middle class and its celebration of 'refinement', one that contrasts with their American counterparts' sense of 'laissez-faire' in the realm of culture. If upward mobility also implies a process of deculturation and acculturation in the United States, these adjustments generally refer to the acquisition of dispositions transmitted at school and in the workplace. On the contrary, in describing the 'codes' of the elite, the French more often evoke a 'hidden agenda', tacit rules as regards ways of being, talking, dressing, etc. It is, therefore, unsurprising that most of our French majority respondents extensively recollect difficulties to adjust to their new social status, best exemplified through a widely shared feeling of 'double-absence' (Sayad, 1999), of being neither part of their group of origin nor of their group of arrival. The two are described as sharply different and antagonist and overall, the narratives convey a vision of society as marked by rigid and impermeable social boundaries. They thus claim that their new social status inexorably urges them to take distance with their group of origin. This fatalism certainly constitutes the main difference with Americans' narratives who, even when they acknowledge the distance they have taken with their parents and their family, often assert with confidence their capacity to maintain strong links with their group of origin.

THE MOBILITY EXPERIENCE FROM A MINORITY PERSPECTIVE

African-Americans' Narratives: The Importance of 'Reaching Back'

The picture is significantly different when one looks into the narratives of upwardly mobile minority members. The extension of the Duboisian concept of '*double-consciousness*'[8] by Pattillo (2007) who forged the concept of *middleman* can help us grasp, beyond the diversity of the collected narratives, what defines the specificity of the experience of upward social mobility among African-Americans. Pattillo reminds us that the concept of 'double-consciousness', understood as a sense of belonging to both the Black community and the American nation, can be applied to all African-Americans, irrespective of their social status: no professional or economic achievement, she indeed argues, will ever erase the racial stigma. Yet, the concept of 'middlemen' allows us to employ a more dynamic approach to the issue as it highlights the tensions that Black individuals caught in-between two groups, the Black poor and the White middle-class, may experience. The condition of the *middlemen* eloquently illustrates what our African-American interviewees express: they remain strongly attached to their community of origin; yet, they permanently have to negotiate their upper-middle-class identity in a predominantly white context. This situation of 'in-betweeness' is the main feature distinguishing the narratives of African-Americans from those of the majority group.

Earl, who graduated from an Ivy League University and is a multimillionaire CEO, does not hesitate to mobilise the repertoire of meritocracy and of the American Dream while asserting that he is strongly attached and committed to his group of origin. Raised by a single-mother, he continues to be marked by an early experience of extreme poverty in a small industrial town of Pennsylvania (he describes his home as one of the poorest of a very poor neighbourhood). Two lines of narration therefore structure Earl's discourse. One clearly privileges the rhetoric of individual achievement, insisting on a constant need to push back the limits of his success. The other pleads for his attachment to his group of origin, emphasising his determination to 'stay grounded' and never forget where he comes from and what he has experienced, back in his childhood and adolescence.

He castigates the beneficiaries of welfare schemes who will never make it in life and simultaneously claims that he 'always tries to give back whatever was given to [him]'. He regularly visits his hometown where he preserved strong ties and remembers that when he first came back there upon graduating, many thought his 'disappearance' was owing to a jail sentence. A very few of his friends had actually imagined that he could have gone to college. This anecdote summarises all the ambiguity of Earl's discourse: there is a certain grievance against his neighbours for whom college is within their scope of possibilities. It also conveys a certain pride in having gone through a trajectory that strongly differs from those of his friends and classmates. Finally, it shows that he is 'authentically' grounded in a Black and poor community. His constant effort to intertwine a narrative of achievement with a repeated assertion of his belonging to the poor African-American community is indeed the most striking aspect of the interview. He regularly helps his family, goes back frequently to the neighbourhood where he grew up and continues to feel he is a full member of a subaltern community. He constantly claims his attachment to his community, such as when he points out that the assistance he brings to his family distinguishes him from most of his white colleagues:

I am the patriarch of my family and I have to take care of things other people may not have to take care of. Sending money home, sending money to my sisters to avoid their house to be foreclosed... Sending money so that my sister can go down to the hospital see her husband who is dying [...] I know there are things I have to do, that other people don't have to do.

Quite revealingly, African-American interviewees declare they financially help their family much more frequently than White-Americans do.[9] Most are indeed very inspired by a moral imperative of solidarity. They feel they share a common destiny with the entire African-American community, fuelled in their common experience of discrimination and stigmatisation. Their sense of solidarity may be tied to a *reaching-back* ideology: they stress a moral obligation to help their fellows whenever they can, through small daily actions that display a constant concern for their community of origin. This corroborates Moore's hypothesis about first-generation middle-class members being generally more likely to develop a 'multi-class' identity than their Black counterparts born in wealthier families (Moore, 2008). In the case of the United Kingdom, Rollock et al. (2013) argue that socially mobile Blacks try to maintain a raced 'moral capital' and that some of them explicitly refuse to engage in White middle-class spaces that they associate with privilege and individualism.

James, a business lawyer, also asserts he strongly feels the need to reach-back to his community. His narrative is centred on a tension between his belonging to the economic elite and his experience of the ghetto. He explicitly refuses any investment in a *bourgeois identity*, claiming that he is 'not a trickle down person'. Committed in various social organisations and NGOs, he wants to reinforce this aspect of his life in a near future. Throughout the interview, he develops a vision of himself as somebody who just does the minimal requirements necessary to be accepted by his colleagues, but he insists on the fact he is constantly 'somewhere else':

> I don't think I'm able to reconcile the two worlds: I just take things as they are. If I did it would require some adjustments, but if I don't it is just the way it is. I think that's the right attitude.

- What do you mean by 'I take things the way they are?'

> If I was only out for my absolute interest, if I was trying to maximize the amount I make, I invest, etc. I think I would have to go some pretty high level mental acrobatics to square that with caring with anybody else. Because these things don't matter with me, I don't have to make that adjustment. [James, 38 years old, juris doctor, business lawyer]

Here, James clearly expresses that he cannot see himself living a life that would radically cut him off from his group of origin. On his side, Orlando recounts how, without even wanting to, he became a role model for a number of people in his building and his neighbourhood of origin:

> I'm being a role model. I live in a building where there are 19 Black porters working, and once people convinced themselves I was a professor and not a drug dealer, one of the guys came up to me and said: 'I tell my grandson about you. If you can be a professor and if you can live here, he can do better!' So in some ways I'm ... not a reluctant ... but a quiet, silent role model. In spite of myself. People look at me and say: 'I can do that!' particularly because I stuttered severely for the first 15 years of my life. I could not utter a coherent sentence. People made fun of me because of that. I literally could not utter a coherent sentence. [Orlando, 64, doctorate in history, professor]

This anecdote that Orlando recounts, clearly shows how spontaneous and essential his attachment to the Afro-American community is for him, even when he does not actively seek it. In addition, this obligation to show his solidarity is often combined with maintaining links within his community of origin. Bill's case allows us to see how these active social relationships are maintained; he has always attached great importance to the neighbourhood he lives in:

> I still prefer to live in working-class neighborhoods. It's still the case today. We'll actually go to my house after. [...] let me give another example: when I bought my house in DC ... because I moved from DC about 20 years ago. When I bought my house in DC 30 years ago it was all-Black, very much working-class neighborhood: it had one White family in about thirty. Today, almost half of them are White families. It's a brownstone house. I stay in the basement when I go to DC and I rent the three storeys. For most of the time I've been in Jersey, 20 years, all the tenants were Black. The last of the tenants is White. Now when I advertise the place for rent, only Whites respond. When previously only Blacks would respond. Gentrification... To tell you the truth I don't like this neighborhood anymore. I am thinking of selling the place... [Bill, 60, MBA, CEO of a consultancy company]

There is clearly a 'memorial' aspect to Bill's attachment to living in poor, Black neighbourhoods. But his manner of choosing his place of residence does not only constitute a way of reassuring himself about his permanency to himself: it also includes him in a web of daily social relationships that are completely different to those he would have experienced if he had lived in a neighbourhood where his neighbours had incomes similar to his (about 500 000$ a year he tells us, although he is single and has no children). His choice of place of residence led him to maintain a very modest lifestyle, far removed from the type of lifestyle he could enjoy. His car is over 10 years old, his clothes are relatively modest (both according to him and from our observations), his manner of speaking still resembles that of his neighbours (with barely disguised pleasure he states that this sometimes scares his business partners). Bill, thus, states he identifies better with people from the working classes than with people from the upper classes as 'I feel the issues working-class people deal with are more real than the issues middle-class people do ...':

> The issues they deal with around relationships tend to be much more ... needy-greedy. It might be about not having enough money to send your kids to schools where they can learn properly. Because the public system is all wrecked. Being over-extended because you live in a house that's three times the size you need and driving a car that is two times the price of the car you need: that's not a real issue to me. That's a self-made issue. [Bill, 60, MBA, CEO of a consultancy company]

In addition to a lifestyle strongly marked by the type of neighbourhood he lives in, Bill regularly sees the members of his family and pays a lot of attention to them. Despite the sacrifices it involved in terms of opportunities to further his career more rapidly, Bill did not allow himself to leave Washington DC as long as his father was alive, to continue to be able to look after him and visit him regularly. He only moved to New Jersey after his father's death. He provides significant financial support to his sister, who is a part-time secretary for an electricity distribution company and a single parent responsible for three children. In addition, in partnership with the Mayor of the town of ***, he intends to create an organisation that would help young people released from prison to find employment.

The recurrent inscription of our informants within a collective history leads us to question the links between race and class in the collected narratives. Is this solidarity with the group of origin class solidarity or the consequence of the belonging to a stigmatised group and of a 'racial socialization' (Constantine & Blackmon, 2002; Lesane-Brown, 2006)?

The literature points to the importance of 'racial socialisation' and insists on the fact that young African-Americans perceive themselves as members of the Black community at a very early age (Coard et al., 2004).[10] The narratives of our interviewees indeed suggest that class influences the way the belonging to the African-American community is experienced. If the solidarity they express is often based on a denunciation of racial discrimination, they often frame it in a way that suggests that their solidarity is mainly directed towards the most dominated fractions of the Black community, towards those who 'stayed on the other side of the fence'. Such an idea is clearly expressed by Leslie who, as she was a lawyer benefiting from high remunerations, abandoned everything to start a PhD in social sciences, with a specialisation on Welfare-State issues:

> My husband says every time you get close to making a lot of money you veer away. I somehow believe that I was not allowed to .... Now we are talking spirituality. I really believe that I was helped along the way both spiritually and directly and that how I show my gratitude is giving

back and using those talents and gifts and blessings so that somebody else's life is better. [...] It informs the way I've chosen to live my life. It works for me. It does not mean hard times don't come for me; but I get great pleasure at the end of my day, saying: 'This is what I have chosen to do with these opportunities I got.' So it's all how you want to hold the experience. It can be a harmful thing or it can be a strengthening thing

This importance of class in the way Leslie defines her group of origin is further reinforced later in the interview when, after saying 'No matter what I do, I get defined by my race', she adds:

Although no one in my family has been involved in unions, I will never cross a picket line. Never, never, never. I just can't do it. Or I get upset if people don't give good tips; or I would either put more money down or I would calculate what I think is a good tip and I would say: 'this is the tip I think we should leave'. Because I come from people ... this is how they've made their lives .... And to short-change someone who is working so hard and whose salaries is tied to these tips ... I am not gonna let anyone treat so these persons who are working so hard for them. And when they would bring water, I would say thank you! And they look surprised because most people treat them like they're invisible. But I come from people who were low service providers. So I guess I am expressing my solidarity by these everyday things. It's really important for me to... not forget where I come from. [silence] [Leslie, 55 years old, PhD in political science, associate-director of a social science research centre]

France: A 'Minority Culture of Mobility' in the Making?

Similar to their majority ethnic counterparts, entry into selective higher education establishments coincides for most of our respondents of North African migrant background with an unprecedented awareness about the breath and width of class-based inequalities. Indeed, upon admission, most of them measure the gulf setting them apart from most of their schoolmates, through first-hand experience of subtle and previously unsuspected dimensions of class inequalities. Lyes, our 22-year-old polytechnique student, describes a one-year phase of 'depression' at the prestigious Parisian *lycée* of Henri-IV, in which he undertook his preparatory classes, as a result of feeling *invisibilised* amid his 'exceptionally wealthy' class-mates. His description relays the recurrent and largely unintentional 'petty mundane everyday humiliations' (Reay, 2005, p. 917) he went through, which targeted the most banal features of his class-based environment:

In terms of cultural references, it may sound pointless but there was this girl who did not even know what the RMI[11] was. She thought that the RMI was the same as the SMIC[12] [...] At that time, my dad was on the RMI so I kept telling myself that she surely did not have anyone in her acquaintances receiving either the SMIC or the RMI [...] There was this other person in my class who did not know Arthur.[13] It's trivial, I know, but then again, I kept telling myself that we just did not have the same lives [...] It was brutal and I did not expect it to be that big a difference.

The obliviousness of Lyes's counterparts of upper-middle-class backgrounds to working-class conditions and lifestyles, and their unequivocally embodying of his prestigious Parisian *lycée*'s sanctioned 'norms of cultural [...] self-presentation' (Carter, 2005, p. 47) served to shape the respondent's status 'as different, lesser, and Other' (Horvat & Antonio, 1999, p. 319). Similarly, Reda, the 19-year-old Sciences-Po student raised in a segregated *cité* of the capital's suburbs evokes a strong sense of alienation as he entered the prestigious Parisian institution.

His narrative describes a stark contrast between the state of euphoria he experienced upon receiving the news of his acceptance and the sense of loss he went through in the first weeks following his admission. Feelings of self-fulfilment and pride were at once replaced by uncertainties as he came to measure the social gap prevailing between his world back home and the environment he had come to inhabit. Managing to 'feel part of the group', he explains, was going to be a daily challenge, one that he had not foreseen. Reda realised that an unpredictably wide social gap set him apart from his counterparts of upper-middle-class background, generating what Mack (2006, p. 56) calls an 'imposter syndrome': feelings of self-doubt about the very appropriateness of his educational choice and about his legitimacy as one of Sciences-Po community's members (Reay et al., 2011, 2005). In assessing his classmates' interactional styles and in determining who fits in and who does not, Reda's account further recalls Bourdieu and Passeron's (1964) evocation of the attitudes, styles and behaviours of the 'inheritors'. In contrast to his own sense of loss and anguish stood his classmates' 'ease, naturalness, aloofness, [...] "brilliance"' (Lareau & Lamont 1988, p. 155):

> I was so excited during the months I spent preparing for Sciences-Po admission. And this summer, once I found out about my acceptance, I was so happy [...] Then I arrived and I think I went through a state of shock. I started daily questioning my choice. I would see how everyone behaved [...] and thought I would never be as good as them, I would never get as good grades as them. Worse, in fact, I was afraid of being excluded [...] I started thinking: 'you won't find your place here, you are not like them' [...] I could not find my marks ('*je ne trouvais pas mes repères*'). Unlike mine, most of Sciences-Po students' parents had also been at Sciences-Po! They [students of upper-middle class background] were therefore familiar with the system [...] so really, what worried me the most was to realise that I was happier about my acceptance prior to admission than when I got here. I kept telling myself, 'I hope this wasn't a mistake', I was not feeling well, I missed my friends [...] I felt lonely, and far away from home, in Paris.

Moreover, akin to their African-American counterparts, another salient dimension of our respondents' sense of class awareness reveals, the moral boundaries they draw between 'us', members of racially minoritised groups coming from socially disadvantaged background and 'them', members of the white elite (Lamont, 2000; Rollock et al., 2012b). While the latter is characterised by a widespread sense of self-centredness, the former, it is argued, has acquired, from an early age, a sense of sharing and empathy, a moral capital which profoundly structures their daily interactions and shape their behaviours, For Lisa, a 30-year-old female entrepreneur and HEC graduate, points out, the ability to easily move between class and educational boundaries and empathise with people located at the bottom of the social ladder is the 'natural skill' at the core moral difference between her former HEC classmates and her. As she recalls:

> They were individualist. When young, they had nannies taking care of everything so for example, they're not used to helping out with house chores etc. see, for example, at the end of our seminars, I was always the only one helping the secretary with tidying the room, etc. I was the only one who had a great relationship with her and she was very appreciative of that

However, in outlining some of the challenges of moving up the educational ladder, unlike Naudet's respondents of non-migrant, majority ethnic background, our informants of North African migrant background point to the painful realisation that the country's elite is unequivocally white. Many of the accounts indeed relay the 'colour' of the budding elites of their institutions. Indeed, if anything, the 'shock of the elite' their narratives evoke has at least partly resulted from realising the 'whiteness', the 'blondness' or, as some of them put it, the fact that their schools' traditional student population has mainly been represented by *Franco-Français*. As Beurgeois, the upwardly mobile blogger and engineering *grande école* graduate notes, as the child of socially disadvantaged, North African immigrants, upon admission, he felt he was a 'stranger in two ways', by virtue of his class and his minority backgrounds. Similarly, Samia, the 26-year-old Sciences-Po Grenoble graduate recollects the discomforting sentiment of being 'an extraterrestrial' in her institution. As she explains, this feeling of estrangement originated from isolation along class lines but it was further exacerbated by the fact that she was one of the school's few 'Arabs':

> I could not recognise myself in the others. I had the feeling that I was an extraterrestrial; in my promotion, we were three Arabs max out of a total of 250 students and that, I thought, was just not normal […] I thought that after all, maybe it would not be too bad … and finally, I get here and no bursar recipients, very few people with immigrant backgrounds, maybe five, six in my promotion, so clearly, I thought, there is something wrong and this situation barely improved during the years I spent there.

The 'race'-conscious description of their institutions' student make-up, marked by the usage of such terminology as 'Whites' vs 'Blacks and Arabs', saturates the narratives of respondents coming from *banlieue* environments that are host to large populations of immigrants from former colonies and their descendants. Their accounts point to an outstanding contrast along racial lines, one that they had largely underestimated. Melya, akin to all of the respondents raised in stigmatised *cités*, highlights a disconcerting feeling as she became aware of the gap along racial lines between the Sciences-Po community and her home population:

> So, first, when you get here, you have the 'week of integration' for all the CEP students, it's cool, it's really people from everywhere, it's mixed. Then, first day of class, it was really intimidating, they put us in Sciences Po's largest amphitheatre, it was huge, and suddenly, you realise that most students are White, blond-haired, blue-eyed …. It's really a strange feeling that you get. When you compare with how it is like back home, it really gives you a weird feeling. I never thought it was going to be that great a contrast.

Additionally, many of the narratives evoke a persistent conflation, among school representatives, teachers, and sometimes even classmates, of their ethnic-based appearances with counter-elite and counter-mobility aptitudes, leading the respondents to recurrently have to make the demonstration of their legitimate presence in their establishments. Nordine, for example, a 25-year-old Polytechnique doctoral student sheds light on his strategy of over-zealousness, which he reflexively ties to his fear of stigmatisation along ethnic lines. As he explains,

> as an Arab, you have to work twice as much as the other students […]it has often happened to me and to my brother, who happens to be his school's top student, to be looked at with astonishment, as if teachers were puzzled over the fact that we are doing great at school, despite being Arabs!'

The evocation of race as a barrier in the respondents' day-to-day higher education experiences unequivocally challenges the dominant colour-blind discourse prevalent in France. We argue that these racially explicit accounts may be, at least in part explained by the increasing, albeit still fragile, attractiveness of the diversity motto as well as a growing national attention, particularly since the 2001 European appeal, to the issue of discrimination (Fassin, 2010; Lepinard & Simon, 2008; N'Diaye, 2008). Additionally, increasing grass-roots anti-racist mobilisations mainly led by upwardly mobile and middle-class racialised youths born and raised in the country's marginalised urban outskirts, have certainly contributed to forging a sense of awareness about racial injustices. Most importantly, these have possibly encouraged racial minorities to voice their concerns about, and experiences with, (perceived) exclusion along racial lines. Interestingly, when compared with Naudet's respondent, Mounira, a second-generation North African immigrant who entered the mainstream two decades prior to Shahrokni's respondents, we note significant differences in the kind of narratives developed. Mounira's account is deeply informed by a Republican discourse equating social success with a process of 'francisation', namely, the process of exceptional intergeneration mobility has been tied to a broader personal enterprise consisting of abiding by the Republican game of 'integration'. It has been accompanied by simultaneously, and forcefully forgetting about one's immigrant legacies and shedding any markers signalling one's ethnic difference from the majority.

In addition to establishing a sense of self-worth and proving one's 'intelligence', Mounira held the deep-seated hope that her admission at the ENA would help her sort out the ambiguous tie she has entertained towards the French nation. She indeed attempts to locate her mobility trajectory in a broader project of integration to the French culture and her social mobility is clearly reconstructed as part of her efforts towards 'francisising'. Her narrative sheds light on the intense dilemma that the Republican ideology brings about in her negotiations. Hopeful that her social mobility would lead her to feel French, she has obstinately played the game of 'integration' to the point of excelling at it. Yet, her efforts have proved unsuccessful in eradicating the stigma attached to her difference, difference that she is condemned to experience as a handicap. Deprived of a competing ideological repertoire enabling her to see her difference as a positive resource, she is indeed constrained to regard it as a burden. This pair integration/success is therefore what is at the core of the specific experience of upward social mobility of individuals of immigrant background of her generation. The latter find themselves in an ideological context leading them to reject any particularistic claim as they move on up socially. The ultimate consequence of this uniformising fiction is embodied in Mounira's incapability to make sense of the 'delta of difference', which still resides in her despite her relentless efforts of integration.

Another central difference from Naudet's majority respondents stems from the kinds of bridge-building strategies descendants of North African descendants have elaborated towards members of their home members 'left behind'. Unlike French majority respondents, who mainly describe their trajectories as the result of individual efforts, for our minority informants, the narratives of our descendants of North African migrants illuminate a sense of continuity between family-based upward mobility aspirations and their personal educational accomplishments. Indeed, mobility is depicted across all of the narratives as the outcome of hard-working migrants' hard work and sacrifices. While most of the informants underline their parents' lack of know-hows about France's educational system, and particularly, about the 'tricks' one needs to know in order to achieve the best academic paths, their accounts shed light on a repertoire of stories, rooted in their parents', and in some cases, siblings' immigrant pasts and serving as powerful moral resources to 'make it'. Lisa, a 30-year-old entrepreneur and HEC graduate explains that her parents had a set of non-negotiable expectations from her and her older sisters: 'Do your homework, be good students, do your sport [...] If we've come in this country, it is only to give you a better future'. Likewise, Nour, a 19-year-old Sciences-Po student, lyrically explains that if she has 'made it', it is mainly because of the high expectations her parents, especially her mother, had set for them:

> To find your way ahead, you have to know where you come from. I have been extremely interested in finding out about their past because this gives meaning to my own life; it is thanks to them that I am where I am today. My mother was the first in her Casablanca village to get the French Baccalaureate, it was a big thing back then but then, things changed when they came to France ... so you keep telling yourself that you have to live up to that, you have to pursue what they have achieved

Therefore, the tension prevailing between their group-based material conditions of existence and their own movement towards an upper-social class is first partly alleviated through what the sense of continuity between familial expectations and personal achievements across this group.

Additionally, as some of the respondents reveal, what they have achieved represents an accomplishment *for* the first generation: mobility contributes to 'giving back' symbolically to hard-working and self-sacrificing migrant parents whose own mobility aspirations often had to be relinquished upon migration. Educational attainment, and ultimately, social success serves to partly repair the injustices that the former generation has endured. This is notably illustrated in the words of Mehdi, a 35-year-old engineer, recently admitted at the prestigious Ecole Nationale d'Administration (ENA):

> We have so many revenges to take: my father leaving Algeria to come and live in exile, his working poorly paid jobs, all the daily humiliations he had to go through, all kinds of efforts to give the best you can to your children despite limited resources [...] that's why I am telling you this is part of the revenges we have to take.

Moreover, the respondents express a sense of concern over 'giving back' beyond symbolic means. As respondents highlight 'giving back' has primarily translated into paying regular visits to parents and demonstrating, though these, that mobility has not been accompanied by a process of self-distancing from those behind. Female respondents, especially, further shed light on a sense of moral obligation to serve as close mentors in their younger siblings' educational trajectories and show them the path. As Mouna, a 27-year-old engineer living in Paris highlights,

[...]success is not an individual concept. If one of my younger sisters does less well than I did, for me, it will mean that I have failed. So, I regularly go back up North, at my parents' to show them that I am there for them; I check their homework, we discuss various postsecondary options, I really try my best and because I have succeeded, I consider it to be my duty, if you will'.

Giving back therefore translates into elaborating a form of mobility-inducing intra-family social and cultural capital readily available to younger siblings. Unlike the majority ethnic respondents, 'giving back', for those who have already entered the job market also takes the form of regular 'financial remittances' to parents and in some cases, younger siblings. In particular, many respondents highlight the fact that they have begun to initiate their parents to a culture of leisure that had largely been denied to them in their day-to-day lives in France.

In many cases, the abovementioned bridge-building strategy does not solely include members of the respondents' family circles. Rather, it encompasses, a broader 'community of struggle' (Lamont, 2000), France's migrants of former colonies and their children, a population that they contend has been consistently targeted by systemic discrimination. Succeeding at school embodies a symbolic reward to them, a form of advancement in the pursuit of racial equality and social justice. Amine, a 20-year-old Sciences-Po student, notably explains that the 'determination and courage' of all first generation immigrants coming from former colonies have been greatly inspiring to *them,* the generation born and raised in France. As he notes, their 'stories are life-changing lessons [...] that's ultimately what gives us the drive to succeed. It gives us the drive to pursue what they've achieved'.

On a more concrete level, some of the respondents point out that through their own achievements in higher education, they may serve as role models and thereby instil a sense of ambition among other minority youths, prompting them to excel in school and move up the educational ladder. To Amine, embodying a 'role model' is nothing short of a 'mission' he has set out to accomplish, upon graduating from the prestigious Sciences-Po. Contrary to the common representation of the successful, he notes, he will dedicate his career to ameliorating the life conditions of youths, mainly of racially and socially disadvantaged backgrounds, living in France's suburbs, the *banlieues.* Through the elaboration of this 'plan', the young man illustrates another common, bridge-building strategy. This operates on two levels: it brings together his current trajectory of mobility with his working class past, and re-connects his personal success story with the collective struggle descendants of North African immigrants experience:

What I really want to get involved in is the social question in France [...] What I would like to accomplish is ameliorating the social conditions in the suburbs. I see that as a mission. We are not 15,000 to get admitted every year at Sciences-Po, in the nation's most elitist institution. So, I think we should be committed to a mission which is to help others, because if we don't do it, nobody will. Because *we,* we know what trouble means, we know what poor social conditions mean, as well as failure. This is not what our power elite has known and experienced in their childhood.

Lastly, if our respondents from the majority group continue to feel a sense of illegitimacy despite having secured the qualifications giving one membership into

France's elite, for descendants of North African immigrants, uncertainty as to their class position was further reinforced by a sense that they could 'easily fall back down' as Lisa puts it. When probed about the reasons behind their sense of anguish and uncertainty about the future and the extent to which they could secure the mobility payoffs they were striving for, most of them pointed to explanations that differed from their white counterparts. The over-representation of descendants of North African immigrants in lower social classes but also the continued threat of discrimination and the fact that, as many highlighted, they needed 'to work twice as much as others with the same qualifications' were commonly outlined as factors which could make their presence into the middle class short-lived and unstable.

CONCLUSION

If the idea of class as a matrix of socialisation producing specific habitus is relatively consensual (Bourdieu, 1984; Lahire, 2011), the idea of race socialisation has been less common, particularly so in the French sociological thought. Building on the works of Moore (2008), Rollock et al. (2011, 2012a) and Rollock (2014), we have, however, showed that the class identities of upwardly mobile individuals in both the American and the French contexts are deeply shaped by race-specific experiences and raced habitus. In particular, we show that upwardly mobile minority members tend to display a stronger sense of solidarity with their group of origin than their majority counterparts. The moral obligation to express solidarity towards those who remain 'on the other side' of the fence is particularly vivid. Our material thus points to the fact that the upward mobility experience of minority members is further complicated by their racial identity. We argue that these racial differences in the way mobility is lived can be read as an avatar of 'White privilege', defined by Leonardo (2004) as a consequence of white supremacy. Our white respondents are indeed much less likely to evoke the felt pressure to financially assist members of their group; additionally, unlike racially minoritised individuals, they further do not have to cope with the issue of racism in their everyday lives. Moreover, as was argued, beyond their class differences, many of them continue to identify with a racial community of struggle. Achieving mobility for minority and majority members is clearly not a process that occurs on equal footing.

This set of circumstances seems to act as a cross-national regularity in the experience of mobility among racial minorities. We argue that they constitute one of the fundamental bases of their emergent class identities. However, we have suggested that these identities are also embedded in specific national and institutional contexts and need to be analysed against the dominant 'national repertoires of evaluation' (Lamont & Thévenot, 2000) prevailing in a given country.

The narratives of our African-American respondents display a stronger sense of solidarity than their white counterparts and seem to be characterised by a stronger sense of being in between two worlds. While they attempt to fit into their new class, they simultaneously emphasise their solidarity towards socially disadvantaged African-Americans 'left behind'. Their narratives recall those of Moore's (2008) multi-class Black respondents, exposing as they do the 'individual and group tension that results from social mobility'. The fact that our respondents are also first-generation middle class, like Moore's respondents, may partly account for this similarity.

In France, the narratives of success have mainly been collected among individuals who have not yet 'completed' their upward social ascension. Furthermore, the data reveals a set of minority-bound issues that may be regarded as nation-specific. The 'minority culture of mobility' we have identified is indeed informed by historically contingent, nationally grounded processes: if anything, indeed, most of our respondents have stressed the necessity to 'give back' symbolically to a former generation of post-colonial immigrant parents whose educational aspirations were largely denied. Additionally, the rise, albeit moderate and uneven, of competing ideological repertoires, such as the 'diversity' discourse seems to play out in the self-presentations of our youngest respondents.

These two distinct configurations show different combinations of the way in which minority members experience their experience of social ascension, in comparison with their majority counterparts. Their efforts to acculturate themselves to their new, predominantly white and upper-middle-class, group leads them to experience much more vividly the tension between their group of origin, while their white counterparts tend to downplay the idea that social mobility implies a radical transformation of oneself drawing on the American Dream national repertoire. In France, descendants of North-African immigrants cannot draw on a collective minority identity as firmly established as is the case for African-Americans. Yet, the fact that they frequently mobilise their family's experience of immigration helps them to root their narratives in a project of achievement. Our data in the French context indeed points to a recent reinforcement of the assertion of difference by minority members. Though French minority members have to face hardships related to both their class of origin and their racial stigma, they conceive their own achievement as a natural consequence of a family project far more often than their majority counterparts do. By frequently drawing on references to the colonial history of France, by showing a desire to help the rest of their community, their narratives indeed reveal a minority culture of mobility that is in the making.

While the minority culture of mobility theory has presented a major advancement in the study of the links between mobility and assimilation among minority groups, one of its shortcomings has stemmed for the little evidence on which its main tenets have rested. In this chapter, through an investigation based on distinctive case studies, we have hoped to contribute to substantiating Neckerman et al. (1999) propositions through an empirically grounded theoretical analysis. Via a cross-national comparative perspective, we have further suggested that far from being exclusive to an analysis of American minorities' social ascent, the theory has proved highly pertinent in appreciating mobility experiences in other national contexts. Moreover, we showed that the kind of strategies deployed by the respondents is deeply shaped by nation-based ideological repertoires. In short, if minority cultures of mobility emerge out of structural conditions transgressing national boundaries, the specific features they espouse may only be grasped through close attention to the historically grounded, nationally bound ideological contexts in which they are embedded

NOTES

1. We define racial minorities as groups that collectively face institutionalized differential treatment across various domains of social life as a result of their skin colour and/or believed cultural differences and ethnic background. This process of racialisation may in turn lead to a re-appropriation of the stigma by members of the group to reverse the meaning attributed to it.

2. Class refers to individuals' position in the socio-economic ladder.

3. In the British context, see the works of Reay et al. (2011); Rollock et al. (2011); and Rollock (2012a, 2012b). In the American context, see Patillo (1999); Moore (2008); and Lacy and Harris (2008).

4. We have explored these intra-group variations elsewhere (Naudet, 2018, Shahrokni, 2015).

5. 'A set of subtle biases and mechanisms of exclusion that are specific to fairly high levels of the occupational structure' (Neckerman et al., 1999, p. 951).

6. As has been showed, admission in these elite institutions translates into the attainment of a highly regarded social status in French society and opens up to the highest positions in administrative, financial, political and academic sectors (Bourdieu, 1989; Draelants & Darchy-Koechlin, 2011).

7. For further discussion on this point, see Shahrokni (2015, pp. 53–74).

8. The condition of 'double-consciousness' leads African–Americans to look at themselves with the eyes of another person. It is a condition in which 'one ever feels his two-ness – an American, a Negro; two souls, two thoughts, two unreconciled strivings; two warring ideals in one dark body whose dogged strength alone keeps it from being torn asunder' (Du Bois, 1996, p. 5).

9. The work of Higginbotham and Weber (1992) on the experience of upward social mobility by both Black and White women in the United States reaches the same conclusion. On her side, Jodi Vandenberg-Daves (2002) observes that African–American women consider their mobility as a resource to help their community while White women rather tend to narrate their achievements as a liberation from family shackles.

10. On their side, Lacy and Harris (2008) have shown that this attachment to a racial identity is not homogeneous and that the class of origin helps understand the variations in the intensity of the attachment to the Black community.

11. RMI: *Revenu minimum d'insertion* represented until 2009 a state-based minimum income support provided to registered unemployed individuals actively searching for employment. It has been replaced by the RSA (*Revenu de solidarité active*).

12. SMIC: *Salaire minimum interprofessionnel de croissance* is France's minimum wage rate.

13. A TV show celebrity.

REFERENCES

Amiraux, V., & Simon, P. (2006). There are no minorities here cultures of scholarship and public debate on immigrants and integration in France. *International Journal of Comparative Sociology*, *47*(3–4), 191–215.

Ball, S. J. (2003). *Class strategies and the education market: The middle class and social advantage*. London: Routledge Falmer.

Beauchemin, C., Hamel, C., Lesné, M., Simon, P., & TeO Team. (2010). Les discriminations : une question de minorités visibles. *Population & Sociétés*, 466.

Benjamin, L. (1991). *The Black elite: Facing the color line in the twilight of the twentieth century*. Chicago, IL: Nelson-Hall Publishers.

Bettie, J. (2002). Exceptions to the rule: Upwardly mobile White and Mexican American high school girls. *Gender & Society, 16*(3), 403–422.

Bobo, L. D. (2011). Somewhere between Jim Crow & post-racialism: Reflections on the racial divide in America today. *Daedalus, 140*(2), 11–36.

Bourdieu, P. (1984). *Distinction: A social critique of the judgement of taste.* Cambridge, MA: Harvard University Press.

Bourdieu, P. (1989). *La Noblesse d'Etat.* Paris, France: Editions de Minuit.

Carter, P. L. (2005). *Keepin'it real: School success beyond Black and White.* Oxford University Press.

Coard, S. I., Wallace, S. A., Stevenson, H. C., & Brotman, L. M. (2004). Towards culturally relevant preventive interventions: The consideration of racial socialization in parent training with African American families. *Journal of Child and Family Studies, 13*(3), 277–293.

Bourdieu, P., Passeron, J.-C. (1964). *Les héritiers. Les étudiants et la culture.* Paris, Editions de Minuit.

Constantine, M. G., & Blackmon, S. M. (2002). Black adolescents' racial socialization experiences: Their relations to home, school, and peer self-esteem. *Journal of Black Studies, 32*(3), 322–335.

Daye, S. J. (1994). Middle-Class Blacks in Britain: A Racial Fraction of a Class Group or a Class Fraction of a Racial Group? Basingstoke and London: Palgrave MacMillan.

Draelants, H., & Darchy-Koechlin, B. (2011). Flaunting one's academic pedigree? Self-presentation of students from elite French schools. *British Journal of Sociology of Education, 32*(1), 17–34.

Dubet, F., Cousin, O., Rui, S., & Macé, E. (2013). *Pourquoi moi? L'expérience des discriminations.* Paris, France: Seuil.

Du Bois, W. E. B. (1996 [1904]). *The souls of black folk.* New York, NY: New American Library.

Fassin, E. (2010). Les couleurs de la représentation: Introduction. *Revue française de science politique, 60*(4), 655–662.

Granfield, R. (1991). Making it by faking it: working-class students in an elite academic environment. *Journal of Contemporary Ethnography, 20*(3), 331–351.

Hajjat, A., & Mohammed, M. (2013). *Islamophobie. Comment les élites françaises fabriquent le "problème musulman".* Paris, France: La Découverte.

Hertz, T. (2005). Rags, riches, and race: the intergenerational economic mobility of black and white families in the United States. In G. Herbert, S. Bowles, & M. O. Groves (Eds.), *Unequal chances: Family background and economic success* (pp. 165–191). New York, NY: Russell Sage Foundation and Princeton University Press.

Higginbotham, E., & Weber, L. (1992). Moving up with kin and community. *Gender & Society, 6*(3), 416–440.

Hochschild, J. L. (1995). *Race, class, and the soul of the nation: Facing up to the American dream.* Princeton, NJ: Princeton University Press.

Horvat, E. M., & Antonio, A. L. (1999). "Hey, those shoes are out of uniform": African American girls in an elite high school and the importance of habitus. *Anthropology & Education Quarterly, 30*(3), 317–342.

Juteau, D. (2006). Forbidding ethnicities in French sociological thought: The difficult circulation of knowledge and ideas, *Mobilities, 1*(3), 391–409.

Lacy, K. R., & Harris, A. L. (2008). Breaking the class monolith: Understanding class differences in Black adolescents' attachment to racial identity. In A. Lareau & D. Conley (Eds.), *Social class: How does it work?* (pp. 152–178). New York, NY: Russell Sage Foundation.

Lamont, M. (1992). *Money, morals and manners: The culture of the French and the American upper middle class.* Chicago, IL: University of Chicago Press.

Lamont, M. (2000). *The dignity of working men.* New York, NY: Russell Sage Foundation.

Lamont, M., & Lareau, A. (1988). Cultural Capital: Allusions, Gaps and Glissandos in Recent Theoretical Developments. *Sociological Theory, 6*(2), 153–168.

Lamont, M., & Thévenot, L. (2000). *Rethinking comparative cultural sociology: Repertoires of evaluation in France and the United States.* New York, NY: Cambridge University Press.

Lahire, B. (2011). *The plural actor.* Cambridge: Polity Press.

Lehmann, W. (2009). Becoming middle class: How working-class university students draw and transgress moral class boundaries. *Sociology, 43*(4), 631–647.

Leonardo, Z. (2004). The color of supremacy: Beyond the discourse of white privilege. *Educational Philosophy and Theory, 36*(2), 137–152.

Lépinard, E., & Simon, P. (2008). *From integration to antidiscrimination ... to diversity? Antidiscrimination politics and policies in French workplaces*. Report for a European approach to multicultural citizenship, European Commission, FP6. EMILIE, Project Report, INED. http://emilie.eliamep. gr/wp-content/uploads/2009/07/emilie-wp4-frenchreport.Pdf

Lesane-Brown, C. L. (2006). A review of race socialization within Black families. *Developmental Review, 26*(4), 400–426.

McNamee, S. J., & Miller, R. K. (2004). *The meritocracy myth*. Lanham, MD: Rowman and Littlefield.

Mack, N. (2006). Ethical Representations of Working-Class Lives: Multiple Genres, Voices, and Identities. *Pedagogy, 6*, 53–78.

Meurs, D. Pailhe, A., & Simon, P. (2006). The persistence of intergenerational inequalities linked to immigration: Labour market outcomes for immigrants and their descendants in France. *Population, 61*(5–6), 645–682.

Moore, K. S. (2008). Class formations: Competing forms of black middle-class identity. *Ethnicities, 8*(4), 492–517.

Naudet, J. (2018). *Stepping into the Elite: Trajectories of Social Achievement in India, in France and in the United States*. New Delhi, Oxford: University Press.

N'Diaye, Pap. (2008). *La Condition noire*, Paris, Calmann-Lévy

Neckerman, K. M., Carter, P., & Lee, J. (1999). Segmented assimilation and minority cultures of mobility. *Ethnic and Racial Studies, 22*(6), 945–965.

Oliver, M. L., & Shapiro, T. M. (1995). *Black wealth/White wealth: A new perspective on racial inequality*. New York, NY: Routledge.

Pattillo, M. E. (2007). *Black on the block: The politics of race and class in the city*. Chicago, IL: The University of Chicago Press.

Reay, D. (2005). Beyond Consciousness?: The Psychic Landscape of Social Class. Sociology Special Issue of Class, *Culture and Identity, 39*(5), 911–928.

Reay, D., Crozier, G., & Clayton, J. (2009). Strangers in paradise? Working-class students in elite universities. *Sociology, 43*(6), 1103–1121.

Reay, D., Crozier, G., & James, D. (2011). *White middle class identities and urban schooling. Identity studies in the social sciences*. Basingstoke: Palgrave Macmillan.

Rollock, N. (2012a). The Invisibility of race: Intersectional reflections on the liminal space of alterity. *Race Ethnicity & Education, 15*(1), 65–84.

Rollock, N. (2012b). Unspoken rules of engagement: Navigating racial microaggressions in the academic terrain. *International Journal of Qualitative Studies in Education, 25*(5), 517–532.

Rollock, N. (2014). Race, class and the harmony of dispositions. *Sociology, 48*(3), 445–451.

Rollock, N., Vincent, C., Gillborn, D., et al. (2013). Middle class by profession: Class status and identification amongst the Black middle classes. *Ethnicities 13*(3), 253–275.

Rollock, N., Gillborn, D., Ball, S., & Vincent, C. (2011). The public identities of the black middle classes: Managing race in public spaces. *Sociology, 45*(6), 1078–1093.

Sayad, A. (1999). *La double absence: Des illusions aux souffrances de l'immigré*. Paris, France: Seuil.

Sennett, R., & Cobb, J. (1993). *The hidden injuries of class* (1st ed., 1972). New York, NY: Knopf.

Shahrokni, S. (2015). The Minority Culture of Upwardly Mobile Descendants of North African Immigrants in France. *Ethnic and Racial Studies, 38*(7), 1050–1067.

Shahrokni S. (2018). The collective roots and rewards of upward educational mobility, *The British Journal of Sociology, 69*(4), 1175–1193.

Silberman, R., & Fournier, I. (2006). Les secondes générations sur le marché du travail en France: une pénalité ethnique ancrée dans le temps. Contribution à la théorie de l'assimilation segmentée. *Revue Française de Sociologie, 47*(2), 243–292.

Simon, P. (2003). France and the unknown second generation: Preliminary results on social mobility. *International Migration Review, 37*(4), 1091–1119.

Torres, K. (2009). 'Culture shock': Black students account for their distinctiveness at an elite college. *Ethnic and Racial Studies, 32*(5), 883–905.

Vallejo, J. A. (2012). Socially mobile Mexican Americans and the minority culture of mobility. *American Behavioral Scientist, 56*(5), 666–681.

Vandenberg-Daves, J. (2002). There's got to be more out there: White working-class women, college, and the "better life," 1950–1985. *International Labor and Working-Class History, 62*(1), 99–120.

WOMEN EXECUTIVES: EMPOWERING WOMEN THROUGH SELECTION IN GERMANY AND BRAZIL

Farida Jalalzai

ABSTRACT

This chapter focusses on whether women heads of states and governments use their powers of selection to empower women. Compared to their male counterparts, do they appoint greater quantities of women to cabinet positions and to more prestigious posts? Examining Germany and Brazil, two countries constituting diverse cultural and institutional settings, this chapter provides in-depth analysis of cabinet appointments and regional breadth. It confirms that women executives do indeed promote more women to their cabinets overall and to higher powered portfolios. This stands in contrast with prevailing findings from within the global literature but generally reinforces those derived from single country and regional explorations.

Keywords: Presidents; prime ministers; national executives; women's empowerment; cabinet appointments

INTRODUCTION

Compared to their male counterparts, do women heads of state and government appoint greater quantities of women to cabinet positions and to more prestigious posts? Research exploring the relationship between executive sex and diversity in cabinet appointments often utilises single case studies (Franceschet, 2016; Jalalzai & dos Santos, 2015; Lee & Jalalzai, 2017). These works provide

Elites and People: Challenges to Democracy
Comparative Social Research, Volume 34, 159–186
Copyright © 2019 by Emerald Publishing Limited
All rights of reproduction in any form reserved
ISSN: 0195-6310/doi:10.1108/S0195-631020190000034008

depth regarding individual leaders and factors affecting the supply and demand for women ministers within the countries they govern. Regional analyses also offer detailed insights into a wider array of countries that may share important features shaping cabinet selection processes and subsequent ministerial diversity (Escobar-Lemmon & Taylor-Robinson, 2005; Jalalzai, 2016; Reyes-Housholder, 2016). Global examinations include a more assorted array of executive institutions and cultural backdrops (Barnes & O'Brien, 2018; Claveria, 2014; Krook & O'Brien, 2012; O'Brien, Mendez, Peterson, & Shin, 2015) but obscure more nuanced factors affecting women's cabinet selection. Analysing Germany and Brazil, two countries constituting diverse cultural and institutional settings, this chapter balances more in-depth analysis of cabinet appointments and regional breadth.

In examining cabinet selection, I track quantities and specific portfolios held by men and women first within each country and then between countries. Within-country comparisons allow for multiple paired analyses of women leaders to one more similar and one more different male case. I also identify common factors affecting patterns of cabinet appointments between the two countries such as multi-party systems and coalition governance but also dissimilar aspects including gendered political opportunity structures.

In spite of the growing quantities of women executives, most literature focussing on gender and elites examine women in parliaments (Alexander, 2015; Franceschet, Krook, & Piscopo, 2012). Scholars, recognising the leading role cabinets may play in policymaking, increasingly consider women's cabinet integration (Annesley, 2015; Barnes & O'Brien, 2018; Claveria, 2014). Research on women prime ministers and presidents has also grown substantially as of late (Clemens, 2006; Franceschet, 2016; Genovese, 2013; Genovese & Steckenrider, 2013; Jalalzai, 2013, 2016; King, 2002; Montecinos, 2017; Skard, 2014; Stevenson, 2012; Thomas, 2016; Waylen, 2016; Wiliarty, 2008, 2010). Women presidents and prime ministers appear particularly poised to utilise their selection powers to promote women to high office compared to their male counterparts. Investigating whether such patterns do indeed surface, this chapter expands the literature related to women cabinet officials as well as presidents and prime ministers (Annesley, 2015; Barnes & O'Brien, 2018; Franceschet, 2016; Jalalzai & dos Santos, 2015; Krook & O'Brien, 2012; Lee & Jalalzai, 2017; Reyes-Housholder, 2016).

This chapter first provides an overview of the political standing of women worldwide in three main positions: legislators, cabinet ministers and national executives (presidents/prime ministers). It then engages literature related to gender and cabinet appointments. Finally, focussing on Germany and Brazil, it explores whether women prime ministers and presidents use their powers to select a greater percentage of women to their cabinets and to less traditional positions than their male counterparts. In doing so, this chapter supports the notion that women executives do indeed promote more women to their cabinets overall and to higher powered portfolios. This finding stands in contrast with the global literature, which does not find that women executives prove particularly more prone to appointing more women to cabinets. It generally reinforces findings derived from single country and regional explorations that, however, do indicate a greater propensity for women leaders to diversify their cabinets. The design of the current study offers in-depth analyses and recognises more specific factors affecting the supply and demand for women in the cabinet in Germany and Brazil. Both countries were led by high-profile women, Angela Merkel and Dilma Rousseff. Compared to their male peers, they both diversified their cabinets, even in the midst of palpable obstacles.

WOMEN IN POLITICAL OFFICES AROUND THE WORLD

As seen in Fig. 1, the lowest portion of women holding national elite positions are national executives. As we move to cabinet ministers and then parliamentarians, gender gaps decrease. Though women struggle to achieve parity in all three posts, this is particularly evident for presidents and prime ministers where women make up far less than 10% of all national executive leaders worldwide. Though women executives comprise the lowest proportion of political leaders among the three main national officeholders explored, I argue that they are especially poised to advance OTHER women to power. While their male colleagues may also empower women through appointment (see Barnes & Taylor-Robinson, 2018, p. 231) women may be more apt to appoint women to positions of power.[1] At the same time, myriad factors shape ministerial selection generally and cabinet diversity specifically, outlined below.

Formal and informal rules involve actors/institutions choosing ministers and those deemed eligible for selection (see Annesley, 2015). Presidents or prime ministers tend to possess formal authority to choose their ministers. In parliamentary systems, a main selector is the prime minister. Parties, however, may institute formal rules that require the party in parliament to select ministers (Annesley, 2015). In presidential systems, presidents play the leading role in cabinet formation.

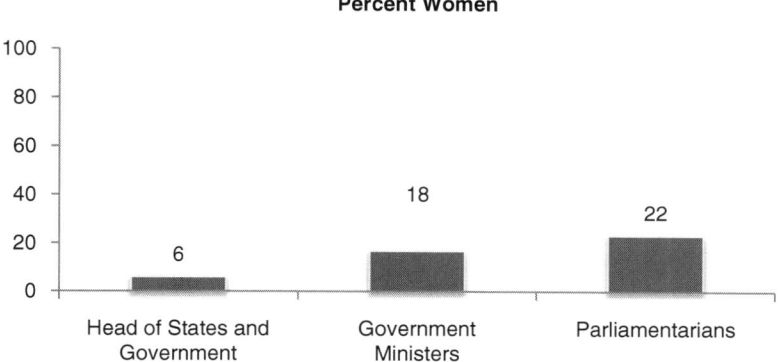

Fig. 1. Women in Political Offices around the World. *Sources*: Ministers and Parliamentarians: UN Women: Facts and Figures Leadership and Political Participation http://www.unwomen.org/en/what-we-do/leadership-and-political-participation/facts-and-figures. *Notes*: Heads of State and Government – Author analysis of approximately 134 presidencies and 118 prime ministerships worldwide. A total of 16 women compared to 236 men were in power in 2017.

Some countries require that legislatures approve presidential cabinet nominees, however, to install their cabinet choices while others are relatively unfettered in their selections.

The eligibility pool varies based on political structure. In most parliamentary systems, only current legislators may serve in the cabinet though exceptions to this exist (Annesley, 2015). In contrast, legislators would normally be barred from simultaneously serving in the legislature in presidential forms of governance. Party systems also matter; countries in which competitive multi-party operate routinely hasten coalition governments. Coalitions can curtail an executive's ability to select fellow partisans since some deference is given to ruling partners (Altman, 2008).[2] Whether cabinet ministers are selected in more generalist or specialist cabinet systems also affects the eligibility pool. In generalist systems, long-term political service such as being a member of parliament may be rewarded with a ministerial appointment (Blondel, 1991). In specialist systems, a driving factor for selection is whether someone has specific policy expertise related to a particular portfolio (Claveria, 2014). Personal friendships and associations also shape the pool of cabinet recruits (Annesley, Beckwith, & Franceschet, 2016; Kopecky, Mair, & Spirova, 2012). Many aspects guiding cabinet selection affect women's incorporation as ministers.

Given that the ministerial pool may be formally or even informally limited to legislators, the percentage of women parliamentarians is usually considered an important factor associated with cabinet appointments. Women's legislative incorporation also indicates the larger political opportunity structures facing women and cultural acceptance of women in power. Women in parliament also may form coalitions to pressure their male peers to select women to their cabinets (Childs & Krook, 2009). Greater quantities of women legislators are indeed statistically associated with higher numbers of women ministers (Arriola & Johnson, 2014; Krook & O'Brien, 2012; Reyes-Housholder, 2016; Whitford, Wilkins, & Ball, 2007).[3]

Women's appointments tended to be higher in specialist versus generalist systems (Davis, 1997) though other broader investigations suggest that this pattern reversed in the last few decades (Claveria, 2014). This may be explained by women's political backgrounds increasingly converging with their male counterparts in more recent periods, being more likely to gain entry to legislative posts. Still, women continue to be underrepresented in feeder institutions such as parliament and or in positions of party leadership in many countries.

While some of the earliest cross-national studies did not verify a connection between ideology and women's cabinet appointments (Davis, 1997; Reynolds, 1999; Siaroff, 2000) the prevailing finding now is that leftist governments tend to integrate more women than do conservative ones (O'Brien et al., 2015). This likely stems from the more gender egalitarian views held by leftist party members compared to their conservative counterparts (Krook & O'Brien, 2012). Presidents representing the extreme left tend to have a significantly higher percentage of female cabinet ministers in Latin America (Reyes-Housholder, 2016). Left-wing parties that adopted gender quotas prove especially likely to promote women to positions (Claveria, 2014).

Scholars generally anticipate that coalitions will limit women's cabinet incorporation. Krook and O'Brien (2012) find more women ministers associated with unified cabinets (see also Claveria, 2014; dos Santos, Gato, & Wylie, 2017). According to Claveria (2014) 'when the senior party trades cabinet seats to other partners for government stability, intra-party competition for the available posts sharpens, thereby increasing the likelihood of men being appointed. Under single-party government, in contrast, the party can fill all cabinet posts, potentially enabling it to diversify the profiles of those appointed' (p. 1161).[4] Higher percentages of women in the cabinet are associated with multi-party systems (Reynolds, 1999) however, and these same settings would be ripe for coalitions. Possibly, women find greater foray into ministerial positions even in coalition scenarios if it incorporates sizable numbers of leftist partners than would be the case otherwise.

Assessments of larger structural and cultural variables yield less definitive findings than institutional factors. Regionally, women in the cabinet fall below world averages in Eastern Europe, Asia, the Middle East and North Africa while well above average in Western countries followed by Latin America (see Paxton & Hughes, 2017).[5] Some studies confirm that Protestant dominated populations tend to have higher levels of women in the cabinet (Claveria, 2014; Reynolds, 1999). Women's educational attainment and workforce participation though tend to be poor predictors of cabinet diversity (Escobar-Lemmon & Taylor-Robinson, 2005). Mixed findings surface regarding egalitarian attitudes and women's appointments. Paxton and Kunovich (2003) demonstrate a connection between national support for women in politics and their legislative incorporation, but Claveria (2014) does not find a similar association for ministerial appointments. Cabinet diversity usually decreases as terms transpire (Davis, 1997; Franceschet & Thomas, 2015; Reyes-Housholder, 2016; Teruel, 2011). Leaders may face more scrutiny regarding cabinet diversity at the start of their governments and leverage their 'honeymoon' periods to symbolise their support for minority groups. Executives face growing international pressure to appoint women to national cabinet posts or to at least not dip below the concrete floor, defined as 'a minimum number or proportion of women believed necessary for a cabinet to be perceived as legitimate' (Annesley et al., 2016).[6]

One main factor explored in this chapter is whether the sex of the president or prime minister affects women's cabinet incorporation. I argue that women executives appear especially positioned to advance other women to power compared to their male colleagues. Rather than stemming from biological differences, gendered social patterns drives these tendencies. Cabinet recruits often arise from among personal associates of selectors (Kopecky, Mair, & Spirova, 2012). As most political leaders are men, they tend to engage within male-dominated networks, leading to men's overrepresentation in the cabinet (Claveria, 2014). When women gain prime ministerial and presidential posts, they may have more female associates, leading them to appoint a higher proportion of women cabinet ministers than their male peers (Franceschet, 2016; Krook & O'Brien, 2012). Symbolism related to being women in an overwhelmingly male dominated office also drives women's greater potential to appoint diverse cabinets. That relatively few individuals comprise cabinets makes it fairly easy for prime ministers and presidents to appoint equal numbers of men and women if they so choose (see Annesley et al., 2016).

The limited body of work focussing on the globe, however, does not confirm that women executives promote more women to their cabinets overall (Krook & O'Brien, 2012) or when women lead coalitions (O'Brien et al., 2015). This is particularly true when analysing female leaders in reference to leftist governments led by their male counterparts. Moreover, women do not necessarily appoint women to higher prestige portfolios. That so few women executives govern at any point in time presents challenges to discerning systematic patterns. While the global literature does not validate the claim that women executives empower women through their cabinet appointments, these studies do not conduct within-country comparisons or offer in depth analyses of the more nuanced factors affecting the supply and demand for women in the cabinet during specific time periods. Regional examinations, particularly in Latin America, do verify women's proclivity to promote other women to positions of power (Jalalzai, 2016; Reyes-Housholder, 2016). Finally, several single country case studies also confirm women's propensity to appoint women to cabinet posts (Franceschet, 2016; Jalalzai & dos Santos, 2015; Wiliarty, 2014). It is challenging, however, to draw more general conclusions outside of the particular country or geographical areas explored in single country and regional examinations.

By assessing two countries in different regions, this chapter attempts to balance the analytical depth of single country case studies (Franceschet, 2016; Jalalzai & dos Santos, 2015; Lee & Jalalzai, 2017) and breadth offered by regional accounts (Escobar-Lemmon & Taylor-Robinson, 2005; Jalalzai, 2016; Reyes-Housholder, 2016) and global examinations (Barnes & O'Brien, 2018; Claveria, 2014; Krook & O'Brien, 2012; O'Brien et al., 2015). The country sample includes two very well-known women leaders: German Chancellor Angela Merkel (consistently ranked as the world's most powerful female leader by *Forbes Magazine*) and former president of Brazil, Dilma Rousseff. Countries in which they ascended share some features though diverge in other respects. The German system is a dual executive system with a federal president and chancellor, a position akin to a prime minister. The chancellor asserts more influence and leads cabinet formation (Helms, 2006; Parks, 1997). Cabinet ministers in Germany are chosen on the basis of both personal and policy factors and usually exercise a great deal of autonomy over their respective portfolios. Brazil is a presidential system, locating the president at the apex of executive authority. Cabinet ministers are typically chosen more on the basis of presidential loyalty rather than policy expertise. The German chancellor and the Brazilian president, though the dominant players determining cabinet portfolios, still face constraints in appointing ministers. A major shared limitation is that they lead within coalition frameworks of governance.

Germany's multi-party system leads to the regular occurrence of coalition governance and increasingly 'grand coalitions' where power sharing transpires between the two largest parties – the left Social Democratic Party (SPD) and the right Christian Democratic Union (CDU/CSU). In 2005, when Merkel first entered office, she governed within a grand coalition which required close collaboration uniting opposing ideological groupings. Though these dynamics presented a challenge, her skill in developing compromises put her in a promising position as she secured a second term in 2009. She led a coalition of the CDU/CSU–Frauen union, a more ideologically cohesive government. Greater internal squabbling, however, characterised this new ruling coalition; the larger, less ideologically cohesive group actually played more to Merkel's strengths of facilitating compromise. In 2013, the CDU/CSU saw their best electoral results since 1990, obtaining nearly 42% of the vote and close to 50% of the seats. Analysts credited this to Merkel's popularity (Schoen & Greszki, 2014). Yet, her party still fell short of a parliamentary majority (Schoen & Greszki, 2014) and her popular support weakened subsequently. As a result of their preferred coalition partner (FDP) not reaching the necessary vote threshold, the CDU/CSU reached an agreement with the SPD to form another grand coalition. Most recently, the results of the 2017 election positioned Merkel to secure a fourth term. She failed, however, to establish a government until March of 2018, nearly six months after the election. The results found a major drop in the CDU/CSU vote share and the rise of Alternative für Deutschland. Following this protracted period of political limbo, another grand coalition ultimately formed (Shalal & Carrel, 2018).[7] Merkel faced an uphill battle, announcing that she would resign as the CDU/CSU leader in December 2018 and pledged not to seek another term in 2021 (LeBlond, 2018).

While grand coalitions coincided with the majority of Merkel's terms, allocating cabinet portfolios in Germany generally requires a high degree of inter-party cooperation between leaders of dissimilar ideological groupings. Based on ideology, we would expect the SPD to integrate more women in the cabinet than the CDU/CSU. While scholars portray coalitions as detrimental to women's cabinet inclusion (Claveria, 2014; Krook & O'Brien, 2012; dos Santos, Gato, & Wylie, 2017), it may be that women find greater foray into ministerial positions when the coalition increases the participation of leftist partners. When the CDU/CSU leads the coalition but shares power with the SPD, women may gain more portfolios than otherwise.

In Brazil, the president must allocate cabinet positions according to negotiated arrangements among coalition parties (Pereira, Bertholini, & Raile, 2016, p. 551). Very different from Germany, however, is that Brazilian parties adhere to very few formal rules. The party system is weakly organised, positioning it as an inherently unstable and inchoate party system (Coppedge, 1998; Mainwaring, 1999). The PT or Workers Party more consistently adheres to an ideology (on the left) but even its distance from other parties has decreased over time (Lucas & Samuels, 2010). It is, therefore, somewhat more challenging to identify clear expectations regarding the effect Brazilian parties and resulting coalitions have on women's cabinet integration though PT governments should generally be accompanied by elevated levels of women than when parties occupying the right hold power. When Rousseff assumed the presidency in January of 2011, the PT held 17% of the seats in the Chamber of Deputies and 26% of seats in the Senate (Jalalzai, 2016). Though the PT held the greatest seat share in each house, they lacked majority status. Rousseff's coalition, which included the right of centre PMDB and several small parties spanning the extreme right and left, formed 60% of the Chamber of Deputies (Pereira, 2011). This coalition dynamic was not particularly different during Lula's presidency (see Pereira, 2011). The coalition, however, fell apart during her second term, as the impeachment crisis period was in full swing. This fundamentally transformed the structure of the cabinet and resulting appointments, a point dissected later.

As far as the formal pipeline from which women cabinet appointees may be drawn, Germany does not require that cabinet ministers hold parliamentary seats. Informally, however, parliamentary careers may signal more general acceptance of women in positions of power and, unofficially, a cabinet pipeline. Women's levels never rose above 10% of the Bundestag until 1987. Over the next three decades their presence grew steadily, reaching a high of 37%. In 2017, it dipped to 31%. Though backsliding occurred, women still form a relatively high proportion of the German parliament. Cultural attitudes toward women's equality in Germany are very positive in the context of global and regional data (Paxton & Hughes, 2017, p. 120).[8] Women do not appear particularly hampered from entering cabinet positions in Germany.

Women's political and cultural standing in Germany presents a sharp contrast to Brazilian women. The pipeline of women in the Brazilian legislature in comparison is very small and this is in spite of having a quota law (Alves, 2009, 2010; Araújo, 2003; Rangel, 2009, Wylie & dos Santos, 2016). In 2003, women's percentages in the Chamber of Deputies were only 9 and 12 in the Senate. Fifteen years later, women comprised 11% of Deputies and 15% of Senators. Women's legislative presence is, therefore, virtually unchanged and very low compared to both Germany and also its Latin American counterparts. Cultural support for women's equality is much lower than in Germany and in Latin America (Paxton & Hughes, 2017, p. 122). As such, these indicators suggest it may be unlikely to see significant increases in the percentages of women in the Brazilian cabinet even under a liberal female president.

METHODOLOGY AND HYPOTHESES

To assess the effect of executive sex on women's cabinet integration in Germany and Brazil, I track both quantities and types of cabinet posts men and women attain. While this chapter assesses numbers of women's appointments, it also examines the extent to which women gain stereotypically feminine posts. Escobar-Lemmon and Taylor-Robinson (2005, 2009) consider 'masculine' ministries as generally involving the public sphere. This encompasses several specific issues, including agriculture, construction, defence/ security, economics/finance, foreign affairs, government and interior, industry/ commerce, science, labour, transportation as well as communication. Other areas prove neither 'masculine' nor 'feminine', including justice, environment, sports, tourism and planning/development, are deemed either unclassifiable or gender neutral (Bolzendahl, 2018). The 'feminine' ministries typically encompass the private sphere. Topics vary from policies related to nurturing as well as advancing women's roles. Specific policies include children and family, health care, welfare, culture, education and women's rights (see also Bolzendahl, 2018). While scholars note that women have tended to be relegated to less prestigious and more stereotypically feminine offices, this no longer proves a hard and fast rule worldwide (Bauer & Tremblay, 2009). This current analysis uncovers whether this also holds true in Germany and Brazil and how having a female national executive in place facilitates this pattern.

In analysing quantities and the quality of women's cabinet appointments, I examine multiple paired analyses of national leaders over time in Germany and Brazil. One female and male pair in each country was affiliated with the same party and the other pairing hailed from different parties. I first focus on the beginning and end of each term rather than total appointments. This provides two advantages. First, scholars suggest that cabinet diversity decreases as presidential and prime ministerial terms progress (Davis, 1997; Franceschet & Thomas, 2015; Reyes-Housholder, 2016; Rodrıguez, 2011). Analysing the beginning and conclusion of each mandate verifies whether these larger patterns also exist in locations explored in this chapter. Second, as prime ministers and presidents often switch ministers to different positions rather than just bring in new people (particularly in generalist cabinet systems), this strategy may paint a more realistic picture of women's cabinet inclusion at particular points in time. The same woman may be selected to three different positions throughout one government term versus three distinct women serving simultaneously; the latter would indicate women's greater cabinet integration.

As far as time frame, I analyse all German cabinets from 1982 to 2018, which includes chancellors Kohl, Schröder, and Merkel. Kohl was a member of the conservative Christian Democratic Union (CDU/CSU) and held power from 1982 through 1998. Gerhard Schröder, of the left-leaning Social Democratic Party (SPD), followed Kohl and held the chancellorship from 1999 through 2004. Merkel, a member of the CDU/CSU, succeeded Schröder in 2005 and, as of this writing, has remained in power for four terms but will not seek a fifth one. For the paired cases, I compare Merkel to her fellow partisan Kohl and then to Schröder. One female and male pair is from the same party and another is affiliated with a different party. The similar pairing offers a benefit holding party constant with the primary difference between the leaders being executive sex (see Shair-Rosenfeld & Stoyan, 2018). Other paired cases in each country prove dissimilar in terms of partisanship, making it more challenging to isolate the effect of sex. Yet, when the woman leader represents the more conservative party (as is the case with Merkel), an important opportunity presents in verifying whether she still appoints women at equal or greater rates than her more liberal male counterpart. Ideology would predict that Schröder should appoint more women. Merkel's gender, however, would drive an expectation that she would select women more than Kohl and perhaps even Schröder.

In Brazil, I analyse three presidents in power between 2004 through 2018. This period includes Luis Inácio 'Lula' da Silva, Dilma Rousseff, and Michel Temer. Lula, from the PT, was in office 2003 through 2010. Constitutionally barred from a third consecutive term, Lula ostensibly selected Dilma Rousseff as the PT presidential candidate in 2010. Rousseff then served one full term from 2011 to 2014 and part of a second mandate that started in 2015 until her removal from power in 2016 on unproven corruption charges (BBC News, 2018). As Rousseff and Lula shared partisanship and her presidency was meant to be more of the same, differences in women's appointments may be influenced by gender. Rousseff was succeeded by her Vice-President from the centre right PMDB, Michel Temer, who led the call for her impeachment. In this paired case, gender and ideology are two important shifts that together might explain variations in women's cabinet appointments.

I hypothesise that Merkel and Rousseff will appoint more women to their cabinets and to more prestigious positions than their male colleagues. Even though Merkel represents a conservative party, I expect that her gender will still positively influence her selection of women even in comparison to her more liberal male counterpart, Schröder. Women's status in Brazil, ascertained by cultural attitudes and women gaining entry to feeder positions such as legislator makes it more difficult to appoint women cabinet ministers in comparison to Germany. Still, Rousseff, from a liberal party, will go above and beyond her male counterparts (including Lula) to enhance women's empowerment in the cabinet. In both systems, coalitions shape leaders' abilities to appoint more women to their cabinets or to more powerful and masculine positions, with ideological aspects being particularly influential.

FINDINGS

Gender and Appointment to the German Cabinet: Start and End of Terms

As seen in Table 1, Kohl integrated few women overall in his early cabinets. Rather than decreasing their percentages as each individual term transpired, women's levels almost always increased. The fourth government seemed to be a

Table 1. Appointments to Positions in the German Cabinet by Government and Gender: Start and End of Terms.

Chancellor	Term	Start of Term % Women	End of Term % Women	Difference
Kohl	1	6	6	0
	2	6	13	+7
	3	11	17	+6
	4	21	26	+5
	5	12	13	+1
Schröder	1	33	27	−6
	2	46	46	0
Merkel	1	31	31	0
	2	25	25	0
	3	33	40	+7
	4	40	−	−

Source: Analysis of German Federal Cabinet webpages.
Note: Only counts ministers in place at the beginning and end of the terms rather than total appointments.

turning point. Four women, including Merkel, held one of 19 portfolios, or 21% of the cabinet spots. Moreover, an additional woman was brought in at the end of the term, raising women's levels to 26%. By Kohl's fifth and last term, however, the proportion of women declined to 12%. Chancellor Schröder appointed a larger proportion of women to his cabinet than did Kohl. Women held 33% of cabinet posts at the start of his first government and slightly decreased to 27% at the end. Even so, women's levels were still higher than during Kohl's most gender diverse cabinet. More strikingly, Schröder appointed record setting percentages of women to his cabinet, 46%, as his second term commenced; and he made no changes to his cabinet, so women remained just below complete parity. Merkel also appointed more women to her cabinet than Kohl, her fellow partisan from the right. Usually, women formed about one third of her cabinet. As Merkel's third term concluded, however, women made up 40% of her government and this held at the start of her fourth mandate. Women's highest levels in the cabinet were still during Schröder's tenure but Merkel approaches his record.

Gender and Total Appointments to the German Cabinet

When analysing the total number of appointments and gender, I focus only on Schröder and Merkel's chancellorships (see Table 2). This is mainly driven by the very few numbers of women during Kohl's tenure and the inability to control for larger shifts in Germany's status in women's status over such a long period of time. Women made up 32% of Schröder's total cabinet ministers during his first term and rose to 46% during the second. Totalling only 13 people, his second cabinet was relatively small and also completely stable. Merkel's total appointments of women ranged from 28% in her second term to 40% in her third. While still not technically a 'parity' government, women's levels approach equality in the German cabinet.

How do party and coalitions affect women's cabinet integration in Germany? Women's inclusion in the German cabinet is greater in governments that either was dominated by the left or combined the left-leaning SPD and right-leaning CDU/CSU in grand coalitions. Women's percentages were smallest during Merkel's

Table 2. Appointments to Positions in the German Cabinet by Government and Gender.

Chancellor	Term	% Women
Schröder	1	32
	2	46
Merkel	1	32
	2	28
	3	38
	4	40

Source: Analysis of German Federal Cabinet webpages, https://www.bundesregierung.de/Webs/Breg/EN/FederalGovernment/Cabinet/_node.html._

Note: Calculations include duplicate appointees if someone was appointed to multiple posts.

second term when her coalition contained other right oriented parties. Grand coalitions have proven more auspicious for women's inclusion during Merkel's tenure but not necessarily because of the SPD leadership's greater inclination than the CDU/CSU to incorporate women. In the current coalition, for example, the CDU/CSU and SPD have equal numbers of women in the cabinet. One of the most important predictors of cabinet appointments is the control of portfolios by coalition partners (Wiliarty, 2014). For instance, typically the party leader of the largest coalition partner assumes the role of the Vice-Chancellor (who always holds another position in the cabinet). Allocation of specific portfolios is party/coalition driven rather than simply a result chancellor preference. During Merkel's three grand coalitions, the SPD has tended to hold the Foreign Affairs and Finance portfolios while the CDU/CSU has controlled Defence. While men filled the first two portfolios, a CDU/CSU woman has occupied the defence role, a point discussed further in the next section.

If cabinet appointments in Germany are driven mainly by party and coalition dynamics, do findings suggest that Merkel's gender played no role in the percentage of female appointees during her tenure? No evidence actually exists that Merkel ever pledged to install a 'parity cabinet' (Wiliarty, 2014). Given her conservative credentials, she would have been expected to appoint women at rates similar to her co-partisan, Kohl, or perhaps marginally higher given changes in women's status over that long period. The fact that she matched Schröder's previous record of women cabinet ministers is noteworthy. Yet, when Kohl governed from 1982 to 1998, executives did not face the same international pressure to appoint sizable numbers of women to their cabinets. While there is no mandate that German cabinet members be drawn from the parliament, we generally do see an increase in the percentages of women in the Bundestag over the time frame examined (1982–2018). In 1998, when Kohl was chancellor, women held 26% of the seats in the Bundestag and their percentages continued to grow over time. It is again worth noting that women's levels in the most current Bundestag actually dropped from 36% to 31%. The fact that women hold 40% of the cabinet seats as their presence in the Bundestag declined perhaps suggests a tendency for Merkel to go above and beyond the norm in her appointments of women to high office. Another observation that does not fit the larger patterns in the literature is that women's percentages in the cabinet tend not to decline over the course of a chancellor's term in Germany.

What types of portfolios have women gained in Germany? Given Schröder's Social–Democratic partisanship, it might be expected for women to serve in more path-breaking capacities. Yet, as a woman, Merkel may have prioritised appointing women to posts beyond the typical 'feminine' ministries. As Kohl's appointments of women tended to be at much lower rates than compared to Schröder's and Merkel's, I make few observations regarding portfolio types when occupied. During Kohl's tenure, women's earliest appointments were to portfolios typically associated with 'femininity' including Youth, Women, Family, Health and Education.[9] When this pattern diverged, this resulted from women's appointments to positions that lacked a prevailing gender slant rather than their selection to head more 'masculine' ministries. Examples of such appointments included

ones to the Justice Ministry as well the Environment, Nature Conservation, and Reactor Security Ministry (held by Merkel, who had previously served as Minister of Women's Affairs).

Appointments and Ministry Gender Slant in Germany

Women gained much more space in the cabinet during Schröder's and Merkel's tenures. Under both of these chancellors, however, the most common cabinet portfolio type held by men was 'masculine', although this tendency largely decreased with each subsequent term (see Table 3). Men almost never occupied feminine portfolios, whereas, until Merkel's third term, women were most commonly gained entry to feminine roles. An equal percentage of women, however, held 'feminine' and gender-neutral portfolios during Merkel's third term. By Merkel's fourth mandate, women are most often positioned in gender-neutral ministries, followed by 'feminine' ones. Moreover, Merkel also started to appoint men to 'feminine' ministries such as health or ones with no particular gender connection. Women still almost never occupy 'masculine' portfolios, though Merkel's appointment of Ursula von der Leyen as the first female Minister of Defence is particularly noteworthy. Compared to Schröder, Merkel has varied the gendered space men and women in her cabinet occupy. Previously, we saw grand coalitions as a potentially positive driver of the percentage of women in the cabinet during Merkel's chancellorships. Merkel's tendency to shift women to less traditionally feminine ministries however, continued in her second term, which was not during a grand coalition. Merkel's varying portfolios men and women hold in her cabinets has occurred in spite of the type of coalition at work.[10] Overall, we see some confirmation of Merkel empowering women through her selection of women to head more varied ministries based on gender roles.

Appointments and Ministry Prestige Slant in Germany

As far as prestige, Schröder's first government saw men appointed equally to high and medium prestige portfolios and women to medium prestige ones. During his second term, men held a greater percentage of high prestige appointments and women mostly gained positions offering medium prestige. Low prestige portfolios were only held by women (never men) and not a single woman gained a high prestige post. Under Merkel's governments, women most often hold posts affording mid-level prestige. However, she also appointed women to high-prestige posts. Apart from her first term when a slightly greater percentage of men held high prestige positions, men most often served in medium prestige offices, just like their female counterparts. As such, Merkel has improved the quality of positions women have held under her governance and this is true regardless of the coalition at work (see Table 4).

Having analysed women's cabinet appointments in Germany, we see some confirmation that a woman at the helm of power has empowered women through her appointment powers. Merkel's appointments of women as a percentage of

Table 3. Appointments and Ministry Gender Slant in Germany.

| | Schröder | | | | Merkel | | | | | | | |
| | 1 | | 2 | | 1 | | 2 | | 3 | | 4 | |
	Number	Percent	Number	Percent	Number	Percent	Number	Percent	Number	Percent	Number	Percent
High male	7	32	4	31	7	37	8	32	6	29	3	20
High female	0	0	0	0	0	0	0	0	1	5	1	7
Medium male	7	32	3	23	6	32	9	36	6	29	5	33
Medium female	6	27	5	38	5	26	5	20	5	24	4	27
Low male	0	0	0	0	0	0	0	0	0	0	0	0
Low female	1	5	1	8	1	5	2	8	2	10	1	7
Unclassifiable male	1	5	0	0	0	0	1	4	1	5	1	7
Unclassifiable female	0	0	0	0	0	0	0	0	0	0	0	0
Total	22	100	13	100	19	100	25	100	21	100	15	100

Source: Analysis of German Federal Cabinet Webpages, https://www.bundesregierung.de/Webs/Breg/EN/FederalGovernment/Cabinet/_node.html.

Note: Coding based on Escobar-Lemmon and Taylor-Robinson (2005, 2009) out of total appointments throughout entire term and accounts for cabinet changes. Calculations have duplicate appointees if someone was appointed to multiple posts. Percentages may not total 100 because of rounding.

Table 4. Appointments and Ministry Prestige Slant in Germany.

| | Schröder | | | | Merkel | | | | | | | |
| | 1 | | 2 | | 1 | | 2 | | 3 | | 4 | |
	Number	Percent	Number	Percent	Number	Percent	Number	Percent	Number	Percent	Number	Percent
High male	7	32	4	31	7	37	8	32	6	29	3	20
High female	0	0	0	0	0	0	0	0	1	5	1	7
Medium male	7	32	3	23	6	32	9	36	6	29	5	33
Medium female	6	27	5	38	5	26	5	20	5	24	4	27
Low male	0	0	0	0	0	0	0	0	0	0	0	0
Low female	1	5	1	8	1	5	2	8	2	10	1	7
Unclassifiable male	1	5	0	0	0	0	1	4	1	5	1	7
Unclassifiable female	0	0	0	0	0	0	0	0	0	0	0	0
Total	22	100	13	100	19	100	25	100	21	100	15	100

Source: Analysis of German Federal Cabinet Webpages, https://www.bundesregierung.de/Webs/Breg/EN/FederalGovernment/Cabinet/_node.html_.
Note: Coding based on Escobar-Lemmon and Taylor-Robinson (2005, 2009).

her cabinet have generally been quite high, though not record-breaking. More impressive is that, under Merkel's governance, women are less relegated to only 'feminine' and less prestigious cabinet positions. Men enjoy greater variability in their placements as well. All of this has occurred with very little change in women's levels in parliament and even backsliding after the 2017 election. Moreover, while Merkel's terms under grand coalitions have been accompanied by women's greatest share of cabinet seats, she has selected many women from within the CDU/CSU. Moreover, many of the women occupying less feminine and more prestigious roles are also co-partisans. Given Merkel's conservative party linkages, her tendency to appoint women as a large share of her cabinet and to more varied positions based on gender roles and prestige is quite notable.

Cabinet Appointment Findings – Brazil

Turning now to Brazil, women's cabinet levels were very low until Lula's presidency. Lula appointed more women than all previous Brazilian presidents. This groups of women included Dilma Rousseff who would later use this experience as a stepping stone to the presidency, similar to Merkel who held different portfolios under Kohl. Lula also created the Special Secretariat of Women's Policies cabinet post (Bohns, 2010). His gestures to incorporate more women into the government are in line with the PT's more liberal ideology. Since Rousseff's impeachment, this chapter takes an advantage of the opportunity to also compare Rousseff's behaviour to that of her male successor, Michel Temer, who hailed from a different party but dealt with similar dynamics that all three presidents shared – the limited supply of women in political positions in Brazil and fairly unprogressive gender attitudes. As before, I first compare cabinet composition at the start and end of each presidential term, a first cut to see the typical percentage of women in the cabinet at particular points in time.

Gender and Appointment to the Brazilian Cabinet: Start and End of Terms

As his first term commenced, 11% of Lula's cabinet appointees were women, and women held this level at his term's conclusion. By the beginning of his second mandate, women's numerical representation dipped to 7%, finishing at 10% by the end of his presidency. Rousseff's first term saw record numbers of women in the cabinet. As she entered office, 26% of her cabinet positions were held by women and only lowered slightly at the end of her first mandate. We see, however, women experiencing a setback at the start of her second term when only 16% of her appointees were women. Recall, however, that this is still a far greater level than women achieved during Lula's presidency. As she approached her crisis period, women's percentages dropped to similar rates to when Lula was president – 10%. After Rousseff's impeachment, President Temer notoriously decided not to appoint a single woman to his cabinet when he took office (Lopes, 2017). Because Temer only managed to ultimately appoint one woman to his cabinet at the time of this writing, I can only compare Lula's and Rousseff's appointments (see Table 5).

Table 5. Appointments to Positions in the Brazilian Cabinet by Government and Gender: Start and End of Terms.

President	Term	Start of Term % Women	End of Term % Women	Difference
Lula	1	11	11	0
	2	7	10	+3
Rouseff	1	26	24	−2
	2	16	10	−6
Temer	1	0	−	−

Source: Analysis of the Official Brazilian Government Portal through the website of the Presidency of Brazil (Ex-presidentes n.d.)
Note: Calculations have duplicate appointees if someone was appointed to multiple posts. Percentages may not total 100 because of rounding.

Table 6. Cabinet Appointments in Brazil by Government and Gender.

President	Term	% Women
Lula	1	10
	2	9
Rouseff	1	18
	2	9
Temer	1	0

Source: Analysis of the Official Brazilian Government Portal through the website of the Presidency of Brazil (Ex-presidentes n.d.).
Note: Calculations include duplicate appointees if someone was appointed to multiple posts.

Gender and Total Cabinet Appointments in Brazil

This section analyse total appointments made by Lula and Rousseff during Lula's first term, four out of his 42 appointees were women, representing nine percent of his total selections. During his second mandate, six of 67 ministers were women, once again nine percent of the cabinet. When analysing his two terms together, women represented 10 of 109 appointments or nine percent of his total appointments. Again, this was still significant at the time since their previous record was three percent under President Itamar Franco.

Rousseff selected women to hold 14 of 77 cabinet appointments during her first term. As such, women represented 18% of all of her cabinet appointments. As Rousseff began her second term in 2015, the country was already experiencing an economic downturn. Moreover, while she was re-elected in a tight runoff, the political crisis was already in progress. Rousseff's ministerial appointments indicated that she was looking for established politicians (mostly male) that could help her address the political crisis. In 2015, Rousseff appointed six women (14%) to her cabinet, keeping four from her previous administration, and brought in another two. In the transition, two women lost their places to men. While the number of women in her cabinet was smaller in 2015 than it was in 2011 when Rousseff first took office, Rousseff continued to maintain more women in cabinets than any other previous president, including Lula.

During Lula's first cabinet, 18% of cabinet posts were offered to coalition parties, 40% went to the PT, and the rest to non-partisans. The four women (11% of all cabinet members) appointed during his first cabinet all hailed from the PT; while the party may be consciously seeking women to fill positions of power, coalition partners may not prioritise the nomination and appointment of women as ministers. The dominance of women hailing from the PT continued throughout Lula's administration, with nine of the 10 women he appointed during his two terms coming from his party.

As far as the partisan distribution among portfolio allocations upon Rousseff's entry, the PT claimed 17 ministries (45%). Its main coalition partner, the PMDB, held six (16%) and another eight ministers (21%) lacked party affiliations (Frayssinet, 2010). As seen during Lula's administration, the women appointed to cabinet positions came overwhelmingly from the PT. Of the fourteen women appointed to Dilma Rousseff's first cabinet, nine hailed from the PT while four lacked party affiliations. As before, no women who represented parties came from outside of the PT in the initial cabinet formation. Over time, however, Rousseff was less likely to appoint women with partisan linkages, a fact that may have cost her support from the PT and coalition partners but potentially demonstrated the importance she placed on diversifying the cabinet.

Rousseff was expected to have Lula loyalists in her cabinet, particularly since she owed him a special debt of gratitude for her election. Thirteen of Rousseff's initial appointees (slightly over one third) served as part of Lula's cabinet, some holding very important posts such as Finance Minister and Chief of Staff (Frayssinet, 2010). Given these cross and intra-party pressures, Rousseff's ability to select women appeared constrained. As such, the proportions of women in her cabinet seem notable. Rousseff's willingness to continue this diversification waned as she entered the crisis period. Many of the early ministers in Rousseff's administration were holdovers from Lula's regime, with several essentially sacked because of corruption allegations against them (Araújo et al., 2016). Other ministers resigned to compete for other offices, a fairly common practice in Brazil.

Because of the nature of Brazil's coalition dynamics, Rousseff's decision to appoint so many women may have exerted a negative effect in her ability to negotiate with the PT's coalition partners. Rousseff was going against recommendations from the PT to fill some of these positions, insisting that the party leaders find women to fill some of the cabinet posts. Second, by appointing a total of ten women with no party affiliation (most of them extremely competent 'technocrats' that lacked the political networks other politicians, especially male politicians, have), the president was arguably putting women's representation in front of coalition management, something that can negative affect governing a presidential coalition (Pereira et al., 2016), which was a particularly unstable and weak one.

The budget crisis forced Rousseff to eliminate eight ministries in 2015, including the Women's Policy Secretary (Matoso, Alegretti, & Passarinho, 2015). As the crisis deepened, budget uncertainties and political wrangling forced Rousseff to eliminate eight cabinet positions, reducing the total number of cabinet positions from 39 to 31. Of the posts eliminated, three are especially noteworthy. Rousseff fused the Women's Secretariat, the Racial Equality Secretariat, and the Human

Rights Secretariat into one cabinet. Women overwhelmingly occupied these three positions during Lula's and Rousseff's administrations. Moreover, these three cabinet posts addressed women's related issues. Combining the ministries meant less money was allocated to address issues related to women's rights. Nevertheless, as the crisis deepened, women still maintained their numerical presence in the cabinet. Six women were in the President's last cabinet, occupying 19% of all cabinet positions available, *even after* the elimination of eight cabinet posts.

When analysing the totality of her presidency, Rousseff selected 14 different women to hold 20 cabinet appointments during her 6 years. Overall, women represented 20 of 143 appointments or 14% of her total appointments. Again, though hardly parity, this still went above and beyond previous records. Again, women only comprised nine percent of all of Lula's cabinet ministers he appointed throughout his two terms. Michel Temer failed to appoint any women to his cabinet and eliminated more ministries including the Ministry of Women, Racial Equality and Human Rights. Instead, all ministries related to women, racial equality and human rights were supposed to also be handled by the Ministry of Justice. With her presidency ending prematurely owing to impeachment, her replacement, Michel Temer, did not appoint a single woman to his cabinet. This was the first time since 1979 that no women were part of the cabinet. While Temer's PMDB became the largest party in Congress, its plurality was not enough to escape a governing coalition. Of his initial cabinet appointments, only two (8 percent of all cabinet positions) were not affiliated with a party. Eight (35%) of his appointments went to his own party; four (17%) went to PSDB, the strongest opposition party during PT's presidencies; and the other nine (39%) were filled by politicians from seven different parties comprising the new coalition established by Temer. Rather than a conscious effort to exclude women, his officials argues that the new government had little time to come up with cabinet member names and that party leaders simply did not propose women to Temer (Amorim, Prazeres, & Marchesan, 2016).

Findings thus far demonstrate that Rousseff promoted a greater percentage of women to the cabinet than all previous Brazilian presidents, including Lula. Moreover, given their partisan connection as well as the fact that Rousseff owed Lula a special debt of gratitude given his central role in her election, we would expect more of the same as she composed her cabinet and even made adjustments over time. Contrary to expectations derived from the cabinet literature, she appointed more women as she made changes during her first term. Even as she received increased scrutiny during her second term, Rousseff did not waver from choosing women that did not hold the typical party credentials to the PT or coalition partners.

Appointments and Ministry Gender Slant in Brazil

Table 7 compares Lula's and Rousseff's appointments based on the gender slant of the ministry. For both Lula's first term and Rousseff's first and second terms, the most common configuration is for men to hold 'masculine' posts. Slightly greater percentages of women hold 'feminine' posts in Rousseff's compared to

Table 7. Appointments and Ministry Gender Slant in Brazil.

| | Lula | | | | Rouseff | | | |
| | 1 | | 2 | | 1 | | 2 | |
	Number	Percent	Number	Percent	Number	Percent	Number	Percent
Masculine male	19	45	22	33	38	49	30	45
Masculine female	1	2	2	3	2	3	1	2
Feminine male	10	24	12	18	5	6	7	11
Feminine female	1	2	1	1	5	6	2	3
Unclassifiable male	9	21	27	40	20	26	23	35
Unclassifiable female	2	5	3	4	7	9	3	5
Total	42	100	67	100	77	100	66	100

Source: Analysis of the Official Brazilian Government Portal through the website of the Presidency of Brazil

Note: Coding based on Escobar-Lemmon and Taylor-Robinson (2005, 2009). Calculations have duplicate appointees if someone was appointed to multiple posts. Percentages may not total 100 due to rounding.

Lula's presidency while a lower proportion of men gained 'feminine' portfolios during Rousseff's tenure. I also note the very large percentage of posts that lack clear gender specifications. Not many differences surface between each president and the gender slant of cabinet positions either men or women occupy. As such, no evidence exists that Rousseff selected women to occupy different gendered space compared to her male counterpart.

Appointments and Ministry Prestige Slant in Brazil
When comparing Rousseff's to Lula's presidencies, we again see few differences between levels of prestige and gender (see Tables 7 and 8). Rousseff tended to appoint a greater proportion of men to high prestige posts than Lula, but this was also the case for women, at least during her first term. A greater percentage of men held positions offering mid-level prestige under Lula than Rousseff, particularly in his second term. Rousseff, on the other hand, tended to select men to hold lower prestige positions than Lula during her second mandate. Therefore, we do have some confirmation that women tended to fare better during Rousseff's administration, at least during her first term than during Lula's. At the same time, these differences proved quite minimal overall. While women formed a larger proportion of Rousseff's cabinet compared to her male counterparts, women's placement was marginally better in terms of prestige compared to Lula and about the same as far as gender stereotypes related to ministries. Of course, as Rousseff's presidency came to a screeching halt nearly two years before the end of her term, her male replacement, Michel Temer, set women back farther than any president in Brazil's recent democratic history.

DISCUSSION

Women still rarely gain access to the most influential executive positions worldwide (Jalalzai, 2016). Germany and Brazil both prove exceptions as Angela Merkel and Dilma Rousseff occupied the highest offices available in these countries, respectively. As lead players in cabinet formation, they possess the power to appoint others, including women, to high office. Their genders would lead us to expect they would strive for greater gender parity in their governments. Rather than biologically driven, this expectation is guided gendered socialisation patterns. We would anticipate the social networks of female leaders to include more women. Greater gender consciousness and awareness of the continued discrimination women face in the political realm also could hasten greater equity within their cabinets. Symbolism related to being women in an almost exclusively male domain also may facilitate patterns of greater inclusivity during women's administrations.

Having analysed Germany and Brazil, this chapter supports the assertion that women executives tend to use their appointment powers to promote women. This challenges the global literature, which does not find women executives more prone to enhance gender diversity in cabinets (Krook & O'Brien, 2012;

Table 8. Appointments and Ministry Prestige Slant in Brazil.

| | Lula | | | | Rouseff | | | |
| | 1 | | 2 | | 1 | | 2 | |
	Number	Percent	Number	Percent	Number	Percent	Number	Percent
High male	61	63	5	7	12	16	16	24
High female	0	0	0	0	3	4	0	0
Medium male	25	26	37	55	33	43	24	36
Medium female	3	3	3	4	3	4	3	5
Low male	5	5	7	10	8	10	10	15
Low female	1	1	3	4	4	5	1	2
Unclassifiable male	2	2	12	18	10	13	10	15
Unclassifiable female	0	0	0	0	4	5	2	3
Total	97	100	67	100	77	100	66	100

Source: Analysis of the Official Brazilian Government Portal through the website of the Presidency of Brazil.
Note: Coding based on Escobar-Lemmon and Taylor-Robinson (2005, 2009). Calculations have duplicate appointees if someone was appointed to multiple posts. Percentages may not total 100 because of rounding.

O'Brien et al., 2015). In contrast, this current study adds to the mounting evidence derived from country and regional analyses that women executives do appoint more women overall and to less traditional ministries (Franceschet, 2016; Jalalzai, 2016; Jalalzai & dos Santos, 2015; Reyes-Housholder, 2016; Wiliarty, 2014). The approach taken in this chapter – examining two countries from different regions – balances the need for a diversity of cases offered by global analyses with the analytical depth afforded by single country and regional explorations. The research design implemented offered breadth by focussing on two distinct regions (Western Europe and Latin America). It also afforded depth by tracking patterns over time in Germany and Brazil between executive sex and key factors in each country affecting the leader willingness and ability to promote women to power.

While gender would lead us to expect female national leaders to use their selection powers to promote other women to high office, myriad conditions shape one's abilities to do so. Merkel's conservative affiliation would not lead to expectations of more progressive patterns of women's appointments under her chancellorship. Merkel's party has mainly governed with the biggest left party, the SPD. Such power sharing configurations may see more women cabinet ministers than compared to other coalitions led by the CDU/CSU. Women's fairly robust incorporation in lower political offices amidst more progressive gender attitudes would not unduly hamper a national leader committed to appointing women to the cabinet.

Germany's first female chancellor, though from a conservative party, has tended to maintain high levels of women ministers throughout her governments. Though not record-breaking, at 40%, the German cabinet approaches gender parity. Merkel's placements of women in particular demonstrate the importance she has placed on women's presence throughout her tenure. Women have started to amass more prestigious as well as more gender-neutral posts under Merkel's governance. The quality of positions women held has improved and this is the case regardless of the type of coalition led. This progress cannot be attributed primarily to SDP leaders selecting more women; Merkel has integrated several women from the CDU/CSU overall, many that hold more prestigious positions. While women's political participation in Germany is fairly commonplace, women's incorporation in feeder institutions such as the legislature has not increased significantly and even fell recently. As such, women's recent strides are not simply explained by the greater supply of women in the political pipeline.

Rousseff's liberal credentials would seemingly offer more potential for gender parity in the Brazilian cabinet. Yet, the PT shares power with a variety of non-leftist parties in a party system characterised by extreme volatility. Brazilian women enjoy very limited numerical representation in political offices and also contend with traditional views of women's role, posing more challenging for leaders to recruit a diverse cabinet. Findings presented suggest that Dilma Rousseff, like Merkel also promoted a greater percentage of women to her cabinet. Unlike Merkel, this was more the case during her first term than as her presidency progressed to a second mandate. Women's placement was marginally better in terms of prestige and fairly similar regarding gender slant when compared to Lula's cabinets. Rousseff's second mandate posed institutional constraints, as noted. Still, quantities of appointments and prestige indicated a substantial improvement compared to previous presidents. This is not simply a by-product of women in Brazil making substantial inroads within the political pipeline; women's legislative levels throughout the time period examined remained very low. Given the relative scarcity of women in politics as well as more cultural resistance to gender equality, it is not particularly surprising that women in Brazil formed a smaller percentage of the cabinet overall compared to Germany even as Rousseff went above and beyond all of her male predecessors in selecting women. Less expected was Michel Temer completely undoing all of the gains women previously had made as he appointed his new cabinet following Rousseff's impeachment. This move seemed especially startling in completely ignoring international norms that leaders need to have some women present in their cabinets for democratic legitimacy (Annesley et al., 2016). Women's utter exclusion became a stark symbol of the unravelling of Brazil's democracy and gender backlash.

While findings are instructive, a limitation of this study is its inability to verify that commitment to gender parity truly motivated Merkel's and Rousseff's more gender equitable patterns of women's cabinet appointments. While interviews with key political players as well as public declarations made by Rousseff herself do support the assertion that the first female president of Brazil consciously promoted women to powerful positions because she viewed gender equality as important (see Jalalzai, 2016), similar studies do not exist regarding Merkel. As Merkel prepares to step down from power, the relationship between gender and motivations for cabinet selection could be clearer by engaging in subsequent investigations. The gender and cabinet literature would be substantially improved with more in-depth interviews tracing the appointments of cabinet ministers during various governments. This would provide a starting point to unpack the gender and cabinet selection process and how specific motivations for gender parity link to actual behaviour of leaders once in power, men and women alike.

Another limitation of this study stems from the fact that so few people occupy cabinet space overall, and this is especially true for women. Accordingly, even the slightest increase or decrease in women's numbers can lead to substantial differences in overall gender composition. Of course, this limitation is not particular to just this investigation, but still worth noting. Finally, though countries examined are diverse, findings still rest on more in-depth analysis of just two cases. Rather than the last word on this topic, however, this chapter adds to the bourgeoning literature linking the sex of the national executive and its subsequent effect on gender composition within the cabinet. Much more research must be conducted to continue to move this line of inquiry forward.

NOTES

1. Former Spanish Prime Minister José Luis Rodrıguez, President François Hollande of France and Prime Minister Justin Trudeau of Canada are all examples of male executives that have appointed 'parity' cabinets.
2. According to Annesley (2015), coalitions rarely surface in Westminster parliamentary systems, affording the prime minister greater authority over his or her cabinet choices.

3. Yet, as Annesley (2015) suggests the pool depends on the particular country. In Germany, only legislators from the lower house are eligible to hold executive portfolios. In the United Kingdom, ministers hail from either the House of Commons or House of Lords (Annesley, 2015).

4. Claveria's study (2014) of advanced democracies worldwide did not find coalitions to significantly affect women's cabinet appointments until later points in time (1996–2010).

5. Women's percentages are slightly above average in Sub-Saharan Africa (Paxton & Hughes, 2017).

6. Annesley et al. (2016) assert their evidence regarding concrete floors is derived from wealthy democracies. As such, this tendency varies worldwide as does the level that constitutes the specific threshold.

7. It should be noted that the percentage of the vote (91%) Merkel received from her three-party coalition in 2018 does not differ significantly from the support she received in 2013, which was 92%. And this is greater than the 89% of the vote that she obtained her first term in 2005 (Shalal & Carey, 2018). https://www.theguardian.com/world/2018/mar/14/angela-merkel-sworn-in-for-fourth-term-as-german-chancellor.

8. As measured by responses to the World Values survey on six questions related to respondent acceptance of women's equality in various arenas including the political, economy/labour, education and the family (World Values Wave 6, 2015).

9. In Germany, education was often coupled with science in earlier administrations, which is a fusion of masculine and feminine areas. Subsequently, the ministry was renamed Education and Research.

10. During Merkel's three grand coalition governments, the SPD has held the Foreign Affairs and Finance portfolios, for example, while the CDU/CSU controlled Defense. These are all considered masculine (and prestigious) and the first two portfolios have been held by men, while a woman in the Defense role. During her second term, her Defence Minister a member of CDU/CSU's more conservative sister party, the CSU.

REFERENCES

Alexander, A. C. C. (2015). Big jumps in women's presence in parliaments: Are these sufficient for improving beliefs in women's ability to govern? *Advancing Women in Leadership Journal, 35*, 82–97.

Altman, D. (2008). Political recruitment and candidate selection in Chile (1990–2003): The executive branch. In P. M. Siavelis & S. Morgenstern (Eds.), *Pathways to power: Political recruitment and candidate selection in Latin America* (pp. 241–270). State College, PA: Penn State University Press.

Alves, J. E. D. (2009, March 8). Mulheres sem espaço no poder. *Folha de S. Paulo*. Retrieved from http://www1.folha.uol.com.br/fsp/opiniao/fz0803200909.htm

Alves, J. E. D. (2010). A Sub-representação da Mulher Na Política No Brasil e a Nova Política de Cotas Nas Eleições de 2010. *In Brasilia*, Brazil.

Amorim, F., Prazeres, L., & Marchesan, R. (2016, October 24). Ministro de Temer justifica ausência de mulheres no governo: 'não foi possível. *Política*. Retrieved from http://noticias.uol.com.br/politica/ultimas-noticias/2016/05/13/ministerio-sem-mulheres-no-governo-temer.htm

Annesley, C. (2015). Rules of ministerial recruitment. *Politics & Gender, 11*(4), 618–642.

Annesley, C., Beckwith, K., & Franceschet, S. (2016). There are three rules of cabinet appointments. Will Donald Trump break them? *The Monkey Cage*, November 25. Retrieved from https://www.washingtonpost.com/news/monkey-cage/wp/2016/11/25/there-are-three-rules-of-cabinet-appointments-will-donald-trump-break-them/?noredirect=on&utm_term=.52f01722249d

Araújo, C. (2003). Quotas for women in the Brazilian legislative system. Paper presented at international IDEA workshop, February 23–24, Lima, Peru. Retrieved from http://aceproject.org/ero-en/topics/parties-and-candidates/CS_Araujo_Brazil_25-11-2003.pdf

Arriola, L. R. R., & Johnson, M. C. (2014). Ethnic politics and women's empowerment in Africa: Ministerial appointments to executive cabinet. *American Journal of Politics, 58*(2), 495–510.

Barnes, T. D., & O'Brien, D. Z. (2018). Defending the realm: The appointment of female defense ministers worldwide. *American Journal of Political Science, 62*(2), 355–368. doi:10.1111/ajps.12337

Barnes, T. D., & Taylor-Robinson, M. M. (2018). Women cabinet ministers in highly visible posts and women's empowerment: Are the two related? In A. Alexander, C. Bolzendahl, & F. Jalalzai (Eds.), *Measuring women's political empowerment around the globe: Strategies, challenges and future research* (pp. 229–255). London: Palgrave Macmillan.

BBC News. (2018, April 8). *Brazil corruption crisis. All you need to know.* Retrieved from https://www.bbc.com/news/world-latin-america-35810578

Bohns, S. R. (2010). Feminismo estatal sob a presidência Lula: O caso da secretaria de políticas para as mulheres. *Revista Debates, 4*(2), 81–106.

Bolzendahl, C. (2018). Legislatures as gendered organizations: Challenges and opportunities for women's empowerment as political elites. In A. Alexander, C. Bolzendahl, & F. Jalalzai (Eds.), *Measuring women's political empowerment around the globe: Strategies, challenges and future research* (pp. 165–186). London: Palgrave Macmillan.

Childs, S., & Krook, M. L. (2009). Analysing women's substantive representation from critical mass to critical actors. *Government and Opposition, 44*(2), 125–145.

Claveria, S. (2014). Still a 'male business'? Explaining women's presence in executive office. *West European Politics, 37*(5), 1156–1176.

Clemens, C. (2006). From the outside in: Angela Merkel as opposition leader, 2002–2005. *German Politics & Society, 24*(3), 41–81.

Coppedge, M. (1998). The dynamic diversity of Latin American party systems. *Party Politics, 4*(4), 547–568.

Davis, R. H. (1997). *Women and power in parliamentary democracies cabinet appointments in Western Europe, 1968–1992.* Lincoln, NE: University of Nebraska Press.

dos Santos, P. G., Gatto, M. A. C., & Wylie, K. N. (2017). Coalitional presidentialism, gender, and cabinet appointments in Brazil. Paper Presented at the 2017 European conference on politics and gender, University of Lausanne, Lausanne, Switzerland.

Escobar-Lemmon, M., & Taylor-Robinson, M. M. (2005). Women ministers in Latin American government: When, where, and why. *American Journal of Political Science, 49*(4), 829–844.

Escobar-Lemmon, M., & Taylor-Robinson, M. M. (2009). Getting to the top: Career paths of women in Latin American cabinets. *Political Research Quarterly, 62*(4), 685–699.

Franceschet, S. (2016). Disrupting informal institutions? Cabinet formation in Chile in 2006 and 2014. In G. Waylen (Ed.), *Gender, institutions, and change in Bachelet's Chile* (pp. 67–94). New York, NY: Palgrave Macmillan.

Franceschet, S., Krook, M. L., & Piscopo, J. M. (2012). Conceptualizing the impact of gender quotas. In S. Franceschet, M. L. Krook, & J. M. Piscopo (Eds.), *The impact of gender quotas* (pp. 3–26). New York, NY: Oxford University Press.

Frayssinet, F. (2010). Politics-Brazil: Continuity, with a woman's Face. *Inter-Press Service*, December 22. Retrieved from http://www.ipsnews.net/2010/12/politics-brazil-continuity-with-a-womans-face/

Genovese, M., & Steckenrider, J. (Eds.). (2013). *Women as national leaders: Studies in gender and governing.* New York, NY: Routledge.

Genovese, M. A. (2013). Margaret Thatcher and the politics of conviction leadership. In M. A. Genovese & J. S. Steckenrider (Eds.), *Women as political leaders* (pp. 270–305). London: Sage.

Helms, L. (2006). The grand coalition: Precedents and prospects. *German Politics and Society, 24*(1), 47–66.

King, A. (2002). The outsider as political leader: The case of Margaret Thatcher. *The British Journal of Political Science, 32*(3), 435–454.

Krook, M. L., & O'Brien, D. Z. (2012). All the president's men? The appointment of female cabinet ministers worldwide. *The Journal of Politics, 74*(3), 840–855.

Jalalzai, F. (2013). *Shattered, cracked, or firmly intact: Women and the executive glass ceiling worldwide.* Oxford: Oxford University Press.

Jalalzai, F. (2016). *Women presidents of Latin America: Beyond family ties?* New York, NY: Routledge.

Jalalzai, F., & dos Santos, P. G. (2015). The Dilma effect? Women's representation under Dilma Rousseff's presidency. *Politics & Gender, 11*(1), 117–145.

LeBlond, J. (2018). German Chancellor Angela Merkel will not seek re-election in 2021. *The Guardian*, October 29. Retrieved from https://www.theguardian.com/world/2018/oct/29/angela-merkel-wont-seek-re-election-as-cdu-party-leader

Lopes, M. (2017). Brazil's political class is in crisis as over 100 are investigated for corruption. *Washington Post*, April 12. Retrieved from https://www.washingtonpost.com/world/the_americas/brazils-political-class-is-in-crisis-as-over-100-are-investigated-for-corruption/2017/04/12/d2832a8a-1f7e-11e7-bb59-a74ccaf1d02f_story.html?noredirect=on&utm_term=.1efeb2edb90e

Lucas, K. D., & Samuels, D. (2010). Ideological coherence of the Brazilian party system, 1990–2009. *Journal of Politics in Latin America, 2*(3), 39–69.

Mainwaring, S. (1999). *Rethinking party systems in the 3ʳᵈ wave of democratization: The case of Brazil.* Stanford, CA: Stanford University Press.

Matoso, F., Alegretti, L., & Passarinho, N. (2015). Dilma anuncia reforma com redução de 39 para 31 ministérios. *Política*. Retrieved from http://g1.globo.com/politica/noticia/2015/10/dilma-anuncia-reducao-de-39-para-31-pastas-na-reforma-ministerial.html

Montecinos, V. (2017). Introduction. In V. Montecinos (Ed.) *Women presidents and prime ministers in post-transition democracies* (pp. 1–36). London: Palgrave MacMillan.

O'Brien, D. Z., Mendez, M., Peterson, J. C., & Shin, J. (2015). Letting down the ladder or shutting the door: Female prime ministers, party leaders, and cabinet ministers. *Politics & Gender, 11*(4), 689–717.

Parks, S. (1997). *Understanding contemporary Germany.* New York, NY: Routledge.

Pereira, C. (2011). Brazilian president Rousseff's first governing coalition: Better, but not good enough. *Brookings*, February 8. Retrieved from https://www.brookings.edu/opinions/brazilian-president-rousseffs-first-governing-coalition-better-but-not-good-enough/

Pereira, C., Bertholini, F., & Raile, E. D. (2016). All the president's men and women: Coalition management strategies and governing costs in a multiparty presidency. *Presidential Studies Quarterly, 46*(3), 550–568.

Rangel, P. (2009). Sex and the city: Reflections on women's parliamentary representation and the 2008 Municipal Elections. *Sociedade e Cultura, 12*(1), 69–77.

Reyes-Housholder, C. (2016). *Presidentas* rise: Consequences for women in cabinets? *Latin American Politics & Society, 58*(3), 1–23.

Whitford, A. B., Wilkins, V. M., & Ball, M. G. (2007). Descriptive representation and policymaking authority: Evidence from women in cabinets and bureaucracies. *Governance, 20*(4), 559–580.

Schoen, H., & Greszki, R. (2014). A third term for a popular chancellor: An analysis of voting behavior in the 2013 German federal elections. *German Politics, 23*(4), 251–267.

Shair-Rosenfield, S., & Stoyan, A. T. (2018). Gendered opportunities and constraints: How executive sex and approval influence executive decree issuance. *Political Research Quarterly, 71*(3), 586–599. doi:10.1177/1065912917750279

Shalal, A., & Carrel, P. (2018). No love match for Germany in Merkel's third grand coalition. *Reuters*, March 12. Retrieved from https://www.reuters.com/article/us-germany-politics/no-love-match-for-germany-in-merkels-third-grand-coalition-idUSKCN1GO1A9

Siaroff, A. (2000). Women's representation in legislatures and cabinets in industrial democracies. *International Political Science Review, 21*(2), 197–215.

Skard, T. (2014). *Women of power: Half a century of female presidents and prime ministers worldwide.* Chicago, IL: Policy Press.

Stevenson, L. (2012). The Bachelet effect on gender-equity policies. *Latin American Perspectives, 39*(4), 129–144.

Teruel, J. R. (2011). *Los Ministros de la España Democrática: Reclutamiento político y carrera ministerial de Suárez a Zapatero (1976–2010).* Madrid, Spain: Centro de Estudios Políticos y Constitucionales.

Thomas, G. (2016). Promoting gender equality: Michelle Bachelet and formal and informal institutional change within the Chilean presidency. In G. Waylen (Ed.), *Gender, institutions, and change in Bachelet's Chile* (pp. 95–120). New York, NY: Palgrave MacMillan.

Thompson, M. P. (2002). Female leadership of democratic transitions in Asia. *Pacific Affairs, 75*(4), 535–555.

Thompson, M. P., & Lennartz, L. (2006). The making of Chancellor Merkel. *German Politics*, *15*(1), 99–110.

Waylen, G. (Ed.). (2016). *Gender, institutions, and change in Bachelet's Chile*. New York, NY: Palgrave Macmillan.

Weeks, G., & Borzutzky, S. (2013). Michelle Bachelet's government: The paradoxes of a Chilean president. *Journal of Politics in Latin America*, *4*(3), 97–121.

Wiliarty, S. (2008). Chancellor Angela Merkel – A sign of hope or the exception that proves the rule? *Politics & Gender*, *4*(3), 485–496.

Wiliarty, S. (2010). *The CDU and the politics of gender in Germany*. New York, NY: Cambridge University Press.

Wiliarty, S. (2014). Frauenpower? Women in the cabinet under Kohl, Schroeder and Merkel. Paper presented at the ECPR joint sessions workshop, Salamanca, Spain.

Wylie, K., & dos Santos, P. (2016). A law on paper only: Electoral rules, parties, and the persistent underrepresentation of women in Brazilian legislatures. *Politics & Gender*, *12*(3), 415–442.

PART III

ELITES AND POPULISM

ELITES, INSECURITY AND POPULISTS IN WESTERN DEMOCRACIES

John Higley

ABSTRACT

History teaches that agreement about the distribution of valued things is seldom deep or widespread in large populations. When distributive issues rise to clear public consciousness, the tendency is towards civil strife. Stable democratic institutions are rarely the result of all or even most social actors cooperating voluntarily, peacefully and with adequate information; nearly always, they are the products of shrewd decisions made by those who are seriously influential – elites. Elites must trust each other to manage politics in ways that prevent distributive issues from reaching acute degrees that impel power seizures. But can elite trust be sustained in advanced post-industrial conditions? The question arises because of steadily declining needs for many kinds of work, exacerbated by large migrations from non-Western countries and a resulting insecurity that populists exploit divisively for political gain. They act as pied pipers offering delusive enticements, making irresponsible promises and exhibiting disdain for rule of law. Disinclined to deal realistically with, or even acknowledge, long-term post-industrial problems of work, populists erode elite trust and weaken the basis of stable democratic institutions.

Keywords: Elite trust; political restraint; stable democracy; work insecurity; demoralisation; populists; migrations

Elite theory tends to be shunned in comparative and historical social science. This is mostly because it is distasteful. Although research on empirical aspects of elites is voluminous (see Best & Higley, 2018), the bulk of it is tied to democratic theory

Elites and People: Challenges to Democracy
Comparative Social Research, Volume 34, 189–202
Copyright © 2019 by Emerald Publishing Limited
All rights of reproduction in any form reserved
ISSN: 0195-6310/doi:10.1108/S0195-631020190000034009

and ways in which elites tread on its precepts. Unlike democratic theory, elite theory focusses on what special groups of people do or don't do in the political world. It doesn't rest on the premise underlying monarchies and aristocracies that certain people ought to rule and ought to have control of what other people do. Elite theory deals, instead, with a practical matter, which is the degree to which what happens politically is determined to a considerable extent by individuals who hold key positions in powerful organisations and movements. These persons may not be better than anyone else, but elite theory presumes it is their behaviour, rather than the behaviour of people in general, that in many respects shapes what happens in politics.

ELITES

Are elites an inevitable aspect of human organisation? Strictly speaking, they are not. Small communities are capable of operating in egalitarian ways. Although history shows they've rarely done so, under special circumstances and with luck when they form, small communities can function without elites. But in societies of a size normal in the modern world – a population of a million or more – elites are inescapable and, one might add, essential. They aren't merely a consequence of population size; elites also stem from urbanisation and at least incipient industrialisation and bureaucratisation. With these qualifications, one can say that modern societies always have a small number of people in them much more able than anyone else to determine political matters.

This assertion also requires qualification. Elites don't have the power to do anything they please – to restore, for example, a medieval religious belief or restrict the incomes of all or most people to subsistence levels. Neither, on the other hand, are they at liberty to make everyone truly equal, because attempting to do so would antagonise persons and groups better positioned to block equality than those pushing for it. Elites depend upon support by segments of populations and aren't capable of determining the attitude patterns on the basis of which segments give or withhold support. Elites who imagine some 'perfect' society and try to bring it about don't remain elites for very long; they lose support and others take over.

Mostly, elite persons try to sustain their individual power and influence as long as they can. In modern conditions, they're usually well along in life before attaining top positions in hierarchically structured organisations and movements. Typically, they don't attain such positions before 50 or so years of age and are unlikely to hold them for more than a decade or two. But so long as they manage to hang on to their positions, what happens politically depends, especially in details, on their initiatives. In societies where elites deliberately mitigate power struggles, the typical elite person usually comes out pretty well after vacating his or her position. This isn't the case where elites fight viciously for power and losers are victimised for defeats. Such elites are too precariously situated to observe rules that keep power struggles limited. A person belonging to them can't just decide, 'Well, I've had enough of this and I'm going to retire now' and expect to be called upon from time to time to influence what happens or at least be consulted about it. But in countries where elite battles aren't winner-take-all, this is what the typical elite person can safely anticipate.

Elites who deliberately mitigate power struggles can be thought of as mutually trusting. In democratic settings, elite trust underlies a wide range of clashing political views and intense competitions for political office. Without adhering to some single viewpoint, the bulk of elite persons are nevertheless in rough agreement about basic political institutions and game rules. Depending on local conventions about what's right and not right to say and do, they can be polite to each other or exceedingly impolite in ways that sound threatening. The question is whether elites carry out threats they sometimes make; where there is underlying trust they normally do not.

Political restraint is the observable manifestation of elite trust. Elites pursue bargains and compromises, emphasise technical and procedural feasibilities instead of ultimate rights and wrongs, agree to disagree when decisions can't or shouldn't be reached, regularly endorse their society's core values and affirm fidelity to existing institutions rather than particular personalities. They adhere to norms of mutual tolerance and forbearance, accept one another as legitimate rivals and exert institutional prerogatives with moderation (Levitsky & Ziblatt, 2018, p. 8). Over time, political restraint enables competing persons and factions to achieve diverging aims, and this inclines them to view the totality of outcomes as positive-sum and uphold institutions that process their bargains and compromises. Political restraint gives elite persons reasonable assurance that even after missteps, scandals or defeats they will retain their lives, reputations and a decent social status. As Robert Dahl (1971, pp. 36–38) put it in *Polyarchy*, a 'well-developed system of mutual security' and a 'system of mutual guarantees' are bedrock features of elites that keep institutions stable.

Elite trust undergirded the stable political institutions that people in Anglo-American and several European societies have long been familiar with, and it is an absolute requirement for stable democracy. One can look through the last three or four hundred years of world history and notice that in any society where there was a reasonable and sustained degree of representative government based on competing parties, and in which persons elected to political office routinely served out their terms peacefully, it is possible to find a circumstance in the society's history that created considerable elite trust. Thereafter, and except when subnational regional conflicts proved irresolvable (e.g. the North–South divide in the US that led to civil war) elites managed to contain major conflicts and did so over long periods. Persons and groups with grievances were either bought off or put in positions from which further contestation was useless. By performing one or the other operation or combinations of them on major issues that arose, elite trust was perpetuated.

The creation of trust depends, however, upon special and unlikely political circumstances. In Western history, local elites who were cautiously operating representative political institutions under home-rule arrangements in separate colonies came to trust and collaborate with each other in the risky, sometimes violent, process of casting off the last vestiges of colonial rule. This was the origin of elite trust and stable political institutions in the US, Canada, Australia and New

Zealand as well as the United Dutch Provinces when elites collaborated to free themselves from Spanish rule late in the sixteenth century and when Norwegian elites gained de facto independence from Swedish rule in the nineteenth century (Higley & Burton, 2006, pp. 107–122).

In a few independent Western countries, circumstances that induced warring elite camps to make peace deliberately and substitute stable institutions for unstable ones unfolded in England's Glorious Revolution of 1688–1689, Sweden's five-week constitutional settlement in 1809 and after Switzerland's brief civil war in 1847–1848. During the half century following World War II, circumstances propitious for basic 'elite settlements' occurred in occupied Austria when socialist and anti-socialist elite camps agreed in 1946–1947 to establish and adhere to a Proporz system for policymaking to prevent deadly interwar conflicts from recurring; in post-Franco Spain when franquist and anti-franquist elite camps acceded to accommodations engineered by Adolpho Suarez during 1977–1978; in Poland and Hungary when leaders of state socialist and anti-socialist camps negotiated extensive roundtable agreements in 1989; and in Slovenia when a 100 state socialist and anti-socialist leaders negotiated a similar agreement upon becoming independent of Yugoslavia in 1990–1991 (Higley & Burton, 2006, pp. 55–106).

Beyond the two foregoing origins of elite trust, a less explicit origin unfolded in the political circumstances of several Western countries when they reached relatively high levels of industrialisation. In them, already partially trusting elites became more fully trusting by absorbing socialist and other dissident factions when electoral pressures led dissidents to tone down proposals for radical social change. Before World War II, elites in Denmark and Norway were the only ones to achieve substantial trust in this way, albeit there were aspects of trust in both elites during the nineteenth century (Gulbrandsen, 2019, pp. 4–5). During the twentieth century's second half, elites in Belgium, Finland, France, Greece, Ireland, Italy, Portugal and West Germany, along with elites in the Czech Republic and Slovakia after 1993, underwent this process and stabilised political institutions that had previously been unstable or totalitarian (Higley & Burton, 2006, pp. 139–180).

In Western history, the creation of elite trust and institutional stability made it possible, though it didn't guarantee, that a voice in government would eventually be spread by suffrage expansions to large segments of populations. The expansions happened gradually and made it possible to speak of 'democracy' without wondering if the term's users were kidding themselves. As this history indicates, elite theory is compatible with something that most relatively well-off and secure people in Western societies have regarded as a satisfactory form of democracy. But that isn't what 'democracy' means theoretically, which is an arrangement in which all or most citizens have equal and decisive political influence. Because elite theory highlights how elites collaborate to muffle explosive issues that gain public attention, it is regarded with distaste by adherents of democracy. Yet, if one looks at the matter closely, it will be clear that this is how stable democracies actually work.

Elite theory embodies this realism, focussing not only on elections but also how such things as restricted, demanding recruitment processes and behind-the-scenes networks of acquaintance and friendship help elites perform essential political functions if they are going to be performed at all. Yet, factual questions that might logically arise in the mind of a visitor from Mars, such as what makes democracy possible and is it a form of political organisation that can be transferred readily from place to place haven't been asked for a long time. Elites in most countries outside the West are not now and have never been mutually trusting. Consequently, efforts to spread stable democracy around the world have been frustrated by the fact that the essential elite prerequisite is usually not present.

Where elites are accustomed to bitter political conflict along lines of 'Grab what you can – never mind the other person', introducing democratic suffrage and competing political parties soon leads to serious disturbances. Various elite persons fear what these aspects of democracy portend. They assume that other elite persons will employ them to take advantage of innocent voters and gain the upper hand. More broadly, people in propertied upper and middle classes fear expropriation by putative democratic regimes. When crises arise, therefore, seizures of executive power by the military or entrenched civilian groups controlling the military are likely, because no serious degree of democratic government has been implanted. It couldn't be implanted unless elites trust each other to deliberately mitigate power struggles so that most influential, often privileged persons and groups feel safe.

How likely is it that elite trust and stable institutions will persist in the advanced post-industrial circumstances of Western democracies? Will it be easier or harder for elites to perform the function of continuous political pacification they require? Because insecurity, rooted in basic problems of work exacerbated by large influxes of culturally alien refugees, asylum-seekers and economic migrants loom large, one can't be sanguine. Insecurity is giving rise to much unhappiness, unrest and distrust of constituted authority. Its exploitation by populists threatens to erode elite trust, stable democracy's *sine qua non*.

INSECURITY

Starting during the 1970s and becoming quite apparent after the cold war ended, post-industrial Anglo-American and European societies have encountered growing structural problems that elites may be unable to contain or manage. In degrees that vary from one society to another, the problems arise, most fundamentally, from a structure of work that fails to provide for the useful employment of all persons who cannot, unlike the very young and very old, be treated as freely entitled to community support. Because the bulk of work has become organisationally and technologically sophisticated, culturally or economically disadvantaged persons and groups – rural dwellers; persons and groups discriminated against on racial, ethno-religious, gender or other grounds; refugees, asylum-seekers and economic migrants from war-torn or failing states outside the West – cannot obtain more than precarious and poorly paid employment. They tend to become endemically idle and dependent upon grudging community support or the takings of criminal actions.

The most distinctive characteristic of post-industrial work forces is the pre-
ponderance of bureaucratic and service ('white-collar') personnel (Bell, 1973,
pp. 123–164). When the US and UK crossed the threshold to post-industrialism
during the late 1940s, when Canada, Sweden and the Netherlands did so in the early
1950s and when Australia, Austria, Belgium, Denmark, France, New Zealand,
Norway, Switzerland and West Germany acquired a post-industrial configuration
in the early 1960s, white-collar personnel accounted for 40% of their work forces,
a proportion that doubled during ensuing decades (Field & Higley, 1980/2013,
pp. 23–25). The initial post-industrial experience was an unexpected general afflu-
ence resulting from increased levels of real income for families headed by steadily
employed, usually male, wage and salary earners. Families in lower occupational
and income categories found themselves with hours, days, even weeks of leisure and
enough money to get some satisfaction from it. As was the case for rich persons and
families historically, leisure diversions became important parts of life, which for the
bulk of adults and dependents was no longer a matter of ceaseless work.

As a result of organisational and technological advances, however, work became
steadily more complex and intellectually demanding. It increasingly required substantial training and some comprehension of the interdependence of work tasks.
Dwindling numbers of farmers and artisans became in many cases educated, prosperous owners of capital-intensive, organisationally and technologically complex
farms and businesses. Trends during the twentieth century's final quarter indicated that work was also becoming less secure. Men with secondary educations
who had, during the 1950s and 1960s, elected to work in manufacturing plants,
confident they could do as well as or better than, university-bound men, began
to suffer layoffs. Many of those armed with university degrees and working their
ways up the career ladders of large business corporations and financial firms began
to be victims of downsizing, out-sourcing or corporate mergers. Unemployment
and underemployment, which had been mitigated during the 1950s and 1960s
by increased access to post-secondary education and by millions of military and
defence industry jobs in response to the Cold War, became more of a problem.
What elites and people in general could not readily grasp was that many good jobs
that had supported a middle-class lifestyle on one income were disappearing.

First noticeable during the second half of the 1970s and dramatised by widespread 'stagflation' (low growth and high inflation) insecurity became more widespread during subsequent decades. Computers increasingly performed much
routine work that had earlier required human decisions and actions, and the
application of computers to ever more complex tasks proceeded apace. With
increasing frequency, profit-maximising business executives shifted manufacturing operations to plants and retail outlets utilising robots and other automated
machines. Since the 1990s, high-speed computers, the internet and an array of
mobile devices for instant communication have accomplished thousands of work
tasks that previously took much time and effort. A globalisation of labour markets has accompanied these developments, with corporations roaming the world
in search of cheap labour. The overall effect is to make full-time employment
increasingly precarious, for there appear to be few job categories that cannot
be eliminated by introducing automated processes, streamlining organisational

structures or relocating them to cheaper labour markets inside or outside Western countries. In these ways, the structure of work in advanced poste-industrial conditions has come to pose threats to humane, orderly and tranquil societies.

There is a plenitude of data documenting steadily declining post-industrial needs for many kinds of work. Between the early 1950s and 2016 in the US, for example, the participation of working-age men in the officially defined work force dropped by 18 percentage points, and the proportion of men aged twenty and older without paid work more than doubled from 14% to about 32% (Eberstadt, 2016, p. 17 and 20). In terms of working-age male participation in its work force, by 2015 the US ranked 22nd among the OECD's 23 original member countries; only Italy ranked lower (Eberstadt, 2016, p. 51). Between 1980 and 2016, the work force participation rate of US men in the prime working ages of 25–54 dropped 6 percentage points, and in 'full employment' conditions during 2017 and the first 10 months of 2018 it declined a further 0.4 points, while 'hidden unemployment' remained above 7% (*New York Times*, 3 November 2018). During 2018 and the first quarter of 2019, 7 million prime working-age men were outside the US work force. Data compiled and adjusted by the OECD to facilitate comparison of the US, Canada, France, Germany, Spain, Sweden and the UK, showed that participation rates for men in prime working ages declined in all seven countries between 1975 and 2013, with the steepest decline in the US and declines of 3 or 4 percentage points in the other six countries (Maximilliano & Shell, 2015, Panel B). Canada, which lost 400,000 jobs in the economic crisis of 2008–2009, currently has a participation rate of prime working-age men only slightly above the US rate.

In the European Union during 2016, 10.4% of the population aged 0–59 lived in 'very low work intensity households', in which the adults worked less than 20% of their 'total work potential', with the highest proportions in Ireland, Greece, Spain, Belgium and Croatia and the lowest in Estonia, Poland and Slovakia. The proportions of Scandinavian populations living in such households during 2016 were 10.6% of Danes, 8.5% of Swedes and 7.7% of Norwegians. Between 2008 and 2016, the proportion of populations in very low work intensity households increased in 18 EU member states and decreased in only seven (Eurostat news release 155, 16 October 2017).

For many years, elites and observers paid little attention to declining male participation in Western work forces because women were entering work forces in large numbers. Starting in the late 1990s, however, tertiary education enrolments began to level off, entrances of women slowed and significant numbers of women began to be pushed out of jobs. Between 2001 and 2016, for example, a half million jobs in the US retail sector, many of them held by women, were eliminated. Until the mid-1990s, the US had one of the highest female work force participation rates; by 2015 it had one of the lowest (Maximilliano & Shell, 2015, Panel B).

During the present century's first two decades, rapidly growing numbers of temporary 'contract' and part-time workers have tended to conceal declining work force participation rates, especially among men. Twenty per cent of all US workers are now contracted to work on a specific project or for a fixed period of time, half of them without health care and retirement benefits and half earning incomes that vary from month to month or seasonally (Noguchi, 2018). In

Canada, temporary workers account for 13.5% of the work force and part-time workers another 19.6% (Sunit & Thirgood, 2015). By 2020, in the US, between a third and two fifths of the work force will consist of freelance and temporary workers, day labourers, contract workers and others performing insecure on-demand and 'gig economy' jobs (MBO Partners, 2015). In Europe, about a third of the work force is now in what are politely termed 'alternative employment arrangements' that depend upon fluctuating demand for goods and services and don't carry the same levels of health care, retirement and unemployment benefits that traditional jobs carry. The European Commission reported in early 2018 that about 40% of EU citizens are part of the 'irregular labor market', which includes the self-employed and those on part-time contracts (*Financial Times*, 14 March 2018). Like their North American counterparts, European work forces contain a 'contractor class' of workers recruited by, and beholden to, commercial labour agencies instead of employers directly (*New York Times*, 19 November 2017).

It is clear, in sum, that sizable numbers of men and women in the leading Western democracies have lost or are losing the ability to claim incomes and social statuses on grounds that the work they do is necessary to economic and soci-etal functioning. It is not that work, especially highly educated and technologi-cally sophisticated work, is dispensable in productive and distributive functions; rather, given the rapid proliferation of goods and services involving automated processes, out-sourcing and often cut-throat 'gig' employment, the need for work serves poorly to justify claims to jobs and related social statuses unless persons have some special skill or knowledge that happens to be in short supply.

An important consequence is demoralisation – loss of individual morale and loss of respect for established social norms – in sizable parts of middle- and working-classes and, more dramatically and sometimes violently, in unemployed or only intermittently employed under-classes, most of whose members are, in effect, surplus to advanced post-industrial needs for work. 'Diseases of despair' – alcoholism, narcotics addiction, opioids and suicide – manifest this demoralisa-tion (Case & Deacon, 2017). In the US, for example, about 20% of the decline in men's work force participation from 1999 to 2015 and 25% of the decline in women's participation is believed to have resulted from recourse to opioids. In 2015 alone, a million Americans of prime working ages were outside the work force because of opioid addictions (*Washington Post*, 27 March 2017). In the US, during 2017, an estimated 72,000 persons died from opioid overdoses, a number that exceeded deaths from car crashes, HIV and guns combined (*New York Times*, 18 August 2018).

POPULISTS

Explanations of contemporary populism tend to have a 'bottom-up' charac-ter. For example, Ronald Inglehart and Pippa Norris (2016, see also Norris & Inglehart 2019) explore mutually reinforcing explanations that emphasise (a) increasing economic and income inequalities in Western populations contrib-uting to feelings of insecurity and vulnerability and (b) cultural backlashes, mainly among older persons 'seeking a bulwark against long-term [post-materialist] processes of value change', made all the more disconcerting by rising numbers of alien immigrants (pp. 11–14). Inglehart and Norris (2016) conclude,

> The rise of populist parties reflects, above all, a reaction against a wide range of rapid cultural changes that seem to be eroding the basic values and customs of Western societies. (p. 30)

However, 'bottom-up' explanations of populism like those pursued by Inglehart and Norris need to be supplemented with 'top-down' ones. Specifically, more attention should be paid to individual populists who act as pied pipers offering delusive enticements, making irresponsible promises and exhibiting disdain for rule of law. They harp on a quartet of evils: victimisation of 'the people'; villainous 'elites'; a scourge of 'others'; and malign external forces. The success of populist parties and movements depends more heavily on the charisma and often unprincipled behaviour of populist pied pipers than bottom-up explanations recognise.

These populists benefit from two immediate circumstances. The first is heightened employment insecurity resulting from the 2008–2009 Financial Crisis and ensuing economic malaise. Double-digit rates of unemployment and underemployment prevailed in most Western countries for upwards of a decade after 2008–2009 and still prevail in southern Europe, where a third of working-age persons 25 years and under are unemployed and the overall jobless rate hovers around 11% (*New York Times*, 27 February 2018). The second circumstance is sudden arrivals of culturally alien migrants fleeing violence and joblessness in non-Western countries and regions. During 2014–2016, some 2.5 million refugees, asylum-seekers and economic migrants entered EU countries (plus Norway and Switzerland), and an additional 160,000 entered during 2017. In the US, where 11 million undocumented migrants already resided, 409,000 were apprehended at or near the southwestern land border during 2016. Possibly as a consequence of the newly installed Trump administration's harsh anti-immigrant threats, US apprehensions dropped to a 40-year low during 2017, but they returned to pre-Trump magnitudes of 40–50,000 per month during 2018 and up to 146,000 a month during 2019's first half. Canada, buffered by the US, experiences comparatively little illegal migration. Yet, in June 2018, Doug Ford was elected Premier of Ontario, the most important province, by stoking fears of crimes and terrorist acts by illegal migrants. Surrounded by forbidding seas, Australia and New Zealand experience only small numbers of illegal migrants, and those whom Australia apprehends at sea have been sent to harsh detention camps on remote Pacific islands.

To win the US presidency in November 2016, Donald Trump exploited employment insecurity and illegal migration from Mexico. He promised to create millions of well-paying and secure jobs by giving corporations and business owners huge tax cuts, levying stiff tariffs on steel, aluminium and other imports, withdrawing the US from 'unfair' trade accords and rescinding environmental regulations said to inhibit job creation. Claiming that large numbers of Mexican 'criminals', 'rapists' and 'terrorists' were entering the country, he vowed to force Mexico to pay for a 'beautiful wall' he would build along the 1,950-mile southwestern land border.

Trump's behaviour and actions are well known and cataloguing them would be superfluous. Let it suffice to emphasise two aspects of his rise and presidency. First, Trump engages in a 'pluto-populism' that diverts attention from gross income and wealth disparities. His endlessly repeated promise to 'Make America Great Again' is best seen as a subterfuge that leaves plutocracy unmentioned and untouched. Manifesting pluto-populism, Trump's initial 15 cabinet appointees were estimated to be collectively worth at least $35 billion in personal wealth (*New York Times*, 4 April 2017) and Trump's refusal to release tax returns that would reveal his personal wealth and shed light on how he obtained it was another manifestation. Second, Trump is a quintessential pied piper who persuades millions of devoted followers (his fabled 'base') to believe they are the victims of nefarious elites. In classic piper mode, Trump shouted to a large audience at one political rally during 2018 'Ah, the elite, the elite! Did you ever see the elite? [loud boos] YOU are the elite!'

In Britain during 2015 and the first half of 2016, the populist anti-EU and anti-immigrant Independence Party, led by firebrand Nigel Farage, along with a populist-nationalist faction in the Conservative Party elite sought to persuade residents of economically ravaged cities and towns that EU membership was the root cause of their insecurity and the 10% fall in average real wages between 2007 and 2015. Arrivals of 1.5 million workers from Poland and other eastern EU countries under the Union's free labour movement provision were denounced, and the spectre of millions of Muslims coming to Britain via the EU was disseminated. The solution was to 'Take back control!' by exiting the EU. Elites who favoured remaining in the EU forecast economic calamity if a 'Brexit' occurred, and they characterised visions of a bountiful future outside the EU as fantasies and unscrupulous deceptions. Since the June 2016 referendum, which went narrowly against continued EU membership, fighting between pro- and anti-Brexit elite camps has been unremitting, elite relations have become 'febrile and unpredictable' (Menon, 2017, p. 126) and adherence to the centuries-long practice of political restraint has been hard to discern.

Contrary to the populist–nationalist elite prospectus, leaving the EU proved hideously difficult. Twenty months of negotiations between Theresa May's Conservative government and the EU Commission produced a 580-page draft exit agreement that satisfied no one and was decisively rejected three times in a deadlocked House of Commons during early 2019. The House defeats forced May to solicit Labour Party support for her agreement, an unusual move that came to naught. The date for Brexit had to be postponed from the original 29 March until 31 October, that is, Halloween, prompting sardonic quips that it would then be 'trick or treat'. With cabinet and ministerial resignations exceeding 30 and Conservative discipline in the House evaporating, the May government reluctantly scheduled participation in European Parliamentary elections, in which Nigel Farage and his new Brexit Party planned to compete. The likelihood of a second Brexit referendum, even more divisive than the first, increased.

Because of strong trade unions, multi-party systems with well-established major parties, extensive welfare states and shorter experiences of post-industrial conditions, employment insecurity has not been as fruitful an issue for populists to exploit in countries on the continent. Continental populists feed primarily on hostilities towards culturally alien refugees, asylum-seekers and economic migrants, on desires to have them repatriated and on fears of new migrant waves. Assorted populist parties and movements are classified as authoritarian, anti-democratic, liberal, illiberal, nativist, nationalist, neo-fascist and radical–rightist (Marguilies, 2018; Norris & Inglehart 2019; Pappas, 2016). As these distinctions suggest, populists on the continent are a conglomeration and their political importance varies significantly across the EU countries (counting Ireland, plus Norway and Switzerland).

Populists are prominent political figures in a number of countries: Geert Wilders, founder of the Party of Freedom in the Netherlands; Matteo Salvini, leader of The League in Italy; Marine Le Pen at the head of National Rally (formerly National Front) in France; Jimmie Akesson, the Sweden Democrats' leader since 2010; Albert Rösti, leader of the Swiss People's Party, which is the largest in the Federal Assembly; Kristian Thulesen – Pia Kjaersgaard's successor – atop the Danish People's Party; Heinz-Christian Strache, leader of Austria's Freedom Party; and on the left, Beppe Grillo, the guiding spirit of Italy's Five Star Movement and Jean-Luc Mélanchon, the founder and leader of Un-Submissive France. Elsewhere, however, populist figures sit precariously astride tumultuous parties and movements: Alexander Gauland and Alice Weidel, the clashing co-chairs of Alternative for Germany (AfD); Lutz Bachman, who comes and goes as leader of the Dresden-based Pegida movement; Luigi Di Maio, who leads Italy's combustible Five Star Movement as a stand-in for Beppe Grillo.

In post-communist East European countries, several populists wield government executive power: Viktor Orbán, Hungary's prime minister; Jaroslaw Kaczynski, who controls Poland's ruling Law and Justice Party from behind the scenes; Milos Zeman and billionaire Andrej Babis, the Czech Republic's president and prime minister, respectively. East European populists stoke political divisions less between left and right than between right and wrong (Sierakowski, 2018), they parade as staunch defenders of national identities and Christian traditions and they depict opponents as unpatriotic and irreligious.

Populist leaders are less conspicuous in other EU states. In decentralised Spain, where 23% of persons 20–34 years of age are not in work, education or training and 27% of all jobs are temporary, no populist other than one or two Catalonians is prominent. Leaders of Podemos ('We Can') are mildly populist, while those of Ciudadanos (Citizens) are principally concerned to oppose Catalan nationalism. Santiago Abascal, leader of the ultra-nationalist Vox party, which won a modest 10% of the vote in April 2019 parliamentary elections, has yet to gain much of a following outside Andalusia. In Portugal, which also suffers from low employment of working-age young people, no prominent populist has emerged. The same is true in Ireland, where three well-established parties dominate the political arena. In Norway, the populist thrust of Progressive Party leaders is tempered by holding important ministerial positions in a centre–right coalition government. In Finland, the populist True Finns joined a government coalition in 2015, but their support for a third Eurozone bailout for Greece triggered so much infighting that The Finns, as they now call themselves, lost political ground until successfully mobilising rural voters against climate change measures in April 2019 parliamentary elections. In Australia, a populist, Pauline Hanson, leads the anti-Asian immigrant One Nation Party and wins sizable numbers of votes, but her party is based in Queensland and Australia's three main party elites collaborate, tacitly but effectively, to keep Hanson on the political fringe. In New Zealand there is no significant populist leader or party, although Winston Peters, an established politician of mixed Maori-Scots ancestry, sometimes sounds like a populist. In Canada, as noted, the only conspicuous populist to date is Ontario's Doug Ford.

Other than in the US, Italy, Hungary, Poland and the Czech Republic, Western electorates have not vested populists with full executive power, and in Italy it is shared, uneasily, by Five Star and League populists. It is worth recalling that in Hungary, Viktor Orbán didn't pose as a populist when he first became prime minister and only later exploited anti-migrant fears to fend off Jobbik, a virulently far-right populist party. In Poland, Jaroslaw Kaczynski doesn't hold formal executive office, and his Law and Justice Party consistently loses elections in urban areas. In Prague, Milos Zeman occupies the presidency, but it is not a powerful office constitutionally, and billionaire Andrej Babis, who purports to be a populist, is unable to form a government commanding a majority in parliament. Elsewhere, populists and their parties score well in elections, but in mid-2019, only those heading Norway's Progressive Party, and the Swiss People's Party held significant amounts of executive power.

Overall, insecurity and demoralisation produced by the disappearance of many kinds of jobs and influxes of alien migrants are explosive issues populist figures enflame. They harness patriotic sentiments and racial–religious identities while portraying competitors as immoral and corrupt 'elites' (Müller, 2016, p. 3). They couch electoral contests in winner-take-all terms and proclaim they alone can prevent national decline. Their operational code is more nearly 'politics as war' than 'politics as bargaining'.

CONCLUSIONS

The question is the effects populist figures have on elite trust. There's little doubt they make cooperative elite management of volatile issues more difficult because they resist bargains and compromises. Trump is a good example. After three times agreeing in January 2018 to budget compromises offered by the Senate Democratic leader to avoid a federal government shutdown, Trump suddenly reneged, prompting the leader to liken negotiating with him to 'negotiating with Jell-O'. In Britain, hard-line Brexiteers declare they will accept only a 'no-deal' exit from the EU, an uncompromising stance that deadlocks the House of Commons. Geert Wilders in the Netherlands, Marine Le Pen in France, AfD leaders in Germany and leaders of the Sweden Democrats are similarly obstinate. Where, on the other hand, populist leaders participate in or informally support coalition governments, as in Norway, Denmark and Switzerland, obstinacy is diluted by the complexities and responsibilities of governing. It remains to be seen if Italy's perilous economic situation will induce moderation in the polar opposite populists leading its government.

Populists throw wrenches into party systems. In the US, Bernie Sanders' quasi-populist 'Feel the Bern!' 2016 primary election campaign against Hillary Clinton weakened her presidential candidacy and helped open the way to a previously unthinkable Trump presidency. In Britain, the Brexit referendum deepened Conservative Party divisions, eviscerated the Liberal Party and helped radicalise the Labour Party. In the Netherlands, Prime Minister Mark Rutte was forced by Geert Wilders and his Party of Freedom to move markedly rightward to eke out a small plurality of seats in 2017 elections. In France's 2017 presidential election contest, efforts to prevent Marine Le Pen from capturing the Eleysée Palace all but destroyed the existing party system. In Germany's 2017 parliamentary elections, AfD weakened the Social Democrats and became the most extreme right-wing party ever to sit in the Bundestag, with footholds in all 16 state parliaments. This left Germany without an effective government for six months until the previous Christian Democrat-Christian Social-Social Democrat 'grand coalition' was reluctantly reconstituted. In Italy, attacks on established parties by populists produced a hung parliament in March 2018 elections and led to four months of political contortions before a schizophrenic government of extreme right- and left-wing populists could be formed. Similar contortions followed the Sweden Democrats' capture of 17.5% of the vote in September 2018 parliamentary elections, and it took five months to circumvent a resulting standoff between mainstream centre–left and centre–right party coalitions, neither of which commanded a parliamentary majority.

The contempt populist pied pipers voice for elites debases elite discourse. Occupying the powerful US presidency, Donald Trump demeans 'elites' as being responsible for the country's ills. In return, many elites pillory Trump and his administration as a mixture of malevolence and incompetence. In Britain, Brexiteer elites and media label anti-Brexit political leaders 'traitors'. In these and other Western countries, contempt and mud-slinging can metastasize into distrust, with institutions long seen as politically neutral coming to be viewed as overtly partisan. Populist intransigence corrodes the workings of parliamentary and presidential systems of representative democracy. The forms of direct democracy populists celebrate are at odds with the principle of parliamentary sovereignty in the former and the constitutional separation of co-equal executive and legislative powers in the latter. Referendums and plebiscites favoured by populists juxtapose parliamentary sovereignty against 'the people's will'. As in the Brexit struggle, if a governing party is deeply divided between populists and moderates, parliamentary havoc results. In presidential systems, populist presidents like Trump, who claim to act on behalf of 'the people', stretch the boundaries of executive power, and efforts to maintain or restore balance lead to legislative-executive confrontations and crises. Populists help make both parliamentary and presidential forms of representative democracy dysfunctional.

In a longer perspective, it may not be altogether wishful to regard populists as antidotes to the elite myopia and fragile social orders that most post-industrial Western democracies have increasingly experienced since the 1970s (Higley, 2016). Populists force elites to think hard about where their democracies are headed and avoid referendums, unrestricted party primary elections, permissive campaign finance laws and other processes that advantage populists.

Similarly, because populists thrive on often deliberately false and malicious social media messages, they edge elites towards limiting what is allowed on social media platforms. By exploiting employment insecurity for political gain, populists push elites to create large numbers of decent and secure jobs to accomplish things that are at present not accomplished or are accomplished inadequately. These include jobs in the area of ecological and environmental safeguards to slow the effects of climate change and conserve scarce resources as well as human service jobs to better care for the elderly, the physically impaired and others who are handicapped. By profiting politically from hostility towards culturally alien migrants, populists force elites to cordon Western countries off in morally agonising and deeply contentious ways while pondering multiculturalism's political limits. Most fundamentally, by violating norms of elite trust and political restraint, populists serve as clarion calls for elites to preserve these prerequisites of stable democracy.

REFERENCES

Best, H., & Higley, J. (Eds.). (2018). *The Palgrave handbook of political elites*. London: Palgrave Macmillan.

Bell, D. (1973). *The coming of post-industrial society*. New York, NY: Basic Books.

Case, A., & Deacon, A. (2017). *Mortality and morbidity in the 21st century*. Washington DC: Brookings Panel on Economic Activity (23–24 March).

Dahl, R. A. (1971). *Polyarchy*. New Haven, CT: Yale University Press.

Eberstadt, N. (2016). *Men without work. America's invisible crisis*. West Conshohocken, PA: Templeton.

Eurostat news release. (2017). Downward trend in the share of persons at risk of poverty or social exclusion in the EU. No. 155/2017.

Field, G. L., & Higley, J. (1980). *Elitism*. London: Routledge & Kegan Paul (Re-issued by Routledge in 2013).

Gulbrandsen, T. (2019). *Elites in an egalitarian society*. London: Palgrave Macmillan.

Higley, J. (2016). *The endangered west. Myopic elites and fragile social orders in a threatening world*. New York, NY: Routledge.

Higley, J., & Burton, M. (2006). *Elite foundations of liberal democracy*. Lanham, MD: Rowman and Littlefield.

Inglehart, M., & Norris, P. (2016). *Trump, Brexit, and the rise of populism: Economic have-nots and cultural backlash*. John F. Kennedy School of Government Faculty Research Working Paper, Series RWP16-026, Boston: Harvard University.

Levitsky, S., & Ziblatt, D. (2018). *How democracies die*. New York, NY: Crown.

MBO Partners. (2015). *The new American workforce*. Herndon, VA: MBO Partners.

Marguilies, B. (2018). Nativists are populists, not Liberals. *Journal of Democracy, 29*(1), 141–147.

Maximilliano, A. D., & Shell, H. (2015). A cross-country comparison of labor force participation. *St. Louis Federal Reserve Bank Newsletter*, No. 17 (July).

Menon, A. (2017). Why the British chose Brexit. *Foreign Affairs, 96*(6), 122–126.

Müller, J.-W. (2016). *What is populism?* Philadelphia, PA: University of Pennsylvania Press.

Noguchi, Y. (2018). Rise of the contract worker: Work is different now. *National Public Radio Marist Poll* (pp. 1–2), 22 January 2018.

Norris, P., & Inglehart, R. (2019). *Cultural Backlash. Trump, Brexit, and Authoritarian Populism*. New York, NY: Cambridge.

Pappas, T. (2016). The specter haunting Europe: distinguishing liberal democracy's challengers. *Journal of Democracy, 27*(4), 22–36.

Sierakowski, S. (2018, January). How eastern European populism is different. *Project Syndicate, 31*. Retrieved from http://prosyn.org/5740Op1q

Sunit, J., & Thirgood, J. (2015). *Working without a net*. Toronto, Canada: Mowat Center.

THE POPULIST ELITE PARADOX: USING ELITE THEORY TO ELUCIDATE THE SHAPES AND STAKES OF POPULIST ELITE CRITIQUES

Marte Mangset, Fredrik Engelstad, Mari Teigen and Trygve Gulbrandsen

ABSTRACT

Critiques of elites define populism, which conceives of power relations as a unified, conspiring elite exploiting the good people. Yet, populism itself is inherently elitist, calling for a strong leader to take power and channel the will of the people. Elite theory, surprisingly overlooked in scholarship on populism, can clarify this apparent paradox and elucidate the dimensions of populism and its risk of authoritarianism in new ways. In contrast to populist ideological conceptions of power relations in society, elite theory points to the possibility that several elites with diverging voices and interests exist. Furthermore, elite theorists argue that such elite pluralism is a necessary component of a well-functioning democracy. Much scholarship on populism, often aiming to understand its causes and focussing on Western Europe and North America, points to the similarities of populist movements. The focus on similarities strengthens the understanding of populism as a uniform phenomenon and populist elite critiques as homogeneous. However, broader comparative studies show that different populist movements target a range of various elite groups. Indeed, the empirical reality of populist elite critiques targeting diverse elite groups is more in line with elite theory than populist ideological

Elites and People: Challenges to Democracy
Comparative Social Research, Volume 34, 203–222
ISSN: 0195-6310/doi:10.1108/S0195-631020190000034010

conceptions of power relations in society. A key to grasping the democratic challenges posed by the power relations between elites and masses in both populist critiques and populist solutions is an understanding of the institutional conditions for elite integration versus elite pluralism. This central discussion in both classical and modern elite theory is applied to analyse populism in this contribution.

Keywords: anti-elitism; authoritarianism; democracy; elite pluralism; elite theory; populism

THE POPULIST ELITE PARADOX

The current rise of populism across the world has revived classical questions about power relations between the elites and masses and the related democratic challenges. Populism, on one hand, is a salient response to the unequal distribution of power and privilege, but on the other hand, populism has its own problematic understandings of the relationship between the people and elites. How does populist ideology conceptualise these power relations, and in what way are these conceptualisations democratically challenging?

Critiques of elites define populism, which conceives of power relations as a group of conspiring elite exploiting the good people. However, populism is also inherently elitist, calling for a strong leader to take power and channel the will of the people. The understanding of the wicked elite as a homogeneous, united group with common interests is bearer of elitism in a very specific manner. So does the populist understanding of a more adequate leadership as a leader who, freed from intermediate elites and institutional obstacles, voices and promotes the people's interests. Elite theory, surprisingly overlooked in scholarship on populism, can clarify the apparent paradox of populist elitism and elucidate the dimensions of populism and its risks of authoritarianism in new ways.

In contrast to the ideal–typical populist conception of power relations in society, elite theory points to the possible plurality of elites: elites at different hierarchical levels of power and elites in different sectors of society – with possibly diverging interests. Furthermore, in contrast to the populist concept of a political leader with an adequate relationship with the people, elite theory argues that a certain degree of separation between different elite groups is necessary for a well-functioning democracy (Aron, 1950). This chapter explores the opposition between populist ideological understandings of elites and elite theory's conceptualisations of elites and their relations with the people in order to shed new light on populism.

However, to grasp populist perceptions of the relationship between the elites and masses, we must look beyond its ideal–typical ideological conceptualisations and explore the more composite empirical reality. Much empirical scholarship on populist movements, often aiming at understanding its causes and focussing on Western Europe and North America, points to their similarities. In particular, several scholars stress the strength of the cultural thesis (in which anti-immigrant voters criticise the liberal political elites) over the economic and institutional theses in explaining the rise of populism. These studies reinforce the understanding of populism as uniform, voicing a homogeneous elite critique. However, broader comparative studies show that different populist movements target a range of elite groups. West European and North American populists attack cultural and political elites for being too liberal, Eastern and Southern European populists criticise their political elites for being corrupt, and South American populists direct anger towards economic elites. Moreover, populist movements often attack different intermediate elites, such as the leaders of political parties, central banks, employer organisations and unions. Broad, comparative approaches uncover the empirical reality of populist elite critiques targeting diverse elite groups. These critiques are more in line with elite theory's conceptualisations of elite pluralism than populist ideologies' conceptualisations of power relations in society.

The key to understanding the democratic challenges of the power relations between the elites and masses in populist critiques and populist solutions is the question of degrees of elite pluralism and elite integration, a question much debated in elite theory. The populist ideological perception of the elite as uniform and conspiring should be taken seriously in the sense that it should be object of empirical scrutiny. Elite theory contributes analytical tools to scholarship on populism that can be fruitfully used to investigate descriptively whether elites are integrated and homogeneous and to discuss normatively how such unity may represent a challenge to democracy. In this chapter, elite theory and new combinations of existing research on populism are used to discuss theoretically the relationship between the degrees of elite pluralism, institutional conditions for such pluralism and elitist character of populism.

Our discussion on populist ideologies' conceptualisations of power relations and politics draws on empirical and theoretical scholarship on populism, and we construct an ideal–typical model of populist ideologies based on this scholarship. The model might not be accurate for all versions of populist ideologies, but it incorporates key features found in the various definitions and versions of populism and serves as an analytical tool for discussing other conceptualisations of elite–mass relationships. We consider these ideological conceptualisations to be narratives on which populist leaders often draw when mobilising voters and followers.

We further compare these populist ideological conceptualisations to elite theoretical conceptualisations of elite–mass relationships initially developed by elite theorists with more descriptive, analytical goals. However, the analytical tools in elite theory are thought to also provide a more informed point of departure for making a normative assessment of elite–mass relationships. Although these two types of conceptualisations have somewhat different statuses, they can be fruitfully discussed in relation to each other. They are both intended to describe the power relations between the elites and masses in ways that enable normative assessment of those relations. We lay out these two types of conceptualisations.

ANTI-ELITISM AS THE DEFINING FEATURE OF POPULISM

Among the numerous approaches and definitions of populism, a basic set of criteria has gained agreement from most scholars: Margaret Canovan's (1981,

p. 294, 1999) minimalist definition that all populist ideologies express anti-elitism and in some way exalt the people, whatever that term may refer to. An elite critique is always part of the definition whether one sees populism as a class-based movement related to large-scale societal transformation, a response to economic grievances and political institutional failures such as corruption or a specific set of ideas about society and how politics work (Silva, 2017, pp. 11–17). Those who focus on the political dimension of populism, perceiving it as a discourse (Laclau, 2005), political style (Knight, 1998), thin-centred ideology (Mudde, 2004) or a form of mobilisation (Meny & Surel, 2001), all incorporate a fundamental opposition between the good people (the majority) and the wicked elite (the minority; Silva, 2017, p. 12). Populism is anti-elite.

Central to the definition of populism is the homogeneity of the people who are good and have a common general will and set of values, interests and desires (Mudde, 2004; Taggart, 2000). It, therefore, follows that there is no room for disagreement or fundamental differences within the people (Silva, 2017, pp. 14–15). Populism, thus, clearly opposes pluralism and the idea of democracy as a space where diverging interests can be debated and decided. Populist ideologies conceiving of the people as homogeneous and good in this specific manner also need the other half of this complementary Manichean whole: the wicked elite minority who exploits the people. The people are the underdog in the power relations, and the goal of the populist movement is to reverse those relations. Populist ideologies present the exploitation by the elite as motivated by the wish to protect the special interests of this minority group considered to be illegitimate and opposed to the people's general will. The elite is perceived as a homogeneous entity, united in the interest of exploiting the people.

POPULISM AS ELITISM

To develop into a broad movement, populism depends on the formation of its own leadership – its own elite. The question is *how* this elite should be shaped and how the power relations between the leader and the movement are conceptualised. Although it might seem paradoxical, populist conceptions of this relationship can be described as *particularly* elitist in a multifaceted way. First, populist movements generally favour strong leaders. When thinking of empirical examples of strands of populism, we generally associate populist movements with strong, charismatic leaders, such as Geert Wilders in the Netherlands, Vladimir Putin in Russia and Jean-Luc Mélenchon in France. Mudde (2004) argues that a charismatic leader does not define populist movements, but that the choice of such a leader generally follows from the defining element of a leader who interprets and expresses the people's general will without debating or confronting their interests and ideas.

Second, an element defining populism and underpinning its elitism is the idea of a direct connection between the people and a leader. Leaders of populist movements should not educate or try to change the people but rather should express their desires and will. Populist leaders should forge policy that directly expresses that will (Canovan, 1999; Kazin, 1998; Mudde, 2004; Silva, 2017). The idea of the people as a homogeneous entity with a common general will is central to populism's conceptualisation of its own leadership. The single person who takes on the leadership role in a populist movement should be able to interpret and appropriately articulate the people's desires and will. The leader should not demonstrate independent or creative leadership but simply embody and transmit the people's general will.

Although this leadership style can be interpreted as anti-elitist and very democratic and is often presented as such by populist leaders, this direct relationship between the electorate and its leader does open to a particular form of elitism. Populist ideologies argue that to be able to channel the people's will, the leader should be free from institutional constrains and interfering intermediate elites thought to be prone to promote their own interests rather than the people's interests. This conceptualisation of adequate policy leadership as based on a direct connection between the people and the leader unmediated by interfering or obstructing elites is itself elitist. It allows for a concentration of power in the hands of the leader and a very narrow elite, freed from possible counter-elites. A feature of populist ideologies and their conceptualisations of legitimate power relations between the leader and the people thus are the dismissal of intermediate elites and a plurality of elites as illegitimate.

A third element underpinning elitism in populist ideological conceptualisations of the relationship between the governing and the governed is the way in which political leaders are legitimised. Charismatic authority rather than rational-legal authority (Weber, 1992 [1921]) is held up as the source of legitimacy for populist leaders. Although populist parties indeed gain legitimacy through democratic elections, this legitimacy is based on a very thin understanding of democracy. The populist idea of the leader as one who directly interprets and channels the will of the people represents a conception of politics markedly different than liberal democracy (Dahl, 1989). Furthermore, this populist understanding of the relationship between the leader and the governed distinguishes itself from the idea of politics as a process in which various groups deliberate and compete for approval of their views and interests – also in the political decision-making and implementation processes after elections. Populist leaders are not expected to deliberate rationally with other power bases in the government apparatus or to limit their own power by rules and procedures because they are thought to be those who truly know what the people want. Charismatic leadership is a central tool for populist leaders to gain legitimacy as the true interpreters of the people's will. They often have an aura of being a godsend akin to kings' divine nature: therefore, their judgment and actions are the most adequate means to detect what the people's general will is (Silva, 2017, p. 15). Such an interpretation of charismatic leadership is quite in line with Weber's (1992 [1921]) understanding of charismatic authority. Giving power to a leader on the top to judge the correct interpretations of the people's will and the appropriate policy to achieve it has a deeply elitist nature. Table 1 summarises these three elements characteristic of the populist ideas of adequate political leadership.

Populist ideology ideal typically thus both describes the political situation as characterised by a united, oppressive elite and suggests making changes in power

Table 1.   Elements Contributing to the Elitist Character of Populist
Ideal-Typical Leadership.

Components of Populist Ideal–Typical Leadership	Pathway to Elitism (Concentration of Power in a Narrow Elite)
1 Image of a strong leader	Legitimises leaders who make decisions and take action based on their own judgment
2 Direct relationship between the people and the leader	Delegitimises counter-voices, deconcentration of power at the top and institutional constraints on leadership
3 Legitimisation by charismatic authority	The image of the leader as the only legitimate interpreter of the people's will hinders exchange of ideas and opinions and protects the leader from critique

relations that also concentrate power in the hands of a narrow, united elite. This is the paradox of populist elitism. This solution, however, is clearly presented as not elitist but as a way of handing power to the people. Analytical tools from elite theory, thus, make clear the elitist character of populism. Before addressing in more depth why the populist solution of political leadership is democratically problematic and whether the populist diagnosis of a united, homogeneous elite is accurate, we look at how elite theory analyses the relationship between the elites and masses.

CLASSICAL CONCEPTUALISATIONS OF ELITE PLURALISM

Classical elite theory, surprisingly overlooked in scholarship on populism, provides analytical tools for discussing the relationship between elite pluralism and power and clarifying the paradox of populist elitism. The opposition between the ruling minority elite and the ruled masses conceived in populism is a core point in Vilfredo Pareto's (1963) and Gaetano Mosca's (1939 [1896]) contributions to classical elite theory. Normatively, the fundamental views of Pareto and Mosca are quite different from populist ideologies and see ruling elites as a necessary, valuable organisation of politics and society. The authors consider all societies to be necessarily hierarchised and believe egalitarian distribution of power to be impossible. Populist ideologies, in contrast, are based on the idea that it is possible and preferable to take power from elites and give it to the people (Coenen-Huther, 2004). Nevertheless, Pareto's and Mosca's understandings of the relationship between the elite minority and the ruled majority analytically resonate with populist ideological understandings of the relationship between the people and elites as both sides consider the people to be dominated by elites. However, elite theory, developed for a quite different purpose than populist ideologies, offers a more nuanced understanding of these power relations.

In addition to the binary opposition between the rulers and the ruled majority, Pareto (1963, p. 1423) is most famous for defining elites as those who possess the knowledge and skills that make them the best in their areas of activity, whether they are the best chess players, the best political leaders or the best thieves. This is a concept of elite delimited to specific occupational fields and can be characterised as expert or professional elites (Mangset, 2015). In many respects, Pareto's (1963) understanding is compatible with a meritocratic understanding of elites as groups that deserve privileges and power in specific fields, a conception clearly opposed to the populist assessment of the legitimacy of elite domination. Pareto wrote that the most able rulers have power over elites in other fields, as well as over the masses. Nevertheless, his specification of capable elites in a range of different fields implies a certain degree of pluralism. A concept connecting elites to excellence within a specific field necessarily implies a plurality of elites.[1] Although Pareto does not necessarily consider this to imply dispersion of power, he provides an analytical tool for thinking of the possibility of such dispersion of power and connecting it to elite pluralism.

Mosca's (1939 [1896]) writings highlight another tension between elites. In addition to the binary opposition among the ruled majority and the ruling minority, Mosca draws a distinction between different levels of elites: the political elites, who are the ones truly governing, and a broader set of intermediate elites between the top group and the general population. These mediators are necessary for governing; without them minority rule, even 'any sort of social organization would be impossible' (Mosca, 1939 [1896], p. 404). Here, too, emerges the germ of a pluralist conception of elites. Moreover, Mosca envisages a counter-elite, 'another ruling class or directing minority necessarily forms ... antagonistic to the class that holds possession of the legal government'. A plurality of elites functions as an opposition that may 'seriously embarrass an official government' (Mosca, 1939 [1896], p. 116).

Conceiving of elites as possibly divided into groups with potentially differing interests, as found in the classical writings in elite theory of the nineteenth century, opens possibilities for multiple voices and dispersion of power – key conditions for liberal democracy (Aron, 1950). Pareto's and Mosca's theories on elite pluralism are applicable to contemporary normative discussions on the legitimacy of elites in democratic societies. The legitimacy of elites depends on whether they are one integrated group or several different elites; Mosca and Pareto show that several elites are possible. These insights into elite pluralism starkly contrast with populist ideological understandings of the oppressive elite as necessarily homogeneous and characterised by converging interests.

Despite overwhelming differences between the types of society envisaged and interpreted by Pareto and Mosca and the variety of stable democracies in the modern world, fundamental asymmetries of power between majorities and minorities persist in contemporary democratic societies. The ubiquity of various sorts of large organisations created by far-reaching social differentiation in modern societies contributes to such asymmetries of power between the masses and elites. These organisations' hierarchical structure concentrating most power at the summit makes their top leaders core members of any type of social elite. These organisations' institutional make-up and relationships with the political and societal systems of which they are part are crucial to the kinds of relationships among the different elites at the top. Are they united and conspiring together, as populists claim, or do they promote different worldviews and interests? Pareto's and Mosca's theories open up imagining the existence of several elites, but more recent elite theory goes further and focusses on the question of how united these different elites are.

THE POSSIBILITY OF ELITE PLURALISM

Nearly all modern elite theorists acknowledge a certain diversity of elites, as indicated by traditional elite theory. Wright Mills (1956), Dahl (1961), Field and Higley (1980) and Scott (2008) subscribe to a definition of elites as those occupying leading positions in powerful institutions, to use a formulation by Giddens (1972). The main debate in modern elite theory concerns the degree to which these various elites constitute highly integrated groups defending common interests or, to the contrary, are more dispersed, characterised by differing recruitment patterns, interests, worldviews and patterns of career mobility. Do they form a closed group, power elite in Mills's (1956) term, or is the image of a plurality of elite interest groups more relevant? Those who view elites as integrated and united are often called monists, whereas those who view elites as split into separate, competing groups are called pluralists (Genieys, 2011). Elite theorists disagree on interpretations of the empirical situation in a given society at a particular time (e.g. how integrated American elites were in the 1950s) but generally agree on the normative stance that a plurality of elites is beneficial for democratic societies (Dahl, 1961; Mangset, 2017; Mills, 1956). The importance of the descriptive and analytical discussions on the degree of elite integration to modern elite theorists are important to this chapter as it allows better understanding these power relations and provides a foundation for discussing the normative issue of elites' legitimacy in democratic societies.

Debates and insights from elite theory thus are relevant to discussing two aspects of populism. First, regarding populist ideological understandings of the problem of how a united elite exploit the people, elite theorists focussing on elite integration, such as Mills, present an analysis similar to populism in some respects. Furthermore, elite theorists focussing on elite pluralism, such as Dahl and Higley, agree with populists – and Mills – that *if* the elites were united and homogeneous, that would represent a problem. Second, modern elite theory is relevant to discussing populist ideological understandings of the solution to replace the current arrangements: undivided political leadership. Monists and pluralists in modern elite theory are both critical of the democratic legitimacy of this populist conceptualisation of political leadership.

Contrary to populist ideological understandings of today's power relations, the degree to which elite groups are integrated and have the capacity for collective action is likely to vary between countries and through history. The institutional structures for recruitment, career patterns and relations between sectors vary by country and time; so do the conditions for elite integration (Hartmann, 2010; Mangset, 2017). Close analyses also show different modes of elite integration (Engelstad, 2018). At the same time, processes of disintegration may be at work.

We find it most fruitful to regard elite integration not as a defining criterion of elite formation but, rather, as an empirical question (see also Higley & Burton, 2006; Scott, 2008, p. 34). The degree to which elite groups are integrated and act in concert in any society at any time must be examined empirically. It cannot be stipulated a priori that they are homogeneous and united, as populist leaders tend to claim in their attempts to rhetorically seduce the masses.

VARIETIES OF POPULIST ELITE CRITIQUES

Although populist ideology ideal–typically conceives of the elite as a united, homogeneous group, populist movements across the world have attacked a range of elite groups and laid different accusations against them. This empirical diversity of elite critiques is interesting as it tells us that populists themselves are well aware that different types of elites exist – in contrast to what their ideological model states. In this section, we look closer at specific versions of populism and populist elite critiques to illustrate this diversity, without aspiring to exhaustivity. After briefly pointing to some features of populist ideologies and organisations that open up this diversity, we examine four types of populist elite critiques.

Several types of populism can be distinguished according to their political orientations and the specific issues at stake. In addition to the common distinctions between right-wing populism generally opposing the state and left-wing populism opposing both the state and advanced capitalism, an intermediate version focuses on the functioning of the democratic system (Kriesi, 2014, p. 362). Populism grows out of a variety of organisations and movements (Aslanidis, 2017; Ciani & Della Porta, 2017), and its ideas are diffused through several channels (Veugelers & Menard, 2017). Despite this diversity, political parties are the most central organisations of populist mobilisation. Even if parties are interdependent with less institutionalised movements, movements that seek to make significant differences have to be visible in the political centre, which generally requires being represented by one or more political parties. Hence, the dynamics of populist movements are closely linked to party politics and the dominant political rhetoric.

The points of departure for this brief description of various types of populism and their elite targets are Canovan's (1981) minimal definition and Mudde's (2004) conception of populism as a thin-centred ideology with a limited core of values. In contrast to a thick-centred ideology covering a wide range of societal issues, thin-centred ideologies have specific, limited areas of concern. Other examples of thin-centred ideologies are feminism and ecologism. In the case of populism, its core values are anti-elitism and exaltation of a unified, homogenous people and their general will. Accordingly, populist parties show a high degree of flexibility in the issues they emphasise and the groups they attack and may shift relatively quickly over time.

Central elements in attacks on elites are political rhetoric and rhetorical strategies deployed in general, mediatised political discourses (Kriesi, 2014). They are launched on a particular vector, closely connected to common sense and the vernacular in opposition to abstract reasoning and specialised modes of speech and academic jargon. Populist rhetorical strategies are intended to debunk subtleties and replace them with efficient, striking, often derogatory metaphors. It, thus, becomes easy to subsume different types of elites under one heading: *The Elite*. In the following sketch of variations of elite critiques, the discussion is based on examples collected by ordinary observations in order to complement current research, which, in some respects, is limited in studies on political parties. Our analysis of these examples, which indeed comprise a range of different forms of elite critiques, results in four overarching categories: critiques of political elites, intermediate elites, economic elites and cultural elites.

POPULIST CRITIQUE OF THE POLITICAL ELITE

The initial impetus for contemporary populism came from tax resistance and the establishment of anti-tax parties in several European countries (Taggart, 1995). The *poujadist* movement emerged in France in the 1950s, followed by similar parties in Denmark and Norway around 1970. Criticism of the state defined these parties. However, the tax issue declined to secondary importance when waves of immigration to Europe in the 1980s resulted in increased electoral support for populist parties. The turn from taxation to immigration led to a different, somewhat positive view of the state as the guardian of national borders and the source of welfare-state provision.

The immigration issue has become central for two reasons. First, it challenges deep cultural notions of us and them. Second, more implicit but not less significant is the complex question of who constitutes the *demos* (Kaltwasser, 2014) and can claim the rights of citizenship. Once brought to the fore, immigration and immigration policies became the dominant issue for virtually all populist parties across central, northern and southern Europe, leading to one the European Union's (EU) most serious crises in 2015. The populist standard view is that politicians defending international conventions on refugees and immigration live in isolated bubbles and betray national interests.

In central and southern Europe, criticism has also been directed against corrupt politicians, producing disillusionment with liberal democracy (Pappas, 2014; Stanley, 2017). Accusations of untruthfulness among politicians had a decisive influence in bringing Fidez to power in Hungary (Lengyel & Szabó, 'The Political Elite and Trust in EU Institutions after the Crisis. A Comparative Analysis of the Hungarian Case', this volume). Distrust in politicians has accompanied protests against welfare policies, motivated by deficits in state budgets in southern Europe and welfare-state chauvinism seeking to deny immigrants the same rights as citizens in northern Europe.

The form of attacks on elites largely depends on the position of populist parties and movements in the political landscape. When operating as opposition forces, some populist parties remain in a challenger position with little formal power, even if they gather considerable electoral support. This situation is the case in France and the United Kingdom owing to their versions of majority elections. However, major populist parties with relatively high parliamentary representation sometimes also remain marginal, excluded from government positions. The most startling case is the Freedom Party in the Netherlands, a party with only one member, leader Geert Wilders. Other parties in similar positions are the Swedish Democrats and the Alternative für Deutschland in Germany. However, their isolation in parliaments does not prevent them from constant pressuring mainstream politics and politicians, thereby exerting considerable influence as agenda setters.

A different situation emerges when populists gain government positions. They must adjust their rhetoric but continue to depict themselves as outsiders of the political system by directing their elite critique at elite groups other than their own government (Silva, 2017, p. 7). Populist parties long have been minorities in government coalitions in several countries, notably Finland, Norway, Switzerland and Austria. Major effects of their political position have been significant adjustments and moderation in these populist parties.

In post-communist Hungary and Poland, populist parties have gained majorities by winning national elections on anti-elite programmes targeting previous governments' political corruption. Majority power has empowered them to set out to transform political institutions to their own advantage, making relatively liberal regimes nationalistic and conservative and placing growing limitations on the critical press and oppositional civil society organisations (Stanley, 2017). Before coming to power, these populist parties directed their rhetoric against national elites, and as incumbents, they redirect their hostility to the EU's bureaucratic elite.

Resistance to the EU and claims of restoring national sovereignty have become hallmarks of populist movements all over Europe. In southern Europe (Greece and Italy), populist parties have especially directed attacks against membership in the eurozone. In France, Front National (renamed Rassemblement National) has voiced general scepticism of the EU for many years (Ivaldi, 2018; Vasilopoulou, 2011, 2017). Resistance to EU membership was even more forcefully expressed in the Brexit slogan of 'Take our country back'.[2] In addition to the assumption that staying outside the EU will benefit the welfare of the people, these attacks reflect profound concerns about political legitimacy. Put simply, the core question of legitimacy is 'Who should rightfully decide over me?' Despite considerable efforts to build a European citizenship, the core of political legitimacy remains anchored in nation-states. This duality of national and European citizenship has created a deep ambiguity that has become a driving force in protests against the EU and its bureaucratic elite.

POPULIST CRITIQUE OF INTERMEDIATE ELITES

The populist ideal of strong leadership by a single person who interprets and articulates the people's will also implies scepticism towards a plurality of institutions and intermediate bodies. In line with Mosca's theory, the anti-elitism in populist movements is not necessarily or not only directed towards the top political elite but also often towards elite groups immediately below the political leader of a country or a political system. Thus, the president or the prime minister, especially if also the head of a populist movement, is not necessarily the main target of elite critiques. The target may well be the leadership of political parties and central institutions such as public agencies, central banks, educational institutions and unions. This is well illustrated by the Greek activists demonstrating before the parliament during the euro crisis, who resolved not to leave the Syntagma Square 'until all those who led us here are gone: governments, the Troika, Banks, Memoranda, and all those who take advantage of us' (Aslanidis, 2017, p. 310). The critique of leaders and bureaucrats in international institutions, such as the EU, has strong connections with the critique of these various types of intermediate elites discussed here.

Rejection of classical political parties and preferences for less formally organised political movements have characterised Europe in our times. In the literature, the lack of trust in political institutions is often cited as a cause and a consequence of populism (Silva, 2017, p. 7). Peter Mair (2002) and Hanspeter Kriesi (2014) tied the rise of populism in Europe to the erosion of political parties' legitimacy as representatives of the voters (Manin, 2012 [1995]).

> The failure of mainstream parties to effectively articulate and represent policy preferences that are salient to a significant portion of the electorate is … a widely recognized source of new party formation[s] … in established democracies. (Roberts, 2017, p. 294)

Among political institutions, the civil service is a main target of populist movements. When institutions – whether public agencies, party organisations, unions or others – are considered to be central components of the political system, it implies that the political system constrains power with bureaucratic rules. The legal–rational authority of central institutions restricts top leaders' power, particularly in the domains which they control and the procedures they must follow to legitimise their exercise of power. A dominant stereotype is inefficient bureaucrats operating without any thought of useful outcomes or consideration of citizen welfare. These bureaucrats are obsessed with rules and regulations, but at the same time, they are thought to fight for their own interests or some version of a 'deep state' (Osnos, 2018). They can continue to do so as the 'government has been captured by powerful special interests that enslave and impoverish the many to enrich the few' (Silva, 2017, p. 3). This view in particular has been expressed in the United States, where then presidential candidate Donald Trump repeatedly promised to 'drain the swamp' of the Washington bureaucracy, as did Ronald Reagan before him (Garcia, 2016). To circumvent bureaucratic obstruction, populists cherish forms of direct democracy, such as referenda, over the lengthier functioning of parliamentary processes and, above all, the civil service. This attitude has been most strongly emphasised by the Italian Five Star and the French yellow-vests movements but is prevalent even throughout more moderate populism in Scandinavia (Widfeldt, 2017, p. 522).

POPULIST CRITIQUE OF ECONOMIC ELITES

In the critique of economic elites, a clear divide between left- and right-wing populism comes to the fore. Left-wing populism remains strongest in Latin America, where populist parties have long held a position taken by social democratic parties in other parts of the world (Roberts, 2017, p. 290). However, the Latin American elite contains a strong coalition of landowners and capitalists. Left-wing populism is also visible in southern Europe, manifested in parties such as Syrizia and Podemos and the spontaneous movement *La France insoumise*. The French yellow-vests movement cannot clearly be defined as left-wing populism as it is composite and expresses a range of elite critiques and political demands. However, key tenets of the protesters are demands to re-establish taxes on wealth and enact more redistributive taxation and economic justice in general. Anti-capitalist agitation and critiques of economic elites, albeit more moderate, are also voiced by the left-wing populist movements and parties led by Bernie Sanders in the United States and Jeremy Corbyn in the United Kingdom.

Although left-wing populism undeniably exits, right-wing populist rhetoric has been the most noticeable in the political scene in central European and north Atlantic countries. Despite considerable populist support in the working classes, the conflicts between labour and capital – stressed throughout most of the twentieth century – are little discussed. For considerable segments of the working class, visions of class struggle have been replaced by the gap between the people and the political elite (Oeusch, 2008). This is noteworthy as large-scale immigration and importation of labour have accompanied dismantling of traditional industries in Europe, both inside and outside the EU. Even amid high unemployment rates, though, economic elites have largely been exempt from right-wing populist attacks.

At the same time, populist do not appear to consider economic inequality to be a serious problem. It is not prominent on the agendas of the French Rassemblement National or the Dutch Freedom Party. The Brexit campaign was initiated by the deeply conservative faction of the Tory Party but would not have succeeded without strong support in regions hit by high unemployment. In the Czech Republic, billionaire Andrej Babiš won the 2017 presidential election. On the other side of the Atlantic, the president is a billionaire, and the present US cabinet members have the highest average income in cabinet history.

Here, one reservation should be noted. Criticism of the economic elites is more often targeted at the financial elite. In the most recent US presidential campaign, Wall Street was a visible target, as was London City in the Brexit campaign. The activities of economic analysts and financial sector employees are not necessarily more mysterious than those in the corporate sector, but they do not produce tangible, useful products or create jobs that most people can fill. Hence, they remain at a distance from the majority of the population and thus may serve as useful targets in populist rhetoric when billionaires compete for political positions.

POPULIST CRITIQUE OF THE CULTURAL ELITE

Populism is a question of not only politics and parties but also political style (Knight, 1998). The distinction between high and low culture emerges as a constant characteristic of populism, transcending variations in political issues or geography: 'despite the very local nature and texture of all populisms, cross-continentally they are characterized by a surprisingly similar affective narrative' (Ostiguy, 2017, p. 75). Focussing on these cultural components enriches understanding of populism as a phenomenon and yields a more comprehensive view of the variety of elite groups targeted by populism. The theoretical approach to cultural expression summarises social identity and political appeal in a notion of populism's affective narrative. 'High' groups comprise a variety of artists, academics, experts and media leaders who share the power of definition in the public sphere. 'Low' groups, in this context, do not embody economic status or social positions but direct-from-the-liver ways of speaking. Examples of rich people and prominent politicians classified as culturally low flourish; Trump and Silvio Berlusconi are only the most visible illustrations. In contrast, intellectuals' contrived sophistication reveals a bloodless elite.

These coarse claims of authenticity are not the only form of anti-elite opposition. Scientists and academic elites, obviously in the social sciences but also the natural sciences, are also targets. Justified by personal experiences and beliefs and accordingly by claims of authenticity, populists reject, if not ridicule, statements on climate change from the United Nations Climate Panel. By implication, statements on climate change may be dismissed not only by pointing to contrasting observations over relatively short periods but also by exaggerating the doubts attached to any scientific findings. The scientific methodology thus is used to invalidate well-established scientific results (Jasanoff, 2010).

Disbelief in various forms of expertise extends from the sciences to other types of professional expertise. The increased complexity of political issues widens the gaps among the people, elites and experts with high academic credentials. 'I think that the people of this country have had enough of experts with organisations from acronyms, saying that they know what is best and getting it consistently wrong', Michael Gove, then minister of justice, declared during the Brexit campaign (Sky News, 6 June 2016). While experts might issue wrong judgements owing to one-sided application of their expert knowledge, the attacks on them have a broader cultural basis than the (in)correctness of their views based on an assumption that their views are formed without consideration of the world's practical demands.

Modern art is under constant attack as out of touch with the people or impossible to understand. For instance, a Norwegian populist politician suggested converting the National Theatre into a bingo hall. A more sophisticated version is an alliance of cultural conventionality with distaste for modern art. The official establishment of a national canon of arts and literature consisting primarily of traditional works from the nineteenth century has been a central cause for the Danish People's Party. An implicit link to immigration emerges: if all citizens are to embrace the canon, then immigrants are forced to accept it as a sign of sincere belonging to the host country. Similarly, the Danish People's Party and the Norwegian Progress Party turned from their former resistance to gender-equality policies – typically an issue supported by the cultural elites – to embrace of gender equality as a national value threatened by immigrants from Islamic countries. Gender-equal attitudes and practices thus became a sign of willingness to integrate into 'our' culture (Dahlerup, 2018; Teigen & Wägnerud, 2009).

In contrast to the cultural elites and their special manners and modes of expression, media messages are relatively easily accessible, both physically and linguistically. The main populist critique of the media is its alleged hypocrisy, selectively presenting, twisting or simply inventing facts as it belongs to the same elite it purportedly critiques. The slogans travel all over the western world, from *fake news* originating in the United States to *Lügenpresse* in Germany: 'Donald Trump calls journalists liars, Geert Wilders tells the critical media to "drop dead", Marine Le Pen calls them a "self-proclaimed elite", and Nigel Farage accuses them of bias' (Ellinas, 2017, p. 269). The unanimous attack on the media has several sources, including the dramatically increased competition from social media and the low investments necessary to set up alternative news media on the internet. At the same time, the media itself has contributed to these attacks. Professional journalistic criteria have given broad coverage to populist parties and groups, disseminating and normalising populist conceptions (Ellinas, 2017, p. 279).

The various types of elite critiques promoted by populists around the world could be categorised differently. However, we consider that pointing to the critiques of these four categories of elites (political, intermediate, economic and cultural elites) highlights the key features and variety of populist elite critiques, supporting further analysis of the elitist dimensions of populism and the relationship between elites and democracy. Discussing political, economic and cultural elites points to different segments of society that may be organised by competing logics and understandings of value and thus breeds different types of elites that do not necessarily cooperate. We also highlight intermediate elites, although these can exist in the three spheres of society (political, economic and cultural). However, by treating intermediate elites as a distinct group, we specifically identify bureaucratic elites central to our political, administrative and democratic institutions and distinct from politicians in their source of legitimacy. Furthermore, we shed light on the specific populist critiques of these power bases that lie between the people and the political leadership. Critiques of these elites are central to populist ideological conceptualisations of the ideal relationship between the people and the leader and are central to the elitist character of populism.

DEMOCRACY AND THE UNITY OF ELITES?

The various forms of populism identified across the world target a range of different elites. In this way, the empirical reality of populist elite critiques accords more with elite theorists' notion of plural elites than the populist ideal–typical conceptualisation of the united elite. Although different populists target different elite groups, the degree of unity among these elite groups remains a question. It has been discussed in depth in modern elite theory, which accordingly can be fruitful in the discussion on populist elite critiques. Furthermore, elite theories' normative discussion on the relationship between elite pluralism and democracy is also relevant to the discussion on the inherent elitism in populist ideas of leadership.

Are the various elite groups in society common, coherent elite or varied competitors? Why does it matter? As briefly mentioned, the monists following the scholarly tradition of Mills (1956) tend to focus on how closely connected various elite groups are. The pluralists who follow Dahl (1961) stress the diversity of elites. Both strands generally agree on the normative stance that elite pluralism is better for democracy than a too integrated and united elite, but they disagree on the descriptive issue of how integrated elites are. With disagreements on both conceptual issues and interpretations of empirical facts, a final conclusion on the empirical realities is difficult to reach. However, they agree on the significance of the degree of elites' integration to the functioning of democracy. Challenges to democracy can come from too integrated elites that largely share life conditions and ways of perceiving the world and their interests.

Furthermore, elite theory demonstrates the usefulness of explicitly discussing which mechanisms can be relevant to increasing, preventing or decreasing integration of elite groups (for more, see Engelstad, 2018; Mangset, 2017). A useful point of departure may be John Scott's (2008) description of the mechanisms of elite integration and power concentration:

> As occupants of a purely formal category, the members of an elite need have few bonds of interaction or association and may not exist as a cohesive and solidaristic social group. Such solidarity occurs only if social mobility, leisure time socializing, education, intermarriage, and other social relations are such that the members of an elite are tied together in regular and recurrent patterns of association. Only then are they likely to show any unity or to develop common forms of outlook and social consciousness. (Scott, 2008, p. 34)

The mechanisms mentioned by Scott can be described as a cultural mode of elite integration, which can be reinforced by career circulation: the more elite members move between jobs, for example, from public agencies to politics and business, the more integrated the administrative, political and business elites are thought to be (Hartmann, 2007, 2010; Mangset, 2017). Dahlström, Lapuente, and Teorell (2011) described yet another form of elite group relations that can be analysed as a form of elite integration. For example, when bureaucrats and politicians, two supposedly distinct elite groups in the governing system, are not separated by clearly different career patterns and motivational structures, they can become too interdependent and develop a unified outlook on their work, world and common interests. Thereby, not only cooperation but also corruption among bureaucrats and politicians is facilitated. This can be analysed as a case of elite integration from merging professional structures. More general sources of elite integration are overarching structures, such as social and political norms and institutions (Engelstad, 2018), and certain ideologies and political orientations more prone to elite integration (Gulbrandsen, 2019).

Our point is that elites cannot a priori be assumed to be a coherent, united group as populist ideal–typical ideology defines them. The degree to which elites meet, socialise and interact in ways that open up the development of common interests and ways of understanding the world should be investigated. Moreover, the institutional structures that can underpin development of common worldviews and interests and the institutional structures that prevent such development should be examined.

CONCLUDING REMARKS

Given the variety of elite critiques, populist movements' failure to always direct their critiques against the same groups and to always level the same accusations indicate that there are different elite groups and different forms of populism. This contradicts populist ideal–typical ideological conceptions of power relations as one between a homogeneous, oppressed people and homogeneous, malevolent and dominant elite. The extensive literature on populism presents a wide variety of perspectives, but all share anti-elitism as a defining characteristic. However, populism is inherently elitist in two senses. First, analytically, populism conceives of power relations in society as existing between a homogeneous, unified, good people oppressed by a group of homogeneous, unified and malevolent elite. Perceiving the holders of power as a small, unified elite group can be said to be an elitist perception of the power distribution in society. Second, normatively, populism prefers a political system in which a strong leader takes power from the oppressive elites and governs with few restrictions from institutional structures and intermediate elites. The populist view on adequate political leadership understands the leader as one who almost singlehandedly channels the people's will through a charismatic capacity for understanding and interpreting the people's wishes. The vision of a political system without institutionalised intermediate elites and counter-elites and with few legitimate counter-voices in the government decision-making processes is especially elitist and a challenge to democracy.

Elite theory, from its inception, has pointed to the existence of different types of elites. Some may argue that those among elite theorists who have insisted on the strong bonds among elite groups have fed populists' conspiratorial understanding of elites as homogeneous, united and fighting for their common interests. We argue that the rise of populism in our times and indeed populist parties' electoral wins and entry into the governments in several countries make it all the more important to seek inspiration from both sides in this debate in elite theory: those focussing on elite integration and those insisting on elite plurality. Doing so is necessary to investigate the degree of elite integration in contemporary societies, as well as the underpinning institutional structures. Social scientists should empirically establish how integrated elites are in different societies in order to inform political debates. If populist ideological conceptualisations of elites as homogeneous and fighting for common interests are accurate – in a specific society at a specific time – they are as challenging to democracy as populist movements themselves. Furthermore, elite studies in the social sciences should renew the debate on the conditions for elite groups to play a more constructive role in securing institutional restrictions on political leadership, the distribution of power and the democratic exchange of ideas necessary to sustain liberal democracy.

Sociological critiques of elites' growing, illegitimate power and privileges (Piketty, 2014; Savage & Williams, 2008) are needed as the widening gap between the elites and people contributes to the unfairness and frustration initially motivating the rise of populism. Indeed, sociologists have a responsibility to shed light on the power held and used by economic elites as these tend to escape much populist critique. However, sociologists should be able to combine a nuanced critique and discussion on certain elite groups' roles in liberal democracies: a role both as a source to legitimate populist protest and of possible counter-voices and a balance of power. Elite groups' legitimacy as counter-voices and powerful actors clearly depends on the degree and form of their access to elite positions.

ACKNOWLEDGEMENT

Open Access Funded by Centre for the Study of Professions, Oslo Metropolitan University.

NOTES

1. One can say that the degree of the plurality of elites is related to the degree of autonomy in each field or the development of institutional boundaries between fields. We return to this question in the discussion on elite integration.

2. After seeing British politicians' struggle to handle Brexit, some EU-sceptical populist parties, such as the French RN (previously the FN), have moderated their demand to leave the EU into a call to change it from within.

REFERENCES

Aron, R. (1950). Social structure and the ruling class: Part 1. *British Journal of Sociology, 1*(1), 1–16.

Aslanidis, P. (2017). Populism and social movements. In C. R. Kaltwasser, P. Taggart, P. O. Espejo, & P. Ostiguy (Eds.), *The Oxford handbook of populism* (pp. 305–325). Oxford: Oxford University Press.

Canovan, M. (1981). *Populism*. New York, NY: Harcourt Brace Jovanovich.

Canovan, M. (1999). 'Trust the people!' Populism and the Two Faces of Democracy. *Political Studies, 47*(1), 2–16.

Ciani, M., & Della Porta, D. (2017). The radical right as social movement organizations. In J. Rydgren (Ed.), *The Oxford handbook of the radical right* (pp. 327–347). Oxford: Oxford University Press.

Coenen-Huther, J. (2004). *Sociologie des élites.* [Sociology of elites.] Paris, France: Armand Colin.

Dahl, R. A. (1961). *Who governs? Democracy and power in an American city.* New Haven, CT: Yale University Press.

Dahl, R. A. (1989). *Democracy and its critics.* New Haven, CT: Yale University Press.

Dahlerup, D. (2018). Gender equality as a closed case. A survey among the members of the 2015 Danish Parliament. *Scandinavian Political Studies, 41*(2), 188–209. doi:10.1111/1467-9477.12116

Dahlström, C., Lapuente, V., & Teorell, J. (2011). The merit of meritocratization: Politics, bureaucracy, and the institutional deterrents of corruption. *Political Research Quarterly, 65*(3), 656–668. doi:1065912911408109

Ellinas, A. A. (2017). Media and the radical right. In J. Rydgren (Ed.), *The Oxford handbook of the radical right* (pp. 269–284). Oxford: Oxford University Press.

Engelstad, F. (2018). Models of elite integration. In H. Best & J. Higley (Eds.), *The Palgrave handbook of political elites* (pp. 439–457). London: Palgrave Macmillan.

Field, G. L. & Higley, J. (1980). *Elitism*. London, UK: Routledge & Kegan Kegan Paul.

Garcia, E. (2016). A history of 'draining the swamp'. *Roll Call.* Retrieved from http://www.rollcall.com/news/politics/history-of-draining-the-swamp. Accessed on November 15, 2016.

Genieys, W. (2011). *La sociologie des élites politiques* [The sociology of political elites]. Paris, France: Armand Colin.

Giddens, A. (1972). Elites in the British class structure. *Sociological Review, 20*(3), 345–372.

Gulbrandsen, T. (2019). *Elites in an egalitarian society: Support for the Nordic model.* London, UK: Palgrave Macmillan.

Hartmann, M. (2007). *Eliten und Macht in Europa: ein internationaler Vergleich* [Elites and power in Europe: an international comparison]. Frankfurt, Germany: Campus Verlag.

Hartmann, M. (2010). Elites and power structure. In S. Immerfall & G. Therborn (Eds.), *Handbook of European societies* (pp. 290–324). New York, NY: Springer.

Higley, J., & Burton, M. (2006). *Elite foundations of liberal democracy.* Lanham, MD: Rowman & Littlefield.

Ivaldi, G. (2018). Contesting the EU in times of crisis: The Front National and politics of euroscepticism in France. *Politics, 38,* 278–294.

Jasanoff, S. (2010). A new climate for society. *Theory, Culture & Society, 27,* 233–253.

Kaltwasser, C. R. (2014). The responses of populism to Dahl's democratic dilemmas. *Political Studies 62,* 470–487.

Kazin, M. (1998). *The populist persuasion: An American history.* Ithaca, NY: Cornell University Press.

Knight, A. (1998). Populism and Neo-populism in Latin America, especially Mexico. *Journal of Latin American Studies, 30*(2), 223–248.

Kriesi, H. (2014). The populist challenge. *West European Politics, 37*(2), 361–378.

Laclau, E. (2005). *On populist reason.* London: Verso.

Mair, P. (2002). Populist democracy vs party democracy. In Y. Mény & Y. Surel (Eds.), *Democracies and the populist challenge* (pp. 81–98). London: Palgrave Macmillan.

Manin, B. (2012 [1995]). *Principes du gouvernement représentatif* [Principles of representative government]. Paris, France: Calmann-Lévy.

Mangset, M. (2015). What does it mean to be part of the elite? Comparing British, French and Norwegian top bureaucrats understanding of the elite concept when applied to themselves. *Comparative Sociology, 14*(2), 274–299.

Mangset, M. (2017). Elite circulation and the convertibility of knowledge. Comparing different types and forms of knowledge and degrees of elite circulation in Europe. *Journal of Education and Work 30*(2), 129–144. https://doi.org/10.1080/13639080.2017.1278903

Meny, Y., & Surel, Y. (2001). *Democracies and the populist challenge.* New York, NY: Springer.

Mills, C. W. (1956). *The power elite.* Oxford: Oxford University Press.

Mosca, G. (1939 [1896]). *The ruling class.* New York, NY: McGraw-Hill.

Mudde, C. (2004). The populist zeitgeist. *Government and Opposition, 39*(4), 541–563.

Oeusch, D. (2008). Explaining workers' support for right-wing populist parties in Western Europe: Evidence from Austria, Belgium, France, Norway and Switzerland. *International Political Science Review, 29,* 349–373.

Osnos, E. (2018). Trump vs. the "deep state". *The New Yorker,* May 21. Retrieved from https://www.newyorker.com/magazine/2018/05/21/trump-vs-the-deep-state. Accessed on July 27, 2019.

Ostiguy, P. (2017). Populism: A socio-cultural approach. In C. R. Kaltwasser, P. Taggart, P. O. Espejo, & P. Ostiguy (Eds.), *The Oxford handbook of populism* (pp. 73–99). Oxford: Oxford University Press.

Pappas, T. S. (2014). Populist democracies: Post-authoritarian Greece and Post-communist Hungary. *Government and Opposition, 49,* 1–23.

Pareto, V. (1963). *Mind and society: A treatise on general sociology.* New York, NY: Dover Publications.

Piketty, T. (2014). *Capitalism in the 21ˢᵗ century.* Cambridge, MA: Harvard University Press.

Roberts, K. M. (2017). Populism and political parties. In C. R. Kaltwasser, P. Taggart, P. O. Espejo, & P. Ostiguy (Eds.), *The Oxford handbook of populism* (pp. 287–304). Oxford: Oxford University Press.

Savage, M., & K. Williams (Eds.). (2008). *Remembering elites.* Oxford: Blackwell.

Scott, J. (2008). Modes of power and the re-conceptualization of elites. In M. Savage & K. Williams (Eds.), *Remembering elites* (pp. 27–43). Oxford: Blackwell.

Silva, B. C. (2017). *Contemporary populism: Actors, causes, and consequences across 28 democracies.* Budapest, Hungary: Central European University, Doctoral School of Political Science, Public Policy and International Relations.

Sky News. (2016, June 6). https://www.youtube.com/watch?v=t8D8AoC-5i8. Accessed on 27 July, 2019.

Stanley, B. (2017). Populism in Central and Eastern Europe. In C. R. Kaltwasser, P. Taggart, P. O. Espejo, & P. Ostiguy (Eds.), *The Oxford handbook of populism* (pp. 140–160). Oxford: Oxford University Press.

Taggart, P. (1995). New populist parties in Western Europe. *West European Politics, 18*, 34–51.

Taggart, P. (2000). *Populism*. Buckingham: Open University Press.

Teigen, M., & Wägnerud, L. (2009). Tracing gender equality cultures: Elite perceptions of gender equality in Norway and Sweden. *Politics & Gender, 5*, 29–44.

Vasilopoulou, S. (2011). European integration and the radical right: Three patterns of opposition. *Government and Opposition, 46*, 223–244.

Vasilopoulou, S. (2017). The radical right and euroskepticism. In J. Rydgren (Ed.), *The Oxford handbook of the radical right* (pp. 122–140). Oxford: Oxford University Press.

Veugelers, J., & Menard, G. (2017). The non-party sector of the radical right. In J. Rydgren (Ed.), *The Oxford handbook of the radical right* (pp. 285–304). Oxford: Oxford University Press.

Weber, M. (1992 [1921]). *Economy and society*. Berkeley, CA: University of California Press.

Widfeldt, A. (2017). The radical right in the Nordic Countries. In J. Rydgren (Ed.), *The Oxford handbook of the radical right* (pp. 545–564). Oxford: Oxford University Press.

INDEX

Note: Page numbers followed by "*n*" with numbers indicate notes.